Dynamics in Digital Information Systems

Festschrift Volume in Honour of Prof. M. Bavakutty

Dynamics in Digital Information Systems

Festschrift Volume in Honour of Prof. M. Bavakutty

Editor

Prof. A. Amudhavalli

Assistant

Dr. V. Chandrakumar

Ess Ess Publications

4837/24, Ansari Road, Darya Ganj,
New Delhi-110002
Tel. : 23260807, 41563444
Fax : 011-41563334
E-mail: info@essessreference.com
www.essessreference.com

Ess Ess Publications
4837/24, Ansari Road,
Darya Ganj,
New Delhi-110 002.

Tel.: 23260807, 41563444
Fax: 41563334
E-mail: info@essessreference.com
www.essessreference.com

Rs.1150/-

First Published - 2008

ISBN: 81-7000-537-X (10 Digit)
978-81-7000-5337-7 (13 Digit)

Published By Ess Ess Publications and printed at Salasar Imaging Systems

Cover Design by W&P Graphics Pvt. Ltd.

PRINTED IN INDIA

Prof. M. Bavakutty

Contents

Preface .... (*xi*)

Foreword .... (*xv*)

Felicitations

Krishan Kumar .... (*xvii*)

C.A. Augustine .... (*xxi*)

An Interaction with Prof. M Bavakutty .... (*xxix*)

T.P.O. Nasirudheen

List of Publications of Prof. M Bavakutty .... (*liii*)

List of Contributors .... (*lxv*)

1. Library and Information Science 1
   Education in India : Some Observation
   K.C.Abdul Majeed

2. Knowledge Management: A Paradigm 23
   Shift in Organizations.
   Ajit Agale
   Sukeshini Horannavar

3. Are Library and Information 40
   Professionals still Significant?
   A. Amudhavalli

4. Traditional Knowledge Organisation 52
   systems in the Electronic Environment
   Lalitha Aswath

5. The Impact of Knowledge Management 62
   on Organizational Development
   Nagappa V.Bakkannanavar

Anju Govindani

6. Knowledge Management 89
G. S.Birdar
R. R.Naik

7. Total Quality Management (TQM) in Library & Information Centres. 99
V. Chandrakumar

8. Knowledge Management in Digital ....112 Information System: Recent Challenges and Solutions
Subarna Kumar Das

9. Dynamics of Information Technology ....124 and Future Librarianship.
Anil Kumar Dhiman

10. Representation of Institutional ....140 Knowledge on Institutional Websites: a case study of University of California's e-scholarship Repository
Hamsa Kalyani
T. D.Kemparaju
T. B.Rajashekhar

11. Knowledge Management in the ....150 Twenty First Century.
Asis Kumar Hazra
Samir Chattopadhyay

12. Role of Libraries in Knowledge ....164 Management
S. Humayoon Kabir

13. Entering Knowledge Society: some ....174 Modest Indian e- initiatives
C. R. Karisiddappa
Iqbal Ahmad Urajgoli

14. Blogging as a Teaching Tool in Library Education 193
Krishan Kumar
Jaideep Sharma

15. Application of Information and Communciaiton Technologies in Special Libraries. 206
K. Mohamed Haneefa

16. Archival of Digital Resources: Challenges and Issues. 223
T. K.Mohammed Sageer
T. A. Abdul Azeez

17. Knowledge Management in Digital Environment: an Overview. 233
M. Nagarajan
P. Sivaraman
M.Surulinathi

18. Competitive Intelligence in the Context of Knowledge Management 249
Santosh A. Navalur
Savita N. Nayak

19. Mobile and Wireless Communication Technologies in Knowledge Management in Marginalised and rural communities 260
A. Neelameghan

20. Globalization, Information Society and the future of Libraries 276
K. S. Raghavan

21. Information Literacy and Digital Libraries in the Higher Education Scenario 290
R. Samyuktha

22. Concept of Bibliometrics, Scientometrics and Informetrics. 301
S. L. Sangam
Keshava

23. Perspective in Digital Preservation 315
N.R. Satyanarayan

24. Current Trends in IT and its application in Academic Libraries. 324
D. Shivalingaiah
K.Manjunatha

25. Sustenance of Libraries in Digital environment: What & How to do?? 341
R. S. R.Varalakshmi

26. Biometric Technology for Network Security 356
Rekha Rani Varghese

27. Digital Library Security and Competencies of Library Professionals. 366
Shilpi Verma
K. L. Mahawar
Rekha Verma

28. Competencies of LIS Professionals in the Digital Age. 375
K. P. Vijayakumar

29. Scholarly Communication in the Networked Environment. 390
V. Vimalkumar

30. Web Based Knowledge Management in digital era. 399
K. Vinitha
S. Kanthimathi
Sampath Kumar

Index 409

Preface

I am privileged to pen down the preface as the Editor of this Festschrift Volume published in honour of Prof. M. Bavakutty, on his departure from his long distinguished career in our profession. A senior professional, teacher and practitioner and a colleague with us for the last three decades as the University Librarian at C.H.Mohammed Koya Library and Professor & Head, Department of Library & Information Science, University of Calicut, Kozhikode, his name never fails to evoke nostalgia. The fusion and synergy with which he successfully completed his career is remarkable. A band of professionals and young researchers have earned their doctorates, under his leadership and guidance. Dr. Bavakutty himself is a prolific writer and contributor to the body knowledge in our discipline and well known in the profession.

The changes in recorded media from paper to digital, the impact of Information & Communication Technology (ICT), pervasion of the Internet in scholarly communication, the changing user perception and self access to information are the challenges before the contemporary Library & Information Science (LIS) profession. To cope with the challenges of digital environment and sustain in the ever changing knowledge society Library & Information Centres (LIC) have to initiate new services. The outcome of the challenges is the 'Digital Divide' which warrants a need for the society to become Information Literate to be economically progressive. There have been several Information Literacy initiatives across the globe. Global resources of Information Literacy and initiatives in India are examined with special focus on role of Information Literacy and digital libraries in the context of higher education.

Knowledge Management will facilitate empowering rural and indigenous communities on the one hand and enable the sharing and use of the wealth of tacit community knowledge for the good of the nation, the global community of nations and states. The concern is not only the need to empower the marginalized communities through information out-reach programmes but also to collect and record the community knowledge, make efforts to understand their cultures, and leverage on the wisdom they possess for the good of the society. Recent developments and extension of ICT applications points to the possibilities of bridging the digital divide and better management of rural community knowledge. Attempts to use ICTs to reach out to indigenous and marginalized rural communities with a view to empowering them through implementation of e-governance, providing access to a variety of government documents relevant to the life of rural communities, village kiosks, land-sat imaging and remote sensing, geographical information systems, etc.

Most of the papers in this volume are in the areas of Knowledge Management, Knowledge Organization, Library & Information Systems, Services and professionals in the digital and networked environment. All these papers are contributed by friends and fellow colleagues of Dr. M. Bavakutty in the field of Library and Information Science.

I consider this Volume brought out in his honour as a befitting tribute for a dedicated and competent colleague of us yesterday, today and tomorrow. It is my pleasure and pride to be the Editor of this Festschrift volume to mark the glorious career of my long standing friend and colleague of mine.

Prof. M. Bavakutty, I wish him further success in all his endeavours and pray the Almighty for a long, peaceful and healthy life.

I thank all the contributors, felicitators and all those who supported us in bringing out this volume. I also thank Mr. Sumit Sethi, Managing Director, Ess Ess Publications for bringing out this significant volume so nicely.

Chennai **A. AMUDHAVALLI**

27th March 2008

Foreword

I am gratified to learn that a Festschrift volume entitled **"Dynamics in Digital Information Systems"** in honour of Dr. M. Bavakutty is being published. Dr. Bavakutty is known to me from his student days. Later he assumed charge of the Farook College Library as the librarian and contributed a great deal to systematize and develop the library. He had shown leadership, ability and enthusiasm in all the fields of activity he engaged in. He has contributed immensely in developing the C. H. Mohamed Koya Library of Calicut University as a modern and well organized library. His passion for promotion of teaching and research in Library and Information Science has earned him the respect and admiration of students and colleagues.

Library and Information Science is a field where changes are taking place with breathless speed. It is a heavy task to keep pace with the marvellous changes. Information explosion and the need for management of information are great challenges to professionals in the field of Information Science. Since writing began in the remote past, more than 3000 years before Christ, intellectual progress has been exponential. Writing passed on new knowledge and technology to succeeding generations with far greater ease and accuracy than oral communication through memory.

Several libraries were established during the ancient civilizations in Babylon, Alexandria, Taxila etc.

The writing materials they depended on were cumbersome before the arrival of paper. The Babylonians used clay tablets, the Egyptians used papyrus and the Indus people used soft soap stone – their system is still not satisfactorily deciphered. In the libraries space required was enormous. In the Babylonian library it is said that the Epic of Gilgamesh consisted of one lakh tablets tied on strings. Stones, bones, parchments and palm leaves were the available medium resorted to. The arrival of paper was a great landmark almost as revolutionary as the magnetic discs and electronic media. Our consumption of paper is enormous. If new media like electronic media did not arrive, our forests would have been denuded before long. Such are the miraculous changes taking place in writing and writing media. Now even books are going to be things of the past, curious decorating material in old world libraries and drawing rooms of the rich. Internet and a variety of other networks are used for dissemination of information. The digitization of information is the latest development and I am sure that this would not be the end of road. Dr. Bavakutty graduated when digitization was not even dreamt of. However he has kept abreast of the developments in information science and Information Communication Technology in the times of knowledge society.

I believe this Festschrift volume brought out in honour of Prof. M. Bavakutty is a befitting acknowledgment for his glorious, dedicated and long library professional career. So, it is my pleasure to write this foreward and I wish him every success in all his academic and professional endeavours.

Feroke
3rd October 2007

Prof. K. A. Jaleel
Former Vice Chancellor
University of Calicut

Dr. M. Bavakutty

A Student to a Scholar

Krishan Kumar

Dr. Bavakutty was born on 15th July 1946, one year before, India became independent. This year is a landmark in the history of library education in India. It was in the year 1946 when a full-fledged Department of Library Science was started at University of Delhi. It was the first independent department of its kind at the university level in the country. University of Delhi was the first university to establish a department just like other disciplines.

He started his library career in 1968. He was a youngman, barely twenty two years, when he joined MES College Library, Ponnani (Kerala). That was the time when libraries were in their early stage of development (there were no computers in libraries) and library education was in its infancy.

Period of growth in librarianship started in early sixties, when there was sudden growth of libraries and library education. The main reason was the allocation of funds for libraries in third five-year plan of Government of India. Another major factor was the support extended by UGC to libraries and library education. Many new libraries and library schools were started in sixties.

Period of modernisation started in early 1990s,

when modernisation of libraries started taking place. Government of India gave a thrust to application of information technology, through various incentives and UGC also gave liberal funding for establishing of computer laboratories. Library schools started revising their curriculum introducing courses on computer application in libraries and also included chunk of information science. It is also during this period that the library schools established computer laboratories for giving hands on experience to their students. This is also a period of consolidation.

Dr. Bavakutty retired from University of Calicut in 2007. Thus, his period of active service covers two important periods in the history of libraries and librarianship in India, namely, period of growth and period of modernisation. When he retired, libraries and librarianship had got well established. Now India is resurgent India. Indian society has entered the stage of knowledge based society. Libraries are getting due notice. Libraries are being modernized. Library education is well-established.

Dr. Bavakutty has been a part of the scene. He has been a witness and a leading participant in giving shape to libraries and library education in the state of Kerala. He was the first university librarian, Professor and Head of Library School at Calicut University. He has left his mark. It goes to his credit that Calicut University Library was the first university in Kerala to be modernized. He has left his legacy, which should be carried forward.

In 1969, he joined Master of Library Science at Department of Library Science, University of Delhi. At that time, I happened to be a lecturer in the Department. He was my favourite student. Since that time, I have been keenly watching his progress in teaching and librarianship. As a student, he was enthusiastic, well-behaved and highly intelligent. I was impressed by his sincerity of purpose and commitment to library profession. He showed early signs of leadership. He has been an ardent follower of Dr. S R Ranganathan. We are proud of his achievements.

He has been a pillar of support to library profession especially in Kerala. He was deeply involved in the activities of Kerala Library Association since his student days. He will be remembered for his contribution. I am sure, he will continue to serve the profession as a senior, giving advice and guidance to young professionals. Young professionals need mentors of his kind.

He has a multi-faceted personality. He has not only contributed to library profession but also in other areas as well. He has written number of articles in Malayalam. He was the chief administrator at Calicut University, being the Registrar, during 2000-2001.

He has served the profession in various positions for about four decades. Over the years, he has created a large following consisting of former students, colleagues, well-wishers and admirers. He richly deserves to be honoured through a festschrift volume, so that a rich tribute can be paid by his well-wishers and admirers. I feel proud to be associated with this venture.

May Almighty bless him with true happiness and long life to serve the profession in various ways.

August 18, 2007
Toronto (Canada)

Dr. M. Bavakutty as I Knew Him Over the Years

C.A. Augustine

Dr. Bavakutty has passed his 60th year of birth on July 15, 2006. In honour of him this festschrift volume has become very much appropriate and desirable. I feel that I am also honoured by the organisers of this project for wanting me to write my reminiscences about him.

I met Bavakutty for the first time when he joined the B.Lib.Sc. degree Course in the Department of Library Science in the University of Kerala in 1968. I was then one of his teachers in my capacity as a part-time Lecturer along with my regular position as Asst. Librarian in the Kerala University Library. But, in 1969 I moved over to the Department as a full time Lecturer in Library Science. Although Bavakutty was a young man of 22, shorter in stature than many, extremely humble and simple in many respects, he had evincive traits of leadership. Teachers as well as his classmates liked him and he was influential among them. His interest and enthusiasm in matters connected with the library profession were especially noticeable. This might be because of his prior working experience in the library of the MES College, Ponnani which gave him a first hand knowledge of the difficulties and disadvantages enjoined on the library staff in academic institutions in Kerala, particularly in a private college library. Perhaps, this gave him a high degree of motivation.

I still remember the enthusiasm he showed when we were working for an amendment to the Kerala University Bill 1968 which was being considered by the then Third Kerala Legislative Assembly. The late Janab C.H. Mohammed Koya was the Education Minister. A team of B.Lib.Sc. students organized by Bavakutty went round with me meeting the Minister and Legislators and educating them about the crucial need of giving teaching status to college librarians in Kerala. For this purpose we canvassed for relevant changes to be made in the Acts governing both the Universities of Kerala and Calicut. The work of Bavakutty and his classmates was the first organized operation in this direction. There were many such subsequent efforts organized by the professional library associations in Kerala but none of them bore fruit in the matter of the teacher status to librarians. I can recall a few names of Bavakutty's team mates in this campaign, like Pattiam K. Kumaran, Jayarajan, P. Ravidran, T.S. Antony, C.J. Kuriappan, M. George, C.P. Mammookoya, and Sr. Selka.

Bavakutty joined the M.Lib.Sc. degree course in the University of Delhi in the very next academic year (1969-70). In December 1969 my wife and I had to attend two conferences in Delhi. One was the Unesco Information Centre Organisers' Conference in the India Information Centre and the other was the National Conference on Information organised by the DESIDOC where we had a joint paper to be presented. This occasion we used to pay a visit to Mr. Bavakutty in the Delhi University Department of Library Science and spent a few hours together. I realized that Bavakutty was the very same personality with active involvement in both studies and professional matters. All his teachers and classmates were found to be specially affectionate towards him.

Immediately after securing the M.Lib.Sc degree, Bavakutty joined the Farook College, Calicut as its librarian. But, in 1972, he joined the Department of Library Science in the University of Kerala as a lecturer, and until 1977 he was there as my colleague and a close associate both in teaching work and organisational matters. At that time the Department was running only the B.Lib.Sc. Degree Course. In 1971 we had given shape to the new professional body called the Kerala Library Association (KLA). Bavakutty began to be actively involved in the work of the KLA and in our efforts at developing it to the status of a state wide professional body of librarians.

By then, our friendship and mutual concern had developed to a great extent. I observed in him, and also enjoyed at, his fast progress as a teacher. He was an ardent believer and follower of Dr. Ranganathan's fundamental ideas that shaped the discipline of Library Science, and it was this factor which made him integrate with the other teachers in the Department. Those in the Department and in the University Library, under the leadership of Prof Isaac who then headed both, worked as a single team for the benefit of the library profession. The Department used to conduct frequent seminars, conferences, short term courses, etc. These were occasions when the teachers in the Department especially could demonstrate their leadership qualities and subject expertise. Bavakutty utilized all these facilities pretty well. At least two important events in which Bavakutty showed his abilities, are: The All Kerala Seminar for School Libraries in Kerala which was held in January 1976 at

Trivandrum under the joint auspices of the Department and the State Institute of Education; and the other was the Indian Library Association South Zone Conference held at Cochin in May 1976. I, specially remember the help rendered by him in the production of the KLA National Library Week Souvenir 1976 which was edited by me.

Bavakutty, as a teacher, was dear to the successive batches of students during his tenure in the Kerala University. Bavakutty and I have travelled together several times while taking the students for their annual study tours. I still value very much his intimacy with me and his sacrificing readiness to shoulder responsibilities and to face the trials and tribulations in respect of the safety and comfort of the students we escorted. There were several crisis situations and risks which we together could very ably meet in protecting one and all of the students in the groups. I do not narrate any of them because I do not want to make this too long. In such study tours his usual complaint, I remember, was about the vegetarian food we often had to choose, and used to argue that at least one meal we should have without this 'eating grass and leaves'. Indeed, he has been a regular non-vegetarian in food habits.

Another aspect, which struck me, in his personality was his firm faith in Islam. He was never a fanatic but a practicing Muslim. Wherever he may be he never misses his prayers and religious observances. Even during conferences and seminars or workshops, in the Ramazan months I have found him abstaining from food while other participants eat and enjoy the rich food served in the venue. Such fasting never affected his activities. There is a passage in the Bible where Jesus preaches that one should not be a hypocrite while fasting: "And when you fast, do not put on a sad face as the hypocrites do. They neglect their appearance so that everyone will see that they are fasting. I assure you, they have already been paid in full. When you go without food, wash your face and comb your hair, so that others cannot know that you are fasting – only your Father, who is unseen, will know. And your Father, who sees what you do in private, will reward you." (Mtt. 6:16-18). Bavakutty reminded me of this Bible teaching as he used to be the same untiring and energetic person he was even during his fasting days.

Bavakutty left the services of the Kerala University in 1977 to join the Calicut University Library as its Deputy Librarian-in-Charge. This was a personal loss for me as he was so much a part of my academic activities. In Calicut, one of his immediate efforts was to start a Library Science teaching programme. He succeeded in this effort in 1978 and the B.L.I. Sc. course began to be offered under his own leadership. I remember that in the beginning years, I was also associated with this programme as a member of the Board of Examiners. At that time it was the practice that external examiners were invited to the University campus for centralised valuation of papers, conducting the viva voce, and finalizing the results then and there. Bavakutty's sincere concern for the academic attainments of the local students who came from mostly a backward environment.

After 1977, Bavakutty started working for Ph. D. as a part-time student in the Kerala University. He was awarded Ph.D. in the year 1984. Bavakutty continued to hold the Headship of the Department until 1997 when he was raised to the position of the University Librarian. He became the Professor of

Library Science in 1998. For some time, during the years 2000-01, he was also the Registrar of the Calicut University. Later, during 2001 and 2002, he functioned as the University Librarian and Professor & Head of the Department of Library & Information Science. In between the above periods, he was for some time, worked as Librarian in a special library in Saudi Arabia.

Thus Bavakutty had a distinguished career throughout. He proved himself equal to whatever position that was assigned to him. Those who knew him intimately will not vouch that his career was smooth and comfortable. He had many opponents and because of that he had to go through severe trials and tribulations which normally would have broken down anybody else in his position. But he could survive all these and come out successful in the end. Was it all due to his political identity, or some personal animosity towards him, or something else? This is not fully understandable. But, as a matter of fact, Bavakutty has been always a very good as a teacher, research guide, or organiser; a prolific writer and an active participant and contributor in professional deliberations, both at the national and international planes. He developed the Calicut University Library to such a status that at a point of time it was the only university library in Kerala having computerized catalogue and operations with Internet searching facilities. He taught many batches of librarians either at B.L.I.Sc. or M.L.I.Sc. level, successfully guided and produced several Ph.D.s, organised several national conferences, summer institutes, refresher courses, etc. He served on the Boards of Studies or Boards of Eaminers of many Universities in India. He authored about ten books at least, and about one hundred papers for journals or seminars/conferences, including international ones. He wrote on almost all subjects of importance for libraries and Library Science education. There were also his contributions in the local language – Malayalam. His long presence in the national and international library scenario has helped to gain due recognition not only for the University of Calicut but also for the whole library profession in Kerala.

Finally, even his so called enemies will agree that he had a very long and checkered professional career having, been a teacher for many librarians in Kerala, a leader in the library profession in many respects, and a person of wide and varied academic connections. Outside Kerala, if anyone ever remembers the University Library and the Library Science Department of Calicut, I am sure, it will be mostly in association with Dr. Bavakutty than anybody else. Such was the personality of Dr. Bavakutty.

Trivandrum

July 25, 2007

An Interaction with Prof. M. Bavakutty

T. P. O. Nasirudheen

Preamble : I should be very thankful to Prof. M. Bavakutty for giving me his valuable time and space in facilitating to gather a few insights into his personal life and distingushed career. I was one among the fortunate students Dr. Bavakutty has guided and supervised in their research work for doctoral degree in the Calicut University. I, am the one, who have closely witnessed the steadfastness and sincerity of our great teacher during all the ups and downs of his life. Hence I preferred, when I was called upon by Professor A. Amudhavalli, the Editor of this Festschrift Volume brought out in honour of Prof. M. Bavakutty, to contribute a brief biodata of his eventful life and career illustrated with consistent pursuit of knowledge and innovation, hard work and perseverance, leadership without compromise and a brilliant teaching profession. This input is drawn from my personal interview I had with Prof. Bavakutty for long hours. This is a humble attempt to share with my fellow professionals the path through which Prof. Bavakutty had travelled to accomplish his remarkable achievements despite odds, adversaries and hardships. I will be more obliged, if our young professionals appreciate this narration in its true professional spirit and come forward to rededicate their life for the cause of library profession as our great teacher and fellow professional Dr. Bavakutty has depicted a role model before us.

T P O NASIRUDHEEN (TPON) : *I would like you, Sir first of all to narrate your early life and education?*

M BAVAKUTTY (MB) : I was born in Ponnani in the North Kerala. I had my primary and secondary school education from the Maunathul Islam School in Ponnani itself and completed my secondary school examination in 1963. It was the last batch of 11 year schooling in the State. It may be surprising that I was the first person passed matriculation in my family. My parents were happy to know I had passed matriculation and were willing to send me for higher studies. But they being illiterate were not able to guide me and not many persons were there around us who had higher education. But I was fortunate enough to avail adequate guidance for higher education from my school teachers. Those who passed matriculation in our area during those days were looking for higher education in Farook College at Calicut, one of the premier colleges established in Malabar immediately after the Independence.

TPON : *Would you kindly explain your experiences while undergoing the graduate programme?*

MB : Fortunately I got admission to Pre-university course in Farook College. I was happy to have an opportunity for higher education in such a premier college in Malabar. An academically disciplined and conducive environment prevailed upon the campus under the Principalship of Prof. K. A. Jaleel who later became the Vice-Chancellor of Calicut University. I was staying in the Main Hostel on the campus which later became Azad Hostel named after Moulana Abul Kalam

Azad, the great scholar, freedom fighter and former Education Minister of Union of India. It was compulsory for all the students admitted to colleges to undergo training in National Cadet Corps (NCC). I was soon selected considering my experience for four years in the Auxiliary Cadet Core (ACC) during my school days as the Under Officer of the newly formed second NCC unit in the College. After passing *B* and *C* certificates, I became the Senior Under Officer of the NCC unit. During my study in Farook College for Pre-University and Degree courses I had attended many leadership camps at many places in India, the noted one among these was at Manali for 29 days in 1966. The training, that I received from ACC in my school days, NCC in the college and leadership camps had by the time made me truly a well disciplined young man. I successfully graduated in Mathematics with second class in 1967.

It was a common trend in those days among the young graduates of Farook College to go to the Aligarh Muslim University for their Master's Degree programmes as it was very difficult then to get admission to Post-graduate courses in any college in Kerala since very few colleges in the State were offering Master's Degree courses. But unfortunately I was not offered admission to the M. Sc. in Mathematics for which I had applied for as my application was misplaced in the University office. It was really a turning point in my life. Had I got admission, I would not have entered into the library profession but I would have become a Mathematics teacher.

TPON : *Would you please explain how did you start career in your life?*

MB : Those days the high schools in Kerala were desperately looking for even untrained teachers in Mathematics as there was scarcity of trained

Mathematics teachers. I applied for such a post in Oriental High School at Edavanna in Malappuram District. I was selected for the post and in October 1967 I joined the school as a Mathematics teacher. But, I could work only until to 31st March 1967 as I was not a trained teacher. However, it was my first appointment and I started my career as a high school teacher drawing monthly salary of a consolidated sum of Rs. 100/- in 1967-68 academic year. This short assignment of teaching for six months in a high school made me more interesting in teaching profession and seriously thinking about to undergo a teachers training programme and to take up the teaching career.

TPON : *Then what made you to acquire the qualifications in Library Science and how did you enter the library profession?*

MB : A Science and Arts college was started at Ponnani (my native place) in April 1968 under the management of Muslim Educational Society (MES), a voluntary charitable society working for the educational empowerment of Muslim and minority communities in Kerala.. I was already associated with the activities of the students' wing of MES and the Principal of the College was very familiar with us. I was the only one among these students having already graduated and others were degree students. One day, the Principal asked me to apply if interested for the post of librarian in the college which was lying vacant. Thus I was appointed as Librarian of the MES Ponnani College on 1st June 1968. That was my entry to the library profession. Soon after I joined the College, I was sponsored by the college for undergoing a Bachelor's Degree Course in Library Science in the University of Kerala at Thiruvananthapuram. Prof. Issac was the then Head of Department and the University Librarian.

Prof. M. N. Ramakrishnan Nair, Prof. C. A. Augustine and Prof. M. M. Job were the faculty.

TPON : *Would you please explain how was the Bachelor's degree in Library Science course delivered by the Department in the Kerala University?*

MB : It was the practice of the Department to conduct the theory lectures in the forenoon sessions and to let the students observe and work in the different sections of the Kerala University Library in the afternoon. This practice made us to properly understand the subject and to get trained thoroughly in the library profession. Such a practice was made possible and facilitated, I do still believe, only because of the one and same person was serving as the Head of Department and the University Librarian. I strongly advocate for the close and strong link to be developed between the Department of Library and Information Science and University/College library as the case may be as the Library and Information Science is a professional and practical oriented subject. Hence the students undergoing this course should be offered maximum practical training during the period of the course itself. Though it was recommended by the UGC and other agencies for these two entities to be separated from one another I still feel very strongly that they should work closer and hand in hand.

Earlier in 1960s and1970s, both the Department and University Library were headed by the one and same person in many universities. For instance Dr. B.V.R. Rao was the Librarian of Delhi University library and also the Head of Department. Prof. Rizvi in Aligarh Muslim University, Prof. Patil in Mysore University, Dr. J. S. Sharma in Punjab University, Prof. D.N. Marshel in Bombay University and Prof. Issac in Kerala University were some other personalities across the country to be cited for heading both the University Library and the Department. It was only later a trend was developed to get the Department separated from the University library system and it assumed an independent identity and status. Such a move has made these two institutions apart and no give and take was made between these two in the development and exchange of professional knowledge and experience. The students undergoing the Library Science course were the ultimate losers as they were not offered any observation and practical training in the library as part of the delivery of the course as it was practiced earlier.

While undergoing the Bachelor's Degree course in Library Science I was very much interested in doing the library classification theory and practice especially the Colon Classification scheme developed by Dr. S. R. Ranganathan, a mathematician turned librarian and library science teacher. The logical approach that I had developed while doing my graduation in mathematics may be one of the factors for my keen interest in Colon Classification. Prof. Issac taught us the library classification - theory and practice. The method of his teaching was excellent and inspiring. Looking at my keen interest and involvement in the classification practice, Prof. Issac often asked for the Class Number, I worked out for the given title in the class and the discussion developed around the Class Number involving the entire students in the class. I was able to obtain maximum marks in the classification practice.

Immediately after completing the Bachelor's Degree course in Library Science from the Kerala University, I resumed the post of Librarian in the M. E. S. Ponnani College where I left to undergo the Library

Science course. But, I was again to leave the College after a stint of only one and half month when I opted for admission to the Master's Degree Programme in Library Science in Delhi University.

TPON : *Sir, may I know of your experiences at Delhi University?*

MB : Yes, I was qualified with the Master's Degree in Library Science from Delhi University and I am proud to say that I am the first in the Malabar area of Kerala to have qualified the Master's Degree in Library Science.

It was my ambition to qualify a Master's Degree in the subject. I had taken much pain and challenges to fulfill the ambition. The interest and involvement I developed while doing Bachelor's Degree course in Library Science inspired me to pursue higher studies in Library Science. I discussed the matter with my teachers in the Department. Prof. Augustine encouraged and guided me in taking admission to Master's Degree course in Library Science which was offered those days only in Delhi University in the country. In June 1969, I applied for the entrance test in Delhi University and received after one month a call letter for an entrance examination required only for the external candidates. But I had only three days left to reach Delhi and train journey on those days was very tiresome. However I started for Delhi and reached Delhi University only in the forenoon of the day of the entrance test after a very tedious train journey. The Classification and Cataloguing theory test conducted in the forenoon session was over by the time I reached the University. On my request showing the call letter delivered to me only three days before, Prof. B.V.R. Rao, Head of Department of Library Science and University Librarian was well convinced and permitted me to appear the afternoon test in the Classification and Cataloguing practical test on condition that I should score 75% marks. Hence the Department arranged a special test for me in Library Classification and Cataloguing theory on the next day. I was one of the three candidates selected from among the external applicants for the year 1969-70, and the other two were Dr. K. S. Raghavan who is now Professor in Documentation Research and Training Centre (DRTC), Bangalore and Dr. V. S. Rasthogi who was the Deputy Librarian of Punjab University, Chandigarh.

During my stay at Delhi, I had visited major libraries such as Parliament Library, Sapru House Library, British Council Library, Jawaharlal Nehru University Library, USIS Library, Delhi School of Economics Library, Delhi Public Library etc. I had also visited on my study tour and closely observed the functioning of several University libraries in Punjab and Haryana such as Punjabi University at Patiala, Punjab University at Chandigarh, Punjab Agriculture University at Ludhiana, Kurushetra University etc. The life in Delhi University had also provided me an opportunity to enhance my communication skills – oral and written - in English language.

TPON : *Would you please explain the professional career soon after completing Master's Degree in Library Science?*

MB : It was my desire to become the librarian of Farook College, the great *Alma Mater* which was always a source of inspiration for my life and had played a significant role in shaping my career. I heard from my friends that Farook College had notified in some Malayalam dailies for the post of a qualified college librarian. Though very late, I sent an application to the Principal. Unexpectedly, I alone was called for the interview by the principal Prof. K.A. Jaleel and selected for the post of Librarian.

I joined Farook College on June 01, 1970. The Principal recommended seven increments and my basic pay was fixed at Rs. 200. I tried my best to reorganise the college library which I treated as my laboratory to practice whatever I learnt in the Library Science courses in Kerala and Delhi Universities. I was assisted by a qualified library professional and some other non-professional staff in all these efforts. The card catalogue was introduced with the entries prepared according to the Classified Catalogue Code of Dr. Ranganathan, who was alive then. The Librarian was given the membership in the Staff Council which usually consists of teachers only. I was also made the Warden of a students' hostel on the campus. Prof. K. V. Abdurahiman, a senior faculty in Economics was in-charge of the library, as per the practice then. I am proud to state that the practice of putting a senior professor in-charge of the library was done away with, after one year as the Management was convinced with my competence.

TPON : *Would you please explain your entry into the teaching profession in Library Science?.*

MB : After serving for a little more than two years as Librarian in Farook College I joined the Kerala University as Lecturer in Library Science on August 1st, 1972, in the leave vacancy of M. N. Ramakrihnan Nair who had left for the Calicut University to take the post of University Librarian. My colleagues in the Department namely, Prof. K. A. Issac, C. A. Augustine and M. M. Job were my former teachers and were very affectionate and kind enough to treat me as a young brother.

On the return of M. N. Ramakrihnan Nair, a vacant Reader post was converted into a lecturer post to accommodate me. Prof. A. Sreedhara Menon, the Registrar of the University and noted historian took special interest in this matter. I worked as a Lecturer in Kerala University for about five years, 1972 - 77. I taught Classification Theory and Practice, the two main subjects which Prof. Issac handed over to me out of his conviction that I would be able to teach these two courses effectively. I was involved in teaching with devotion and commitment. The *'Prolegomena to library classification'* by Dr. S R Ranganathan was a little difficult to understand by the students. This prompted me to write a text book *'Canons of Library Classification'* mainly based on class room teaching experience. This first book of mine also happened to be the first book to be published by the Kerala Library Association. The book was released by the Hon'ble Chief Minister of Kerala Sri. E. K. Nayanar in 1981.

TPON : *What about your association in the activities of library professional organisations?*

MB : Kerala Library Association (KLA), an association of library professionals in Kerala was in the formative stage during 1968-69. We, the students of Library Science of Kerala University were actively involved in the activities of KLA. I still recollect the good old days when the teachers and students under the leadership of Prof. C A Augustin had pooled all our energy and efforts to canvass for getting academic status to the college librarians when the Kerala University Bill was introduced in the Kerala Legislative Assembly for enactment. In early 1970s I was Joint Secretary of the Association for three years and M. M. Job, a senior lecturer in the Department was the secretary of the Association.

TPON : *Would you please explain your professional career in the Calicut University?*

MB : I had attended the interview for the lecturer post at the Calicut University in 1974. Unfortunately I was not selected for the post. This persuaded me to enhance my academic merits. Meanwhile, I was married on May 25, 1975 and planned to move near my hometown.

Prof. A. P. Srivasthava was the University Librarian of the Calicut University during 1974 -75. In fact, his initiatives to start a Department of Library Science could not be accomplished. Soon after his departure to Delhi University to take charge of University Librarian in 1975, Calicut University notified the posts of University Librarian and Deputy Librarian. M. M. Job and myself applied for the posts of University Librarian and Deputy Librarian respectively. Many candidates were called for the interview and only we two were selected for the respective posts. But, later Mr. Job preferred to continue in Kerala University itself and I could not join the Calicut University immediately as my appointment was stayed by the Hon'ble High Court of Kerala on a petition filed by one of the candidates. When the stay was vacated, I joined as Deputy Librarian holding charge of the University Librarian on March 28, 1977 and continued in that post for 10 years until appointed as University Librarian. It was a great opportunity for me to reorganise a University Library. One of my prime requests to Dr. Noor Mohamed, then Vice-Chancellor was to constitute an Expert Committee for preparing a long-term development plan of the University Library. An Expert Committee was formed with Prof. K A Issac as the Chairman and Mr. A. B. George, University Librarian of Cochin University of Science and Technology and myself as members. The University library was developed in the course of time as per the recommendations of this Committee. A staff structure was envisaged with nine Assistant Librarians and many other professional and non-professional posts were created for rendering a variety of library and information services.

Kerala University only offered the library science course in the state during those days. This prompted us to start teaching programme in library science in Calicut University in 1978. It was really a challenging task. The Board of Studies was constituted with Prof. K. S. Deshpande, Librarian, Karnataka University as the Chairman. Myself and the lecturer appointed earlier and a selective set of Assistant Librarians with Master's Degree were associated with the teaching. Prof. K A Isaac, Dr. K. S. Raghavan, Prof. C A Augustain and Prof. K. S. Deshpande were on the visiting faculty. I was very happy that I was able to start the Library and Information Science course within one year after I joined the Calicut University. My experience as a lecturer in Kerala University helped me in conducting the course. I continued to be the Head of the Library and Information Science teaching programme till 1985 when an independent Department of Library Science was established. During this period, the students had the benefit of having library work experience as an integral part of the course. Since 1986, after the bifurcation of the Department and the University Library this practice was dropped.

Meanwhile I was selected for the post of University Librarian in the Cochin University of Science and Technology in 1986. But I declined the offer due to my commitment to develop the Calicut University Library and make the Calicut University Library the first computerized University Library in Kerala. But, to my surprise my application for the post of University Librarian was rejected by the Calicut University authorities on the ground that I did not possess

Master's Degree in any other subjects, though I possessed Master's degree in Library Science and also a Ph. D. degree. The academic qualifications prescribed for the University Librarian was Masters degree in any subject with bachelor's degree in Library Science. I challenged the decision of the University in the Hon'ble High Court of Kerala. The Court stayed the selection process to the post and the matter was in the Court for one year. After a great legal battle, the University as per the UGC directions again notified the position of University Librarian and I was selected for the post in August 1987. Meanwhile, I had also obtained Master's Degree in Sociology through external study.

TPON : *Would you, please, like to share your research experience?*

MB : Over the time, competition and career opportunities grew. This motivated me to pursue my doctoral programme. Only a few library professionals and teachers with doctoral degree were available during 1970s in India. I tried in vain to register for Ph. D. under the supervision of Prof. C. D. Sharma of Punjab University who has got Ph. D. from U.S.A. and Dr. D. B. Krishna Rao of Madras University who was the first to have been awarded Ph. D. Degree in Library Science in India. Hence, I got registered for Ph. D. in 1976 in the Faculty of Education of Kerala University, as the Department of Library Science was not recognized as a research centre and no research guide was available in Library Science over there. I completed the research work for Ph. D. Degree on the topic "The Organization and Utilization of Libraries in Higher Education in Kerala" under the supervision of Dr. Gomathi Ammal, a senior member in the Faculty of Education of Kerala University. Prof. Issac offered me all the help and consented to be an informal co-guide for my research work. I had collected a large amount of data on the organization and services of college libraries in Kerala with a special reference to the colleges offering post-graduate courses. I owe very much to Prof. A. Sukumaran Nair who was then in the Faculty of Education in Calicut University and later became the Vice-Chancellor of Mahatma Gandhi University for having guided me in the research work and helped me to work out a pattern of data analysis, in the absence of doctoral theses in Library Science to rely upon. The research pattern of doctoral work is being widely adopted and referred to even now by many researchers and students of Library Science. I was awarded Ph. D. Degree by the Kerala University in 1984 and this happened to be the first doctorate in Library Science in Kerala. I became a research guide in Calicut and Kerala Universities in 1986.

Many professionals like Mr. S. Rajendran, Chief Librarian of Vikram Sarabahi Space Centre, Trivandrum, Mrs. Rosamma, Deputy Librarian of Calicut University, Mrs. M. D. Baby, University Librarian of Cochin University of Science and Technology, Sri. N. Sukumaran Nair, Deputy Librarian of Kerala University etc. registered for Ph. D. degree under my supervision. A total number of 12 library professionals and library science teachers were awarded Doctorate Degree under my guidance and supervision. Mr. Mohamed Tahir who was Assistant Librarian in American Studies and Research Centre, Hyderabad was the first to have been awarded Ph. D. Degree under my supervision by the Calicut University in 1989 and thus I happened to be the first research guide to bring out a Ph. D. awardee in Library Science in Kerala.

TPON : *You were offered a foreign assignment.*

Would you please share your experience abroad?

MB : In Saudi Arabia, I was assigned in October 1990, as chief librarian of the Research, Development and Training Centre of the Saline Water Conversion Corporation (SWCC), a Saudi Government undertaking located at Jubail, an industrial township developed about 600 KM north west of the capital city Riyadh. A large workforce of about 5000 men of different nationalities like Egyptians, Palestains, Indonesians, Pakistanis, Indians, Bangladeshis, Europeans, Americans etc. were working in the plant round the clock. We were provided all the living facilities with well furnished quarters and a good working environment. The assignment at SWCC gave me an opportunity to work in a highly sophisticated work environment where I had a plenty of experience of working with computers in Subject Indexing, Information Storage and Retrieval. The library was using a Canadian software for the database creation and other in-house library operations. I could create a bibliographical database of a large number of desalination research and project reports. The library had also a direct online connectivity with the King Abdul Azeez City of Science and Technology (KAACST) at Riyadh that provided us a direct link to the DIALOG on line information storage and retrieval system. The experience of working with the on line information retrieval systems provided me a very good exposure to such online systems and confidence to work in a computerized modern library environment. I worked in the Research, Development and Training Centre of SWCC for about five years.

TPON : *You were instrumental in organizing an All India Library Conference and many national seminars at Calicut University?*

MB : I had attended several All India Library Conferences organised by the ILA, IASLIC, UGC etc. at many places in the country and presented papers in many conferences. I was thinking all the time to organise such an all India conference of library professionals at Calicut where no such conference was held in the past. When I came back from Saudi Arabia in 1995, I did not fail to attend the annual ILA conference for the year held at Vijayawada where I had an opportunity to discuss with newly elected ILA functionaries the feasibility of conducting the next annual session of ILA at Calicut. Prof. P. N. Kaula, the honourable President and Dr. R. P. Kumar, Chief Librarian of AIIMS, New Delhi, the Secretary of ILA accepted my request and it was decided to organise the 42th Annual Session of ILA conference at Calicut University on 21-24 December 1996 on the theme '*Role of Libraries in National Development*'. I was the Organising Secretary of the conference. With the support and cooperation of the then Vice-Chancellor, academic and ministerial staff of the University the Conference was a great success in terms of number of participants and number of papers presented for discussion. The Calicut University campus witnessed for the first time such a large gathering of library professionals from across the country. Dating back in 1978, ILA had conducted one such Annual Session in Kerala at Trivandrum. The conference enabled us to save a pretty good sum of Rs.2.5 lakhs , thanks to a good number of sponsorships. This amount was placed as a separate library endowment fund maintained by the University with a set of guidelines to handle the fund. One was to facilitate with the dividend collected from this fund to sponsor two professionals of the University Library every year to participate in the annual session of ILA conference. Since then, several professionals in the Calicut University Library system could attend in rotation the annual session of ILA conference and present their papers. Second provision was to contribute substantially from this fund to meet the expenses of conducting an annual national seminar of library professionals at Calicut University. We had successfully organised four national seminars in subsequent years from 1999 to 2002 and we got published the volumes of the seminar papers.

The University Library organised a series of training programmes with 15 days duration for the selected school teachers in charge of school libraries. The programme was sponsored by the Department of Education, Govt. of Kerala. We could organise 15 such programmes with 50 school teachers being selected for each course during my tenure as University Librarian in 1980s. The course content includes library organization, management, classification and cataloguing, both theory and practice resulting in enhanced performance of these participants on their return back to school.

I was sponsored by the Calicut University to attend and present papers in many national conferences and seminars organised by the professional associations such as ILA, IASLIC, IATLIS and INFLIBNET etc. I attended and presented a paper in the Third World Congress of Muslim Librarians and Information Scientists held in October 1986 in Malaysia. I have also got opportunities to be Rapporteur/Chairman of several seminar sessions. I was very much associated with the annual CALIBER international conferences organized by the INFLIBNET. I also chaired one session in CALIBER at Madras in 2000.

I am associated with the recruitment of library professionals and Library and Information Science teachers by UPSC, UGC, Kerala Public Service Commission, several universities and other statutory bodies, organizations and institutions as an Expert for interview and evaluation. I am also associated with the UGC in conducting the NET examinations

TPON : *I understand that Calicut University pioneered in computerization of university libraries in Kerala under your leadership. Would you please share your views on this?*

MB : Computerisation of the Calicut University Library started immediately after the 42nd annual session of ILA conference in 1996. The exposure and experiences at SWCC in Saudi Arabia encouraged me to approach the Calicut University authorities with a proposal for computerization of University Library. The proposal was appreciated by the University and was sanctioned a sum of Rs. 10 lakhs from the plan fund for the first phase of computerisation. We started computerisation project with data entry. A few professionals in the library staff who are computer literate and really interested were put into force for library automation. Dr. Mohamed Salih, Information Scientist of the Calicut University Library and a couple of library professionals in the library were very actively involved in this computerization project. Not many software were available in those days for library automation and the available ones were too costly. With the limited funds available, we opted for the CDS/ISIS software designed by UNESCO for data entry that was available free of cost. The project almost took an year to complete the bibliographic database. The CDS/ISIS software does not have provisions for other library operations like issue, return, acquisition, serial control etc. So we converted the database into an integrated library software. LibSys was purchased in the second phase of computerization. We could purchase a few more computer systems and thus extend the computerization to some more service points in the different sections of the library. I could contribute substantially towards the computerization of the University Library and made it the first computerized University Library in Kerala. Now the library provides all the computerised library services including Infonet e-journal consortium services.

TPON : *May you please discuss your publication activities in your long professional career?*

MB : As stated earlier, the '*Canons of Library Classification*' was my maiden text book based on my teaching notes of Library Classification in the Kerala University. My second book '*Libraries in Higher Education*' was based on my Ph.D thesis. The third one in the series was a monograph on '*College libraries in India*' published by the MCT University Publications, London.

I had published several articles on various topics such as organisation, administration, public library movement in Kerala, public library legislation in Kerala, public library bill etc. in Malayalam dailies and journals. An article written on the life and work of Dr. S. R. Ranganathan on the occasion of his demise in 1972 and published in the weekend edition of Mathrubhumi daily was worthy to be noted. I had presented a good number of papers in national conferences/ seminars on different areas . I had edited along with my colleagues the five national seminar volumes that we could conduct after the 42th Annual Session of ILA Conference at the Calicut University and got them published. I also authored with my research students several books on a variety of topics we have selected for the research leading to Ph. D. Degree. I have so far brought out 12 books and monographs and more than 100 research papers in international and national journals and seminar volumes.

TPON : *Can you please share your experiences as University Registrar?*

MB : In December 1998, I was made Professor & Head of the Department of Library Science and also asked by the University to hold the charge of the University Librarian. I continued to hold both the positions of Professor of Library Science and University Librarian till I was relieved to take up the charge of Registrar by the University Syndicate on May 19, 2000. The Syndicate had unanimously decided to give me the charge of Registrar and had full confidence in me that I was capable of discharging the duty of Registrar. As I was in the office of the University Librarian and Head of the Department for a long time and as a Member/Chairman of Board of Studies, member of the Academic Council, Dean of Faculty of Humanities and member of University Senate, I was well aware of the University statutes and regulations.

During my tenure as the Registrar, I observed two main problems in the University administration. The first problem I noticed was that a majority of the administrative staff was not familiar with the University statutes and regulations. As a result the files put up from the sections before the higher authority was not furnished with the enabling provisions of statutes and regulations to support the notes drafted in the files. So every time I had to do a lot of home work going through the issues given in the file and referring to the University statutes and rules in appropriation to resolve the issues. As a result the decision to be taken by the higher authority was often delayed. The second problem I noticed was that staff was not adequately trained to make use of computers in the administrative routine. With the backdrop of a good exposure and training I had obtained in the application of computer and information technology in library field, I was well convinced of the immense potential of computer technology in the administration too. Hence, I initiated two types of training programmes for the administrative staff. One programme was meant to get the section clerks, section officers, assistant registrars, deputy registrars etc, acquainted with the university ordinances, statutes, regulations etc. and the other programme was meant for typists and stenographers working in the University administration to get trained in computer literacy skills and operation. The proposal for these two training programmes was approved and the training was delivered to the target groups in rotation without disturbing the normal office work. I am still proud to note that these two programmes I proposed and then organised for administrative staff have gone a long way in improving the quality of administration of the University. I consider, personally, that these were the two significant achievements I could bring about during my short tenure as the Registrar.

Meanwhile the Syndicate appointed a three member committee to look into the steps to be adopted as part of the austerity measures ordered by the Government of Kerala in the governance and administration of government departments, establishments, universities etc. On the recommendations of the Austerity Committee, the University decided to merge the two posts of Professor of Library Science and University Librarian into one inter alia the other measures adopted to maintain the austerity in the University administration such as to cut in the number of unnecessary posts. Similarly some other identical posts were also combined. I happened to sign this order of the Syndicate on the merger of these posts *inter alia* the other austerity measures.

I was in the post of Registrar for a short stint of one and half years. When a new Registrar took charge on 9th November 2001 I was relieved from the post to take up the responsibilities of Professor of Library Science and University Librarian.

The merged posts were again bifurcated in December 2002. Consequently, I relinquished the post of University Librarian and opted for the post of Professor of Library Science and continued the office till retirement on 31st March 2007.

TPON : *How do you evaluate the trend in Library Science teaching and research programmes in the country and the profession?*

MB : The syllabus of Library and Information Science courses in India ought to be revised and updated keeping the changes in the information environment across the nation and globe. It should be modified to give more importance in practical training in library and information services and to incorporate adequate content in subjects such as organisation of knowledge, structure of universe of knowledge, organization of bibliographic records, application of Information and Communication Technology etc. Special emphasis has to be given on web resources. I have got a genuine doubt why should we still teach the cataloguing rules to our library science students when some good library automation software are available in the field with adequate provision for entering the bibliographic data in the AACR, MARC, CCF etc. formats. Therefore course contents have to be thoroughly revised and updated and latest developments in the field have to be incorporated.

To be frank, there is a sharp decline in the quality of research work and in terms of production and evaluation of the theses. This is unfortunate. I strongly advocate that both the research student and the supervisor need to be sincere and committed in their work keeping themselves abreast with the latest developments in their research field lest the entire efforts put in would be in futile. I have always tried my best to be serious in the research work and to keep the quality of Ph.D. theses prepared under my supervision.

Library is a service oriented institution and the service is the watch dog of a library. Every effort in library profession and research should be focused mainly to improve the quality of service. One of the important areas in library and information science research to be identified therefore is the application of the appropriate measures and tools to sharpen the library services. ICT is one such tool being applied widely in library and information services. The main thrust of library science research should be always to provide the best services to the clientele. One should also understand the rapid changes taking place in the approaches of the users for information. Electronic information resources are becoming popular among users. Hence, detailed studies of various aspects of these resources have to be conducted.

TPON : *Lastly, your views on ICT, Please?*

MB : ICT, is of course, one of the important tools to provide an effective and efficient library and information services. Its merits and demerits are relative and take the merit of it and try to overcome its demerits.

TPON :Thank you Sir, for giving me your valuable time in sharing your professional experiences in your long and distinguished career of 39 years. I wish you and look for further fruitful contributions and pray for you and your family to be blessed with a long, happy and healthy life.

Calicut
October 01, 2007

List of Publications of Prof. M. Bavakutty

I. BOOKS & MONOGRAPHS

1. Canons of Library Classification. 1981. Kerala Library Association. Trivandrum.
2. Library Manual. 1982. Library Council. Calicut.
3. College Libraries in India; A case study. 1986. M C B University Press, London.
4. Libraries in Higher Education. 1988. Ess Ess Publications. New Delhi.
5. Management of Libraries in 21st Century, Ed. 2000. Ess Ess Publications. New Delhi.
6. Organisation of Libraries and Information Centres in 21st Century, Ed. 2001. Ess Ess Publications. New Delhi
7. Library Co-operation in a Networked World, Ed. 2001. Ess Ess Publications. New Delhi.
8. Information: Access, Management and Exchange in the Technological Age, Ed. Ess Ess Publications. New Delhi
9. Methods for Measuring Quality of Libraries. 2005. Ess Ess Publications. New Delhi.
10. Research on Computerisation of Libraries. Ed. 2006. Ess Ess Publications. New Delhi.

11. Information Search Pattern in the Electronic environment. 2007. Ess Ess Publications. New Delhi
12. Future Librarianship in Knowledge Society. 2007. Ess Ess Publications. New Delhi

II. PAPERS PUBLISHED IN INTERNATIONAL JOURNALS

1. "College Libraries in India." *International Library Review* (London). 1982. Vol. 14. pp 391-397.
2. "Library Movement in Kerala". *Libri* (Denmark). Vol.32(3), pp 251-255.
3. "School Libraries in Kerala". *International Library Review* (London). 1981. Vol. 13, pp 447- 451.
4. "College Libraries in Kerala; A Survey Report." *International Library Review (London).* 1982. Vol. 14, pp 437- 446.
5. "College Library Personnel in Kerala". *International LibraryReview* (London). 1986. Vol.18 (2). pp 187-193.
6. "Pay, Status, and Qualifications of Library Professionals in Indian Universities." *International Library Review* (London). 1987. Vol.19, pp 156 - 161.
7. "Acquisition of Scientific Literature in Developing Countries, India." *Information Development* (England). Vol.7(3). July 1991, pp 156 -163.

III. PAPERS PRESENTED IN THE INTERNATIONAL AND NATIONAL CONFERENCES / SEMINARS:

8. "Kerala Public Library Bill, 1974; A Critical Evaluation". Paper presented in the XII All India Library Conference. University of Delhi, New Delhi. 1976.

9. 'Organisational Pattern of School Libraries' Paper presented in All Kerala Seminar for School Libraries. Trivandrum. 5th – 7th January 1976.
10. 'Organisation of College Libraries. Centralisation Vs Decentralisation.' Paper presented in the Indian Library Association South Zone Conference. Cochin. 7 – 9 May 1976.
11. "Development of Public Libraries in Kerala; A Review Report". Proceedings of the 28th All India Library Conference. Lucknow. 1982. pp 141-147.
12. "College Libraries in India; Some Observations". Proceedings of the 29th All India Library Confeence. Mysore University, Mysore. 1983. pp 10-18.
13. "Development of Book Collection in College Libraries in Kerala". Proceedings of the 30th All India Library Conference. Rajasthan University, Jaipur. 1985. pp 177-180.
14. "Staff Pattern in College libraries in Kerala." Proceedings of the 31st All India Library Conference. Baroda. 1985. Pp 251-254.
15. "LIS Education in India; an Evaluation." Proceedings of the 16th IASLIC National Conference. Tirupathi. 1987. Pp 7-12.
16. "Microforms;Types and Uses." UGC National Seminar on Microforms. Sree Venkiteswara University. Tirupati. 1984.
17. "Flow of Islamic information Through Periodical Articles." COMLIS II International Conference. University of Utara Malaysia. Alorstar (Malaysia). 1986.
18. The Status, and Qualifications of the University Library staff. Conference of University Librarians. Osmania University. Hyderabad. 1986.

19. Quality of Library Collection in College Libraries. Proceedings of the 33rd All India Library Conference. S K University, Anantapur. 1987. pp 203-207.
20. Library Automation; Problems and Pitfalls." Proceedings of the 34th All India Library Conference. Bharathidasan University, Thiruchirapally. 1987. pp 73-79
21. Towards better LIS education. LIS Education Centenary National Seminar. Nagpur University, Nagpur. 1987.
22. Library and Information Science education in India; an evaluation. Proceedings of the 16th National IASLIC Conference Sree Venketeswara University, Tirupati. 1987. pp7-12.
23. The College Library. IATLIS National Seminar on Academic libraries. Gulbarga University, Gulbarga. 1988.
24. Techniques of evaluation of libraries. Proceedings of the 34th All India Library Conference. Calcutta. 1988. pp174-178.
25. Role of University Libraries in Distance Education. National Seminar on Distance Education and Libraries. Quilon. 1988.
26. College Libraries in Kerala, State of the Art. National Seminar on College Libraries. Delhi University, Delhi. 1988.
27. Role of National libraries in International Muslim Information Network. COMLIS III International Conference. Istambul (Turkey). 1989.
28. Continuing education for Medical Library Professionals. National Symposium and Workshop of Medical Librarians. New Delhi. 1995.

29. Management - Theme for Continuing Education Programme in Library and Information Science. IATLIS Annual National Seminar. Aurangabad. 1996.
30. Human relations in Resources Sharing Among Libraries. Proceedings of the 41st All India Library Conference. Vijayawada. 1996. pp. 269 – 272.
31. Retrospective data conversion in CHMK Library; A case study. Proceedings of the IV National Convention for Automation of Libraries in Education and Research. 1997. Thapar Institute of Engineering and Technology, Patiala. pp.72 - 74.
32. Internet services in Calicut University. Proceedings of the VI National Convention for Automation of Libraries in Education and Research. 1999.Nagpur University, pp 37- 44.
33. Application of Information Technology in Libraries: Practical experience in a University Library, Proceedings of the 45th All India Library Conference, 23-26. December 1999. Hissar, Haryana. Indian Library Association 1999, pp. 335 - 342.
34. Resource sharing through a computer based network in Calicut University campus, Proceedings of the VII National Convention for Automation of Libraries in Education and Research. 2000, University of Madras. Chennai, pp. 120 - 123.
35. Resource Sharing Among Academic Libraries in Calicut Region: a Proposal, Paper presented in the National Seminar on Organisation of Libraries and Information Centres in the 21st Century, held at University of Calicut May 26-27, 2000. pp. 39-46.

36. Library networks in the Internet era: In pursuit of strengthening resources and services, Paper presented in the National Seminar on Organisation of Libraries and Information Centres in the 21st Century, held at University of Calicut May 26-27, 2000. pp. 133 - 147.
37. Wireless networking in Libraries: a conceptual introduction. Paper presented in the National Seminar on Library Co-operation in a Networked World, held at University of Calicut May 25-26, 2001. Pp. 132-145.
38. Networking of public libraries in Kerala. Paper presented in the National Seminar on Library Co-operation in a Networked World, held at University of Calicut, May 25-26. pp. 175 – 183.
39. Public Responsibility for Public Library Funding and Networking: a case for the Kerala state. Paper presented in the National Seminar on Library Co-operation in a Networked World, held at University of Calicut. May 25 - 26, 2001. pp. 184 – 199.
40. Assessing the Quality of Information Sources and Services in Academic Libraries: a new Management Technique for Librarians. Paper presented in the National Seminar on Information Access, Management and Exchange in the Technological Age held at University of Calicut, May 28 – 29, 2002. pp 150 – 189.
41. Consortium of University Libraries in Kerala: a proposal. Paper presented in the National Seminar on Information Access, Management and Exchange in the Technological Age held at University of Calicut, May 28 – 29, 2002. pp. 211-222.

42. Measures for effective information services for the promotion of distance mode of learning. Paper presented in the National Seminar on Information Access, Management and Exchange in the Technological Age held at University of Calicut, May 28 – 29, 2002. pp 349 – 375.

43. Online information sources in Special Libraries in Kerala. Paper presented in the National Convention on Library and Information Networking (NACLIN 2004) held at University of Pune. November 23 – 26, 2004.

IV. PAPERS PUBLISHED IN PROFESSIONAL JOURNALS, FESTSCHRIFTS ETC.

44. Critical study of Kerala library Bill. *Yojana,* V 1 No (23), 15th June 1967', pp 6 -7.

45. Textbook productions in India. *Grandhalokam* V 22 (11). 1971, pp 35-36.

46. Library catalogue; Its use and functions. *Grandhalokam,* 1973, V25 (1&2). pp.17-20.

47. Books for all. *Chandrika Weekend Edition,* 22nd July 1972.

48. Books for all. *Grandha Logam,* V 24, p (3), July 1972. pp 19 - 20.

49. International Book Year. *Chandrika Weekly,* V 23. (5), 2nd Sept., 1972 pp 19-20.

50. Dr. S R Ranganathan, The father of Library Movement in India, *Mathruhumi Weekend edition.* Oct 15, 1972.

51. Books for all. *Grandhalokam.* V 24 (3). July 1972. pp. 19 - 20.

52. 'Nationalisation of Books import in India'. *Yojana,* V2. (8). pp 5 - 7.

53. Library Catalogue its use and functions. *Grandhalokam,* v 25 (12). 1973.

54. Role of Libraries in Education. *M. E. S. Students and Youth WingSouvenir,* 1974. pp. 65 - 66.

55. Paper Shortage in India. *Yojana.* V5 (6) 6 1974. pp. 18-20.

56. Tips for using Libraries. *Trivandrum Public Library Platinum Jubilee Souvenir,* 1974, pp 73-76.

57. Kerala Public Libraries Bill 1972: An Evaluation. *Library Herald* .V15, (3 & 4). March 1974 - Oct 75. pp. 146-50.

58. Evaluation of Libraries. *Kerala Library Association: National Library Week Souvenir,* 1974, pp. 73-76.

59. Treasures of Knowledge in Muslim India *Voice of Islam* V11. (20). 1975. pp. 25-26.

60. Requisite for an Ideal Public Library system in Kerala'. *Journal of Kerala Studies,* 1976, V 3, (3) pp. 169-178.

61. International Book Year. *Viswavignana kosham*— Malayalam Encyclopedia. V3.

62. Book Publication in India *M E S Journal.* V7, (6). Sept 10. 1976. pp. 5 & 6.

63. Super Imposition in Decimal Classification'. *Herald of Library Science.* V 15. (4). December 1976.

64. Partial takes over of the books import: Implications. Published in *Venkatappaiah, Ed. March of Library Science, Kaula Festschrift Volume.* Vikas, 1979. pp. 313 -319.

65. Classification of Bilingual Dictionaries according to Dewey Decimal Classification. *Herald of Library Science,* Vol. 18.(4). 1979, pp 255-259.

66. Organization of Newspaper cuttings *International Library Movement*, 1980, V 2. (3 & 4), pp. 86-90.

67. Structure of School Libraries. *Herald of Library Science*, Vol 20 (3 & 4), 1981, pp 230 –234.

68. Organization of College Libraries. *ALIS Bulletin*, 1981, V28 (1). pp. 28-32.

69. Library Classification *Grandhalokam*, Vol 33 (11). 1981, pp 15-18.

70. Libraries the Centre for Education, *Grandhalokam* 1982, V 34. (1), pp. 52-55.

71. Books the Friends of Wisdom *Grandhalokam*, 1982 V 34 (4). pp. 31-32.

72. Britannica 3: Treasure of Knowledge *Grandhalokam*, 1982, V34 (8). pp. 31-42.

73. Role of Libraries in Higher Education. *ALIS Bulletin* Vol.7. 1983. pp 6 – 10.

74. College Libraries in India. In : *Gupta B M et al., Ed. Handbook of Libraries, Archives and Information Centres in India.* Vol. 1, New Delhi. Information Industry Publishers, pp. 81-91.

75. Expenditure of the College Libraries in Kerala, *ILA Bulletin* 1984, V19(4), pp. 128-131.

76. Incentives to Teachers for using College Libraries in Kerala, *Herald of Library Science*, 1985, V24, (1 & 2). pp. 22 – 25.

77. Incentives for the use of College Libraries, *IASLIC Bulletin*, 1985, V30(2). pp. 55- 59.

78. Public Library setup in Kerala In : *Rout R K Ed. Library Legislature in India.* New Delhi. Reliance Publishing House. 1986. pp. 223 -229.

79. College Libraries, How it should be? *Library Herald*, 1986, V24 (3&4), pp. 219 - 226.

80. Librarianship and Library Science Education in Kerala' In : *Souvenir on Library Movement in India published in connection with 34th All India Library Conference,* Calcutta, December, 1988.

81. Public Libraries in Kerala In : *Rajagopalan T S, Ed. Years Work in Indian Librarianship.* 1987. Delhi, Indian Library Association. 1988. pp. 37-40.

82. Status and qualifications of University Library Staff. In : *Inamdar, B and Ramaiah, L S, Ed. National Policy for University Libraries in India.* New Delhi, Concept, 1988. pp. 129-136.

83. School Libraries. In : *Mangla, P B. et.al., Ed. Fifty Years of Library and Information Services in India.* New Delhi, Shilpra. 1988. pp. 101 -104.

84. College Library finance. In : *Sewa Singh, Ed. Librarianship and Library Science Education.* New Delhi, Ess Ess Publications. 1988, pp. 101-106.

85. Use of library by the students In : *Shukla. K H and Majumdar, K J, Ed. Trends in Library and Information Science.* Jaipur, RBSA Publishers. 1995, pp. 91 -96.

86. School Libraries in Kerala In : *Vijayakumar, K P and Sukumaran Nair, N, Ed. School Libraries and Educational System with School Library Compendium.* Trivandrum, Kerala Library Association. 2001. pp. 51-57.

87. Library and Information Services in Kerala, In : *Jain, M K, Ed. Library and Information services in India, states and territories,* New Delhi, Shipra, 2001. pp. 183-190.

88. Web Authoring; A 'must' skill for the information professionals at the dawn of the new millennium.

Annals of Library and Information. 2002. V49(4). Pp. 151 - 165

89. Radio Frequency Identification in Libraries; Prospects and Retrospect. In 'Knowledge Organisation in Digital Environment in Libraries'. Delhi. ILA. 2004. pp. 377 – 381.
90. Restructuring Library and Information Science Curriculum, In : Library and Information Studies in Cyber age: *Essays in honour of Professor J L Sardana.* S M Dhawan, Ed. Delhi, Authors Press, 2004. pp. 29-34.
91. Library Consortia in India; Initiatives and concerns. *SRELS Journal of Library Management.* 43(2), June 2006, pp. 177 –184.
92. Who has to judge the quality of College libraries? Librarians or users? *Kelpro Bulletin* Vol. 10 (1). June 2006. pp. 52-55.
93. Measuring the quality of libraries; Role of SERVQUAL . In : Bavakutty, M et. al, Ed. *Future Librarianship in knowledge Society* .New Delhi. Ess Ess. 2007. pp.187- 97.
94. Knowledge Management System for a Multi Campus University. In : Bavakutty, M et. al, Ed. *Future Librarianship in knowledge Society.* New Delhi. Ess Ess. 2007. pp. 349 -60.

List of Contributors

Abdul Azeez, T A
Dy. University Librarian
Sree Sankaracharya University of Sanskrit
Kalady, Kerala.

Abdul Majeed, K C
Lecturer Selection Grade,
Dept. of Library & Inforamtion Science
Farook College, Feroke, Calicut.
kcamajeedfc@tcs.com

Agale, Ajit
Information Officer,
Library & Info Centre,
Tata Consultancy Services, Mumbai
ajit.agale@tcs.com

Amudhavalli, A
Professor & Head
Dept. of Information Science,
University of Madras, Chennai.
amudha75@yahoo.com

Augustine, C A
Retd. HOD,
Dept. of Library & Information Science
University of Kerala, Trivandrum

Aswath, Lalitha
Professor, Dept. of Library & Information Sc., University of Bangalore, Banglaore.

Bakkannanavar, Nagappa V
Branch Head, Library & Information Centre
Tata Consultancy Service
Hi-tech City, Madhapur, Hyderabad.
nagappa.b@tcs.com

Birdar, G S
Asst. Librarian
Gulbarga University P.G. Centre, Raichur.
Gurusb75@yahoo.co.in

Chandrakumar, V.
Lecturer, Dept of Information Science
University of Madras, Chennai-600005

Chattopadhyay, Samir
Documentation Assistant, Rabindra Bhavana, Visva-Bharati, Santiniketan-731235

Das, Subarna Kumar
Senior Lecturer, Dept. of Library and Information Science
Jadavpur University
Kolkata-700032

Dhiman, Anil Kumar
Information Scientist
Gurukul Kangri University
Hardwar (Uttarakhand).
akvishvakarma@yahoo.com

Govindani, Anju
Assistant Librarian
Medi-cps Institute of Technology &
Management, Indore.
anjugovindani@rediffmail.com

Hamsa Kalyani
Assistant Librarian
National Institute of Advanced Studies
Indian Institute of Science Campus, Bangalore

Hazra, Asis Kumar
Library-in-Charge, Rabindra-Bhavana,
Visva-Bharati, Santiniketan-731235

Horannavor, Sukeshin
Information Specialist, Global Consulting
Tata Consultancy Services, Mumbai.
sukeshini.horannavar@tcs.com

Humayoon Kabir, S
Assistant Librarian (Senior Grade)
Cochin University of Sc. & Tech., Kochi
humayoonkabirs@yahoo.co.in

Jaideep Sharma
Associate Professor,
Department of Library and Information Science
IGNOU, New Delhi.
j_sharma2002@yahoo.com

Kanthimathi, S
Librarian (Senior Grade)
Rani Anna College, Tirunelvelli, T N

Karisiddappa, C.R.

Professor & Chairman
Dept. of Library & Information Science
Karnatak University, Pavate Nagar, Dharwad.
karisiddappa@yahoo.com

Kemparaju, T D

Chairman, Dept. of Lib. and Information Sc.
Bangalore University, Bangalore.

Keshava

Dept. of Library and Information Science
Karnatak University, Dharwad .

Krishan Kumar

Retired Professor and Head
Department of Library and Information Science
University of Delhi, Delhi.
krishan14@hotmail.com

Mahawar, K L

Reader & Head,
Dept. of Lib. & Infor. Science
BBA University, Lucknow.

Manjunatha, K

Librarian,
T.A. Pai Management Institute, Manipal.
manjunath@mail.tapmi.org

Mohamed Haneefa, K

Librarian,
T K M College of Engineering, Kollam.

Mohammed Sageer, T K
Asst. Librarian
Sree Sankaracharya University of Sanskrit
Kalady, Kerala

Nagarajan, M
Professor, Dept. of Library & Inforamtion Sc.,
Annamalai Uni., Annamalai Nagar-608002

Naik, R R
Gulbarga University P.G. Centre,
Gulbarga University, Gulbarga, Karnattaka.

Nasirudheen, T P O
Head, Dept. of Library & Inforamtion Science,
Farook College, Feroke, Calicut.

Navalur, Santosh A.
Information & Knowledge Management Trainee
National Centre for Science Information (NCSI)
Indian Institute of Science, Bangalore- 560012
santosh@ncsi.iisc.ernet.in

Nayak, Savita N
Consultant, Tata Consultancy Service (TCS)
Hyderabad.
savi2606@gmail.com

Neelameghan, A
Hon. Visiting Professor, DRTC/ISI
Bangalore 560 059
anm2002@vsnl.net

Raghavan, K S
Professor, DRTC/ISI, Bangalore 560 059
raghavan@drtc.isibang.ac.in

Rajashekhar, T B (Late)
Former Chairman
NCSI, Indian Institute of Science, Bangalore.

Rajgoli, Iqbal Ahmad U
Scientific Assistant
Library, ISRO HQ, Antariksh Bhavan
New BEL Road, Bangalore.
iqbal786@isro.gov.in

Sampath Kumar
Head, Dept. of Statistics
Manonmaniam Sundaranar University
Tirunelvelli, TN

Samyuktha, R
University Librarian I/c,
Madras University Library, Guindy Campus,
University of Madras, Chennai.
Sam007@yahoo.co.in

Sangam, S L
Professor, Dept. of Library and Information Sc.
Karnatak University, Dharwad .

Satyanarayana, N R
Professor, Dept. of Library and Information Sc.
University of Lucknow, Lucknow.

Sharma, Jaideep
Associate Professor
IGNOU, New Delhi
J_sharma 2002@yahoo.com

Shivalingaiah, D
Professor, Dept.of Lib. & Infn. Science,
Mangalore University,
Mangalagangotri, Mangalore.
d_shivaling@yahoo.com

Sivaraman, P
Dept. of Library & Inforamtion Science
Annamalai University,
Annamalai Nagar-608002.

Surulinathi, M
Research Scholar, Dept. of Library &
Inforamtion Science, Annamalai University
Annamalai Nagar-608002.

Varalakshmi, R S R
Professor, Dept. of Lib. & Info Science
Andhra University, Visakhapatnam 530 003

Varghese, Rekha Rani
Guest Lecturer, Dept. of Lib. & Infor. Science,
University of Kerala. Thiruvananthapuram.
rekha_tcr@yahoo.com

Verma, Rekha
Librarian, M.B.P. Govt. Degree College,
Lucknow.

Verma, Shilpi
Lecturer, Dept. of Lib. & Information Science,
BBA University, Lucknow.

Vijayakumar, K P
Lecturer (Selection Grade)
Dept. of Library and Information Science
University of Kerala, Thiruvananthapuram

Vimalkumar, V
Asst. Librarian, Asian School of Business
Technopark, Thiruvananthapuram
Vimal0212@yahoo.com

Vinitha, K V
Librarian, NEC, Tirunelvelli. T N

1

Library and Information Science Education in India

Some Observations

K.C.Abdul Majeed

ABSTRACT

Library and Information Science (LISc) education is aimed to develop competent professionals to manage libraries and information centers scientifically. The quality of LISc professionals depends upon the quality of the professional training offered in LISc schools. This paper is an attempt to discuss the existing LISc education systems existing in India. It discusses the history and existing condition of LISc schools, the level of education, course content, important studies already conducted and the competency of the professionals developed in the country. The paper concludes with some observations.

1. INTRODUCTION

Library and Information Science (LISc) courses are aimed to develop and supply library and information managers with adequate knowledge and skills for doing necessary library and information works and services with the support of modern information and communication technologies. The basic aim of LISc education is to provide students with the appropriate knowledge and skills that will enable them to perform in a satisfactory way as professional librarians. UGC Library Science Review Committee [1] viewed that the aim of LISc education is to give a sound professional education to graduates in the scientific management of Libraries and Information Centers (LICs).

LICs are aimed to collect, process, organise, retrieve and disseminate information needed for the users. It is the place where the people visit for getting their information or documents. LICs, in general, are aimed to meet the information requirements of the users. There are many kinds of LICs with varying aims and objectives. Broadly, LICs can be categorized into three groups: viz., 1. Public libraries; 2. Academic libraries; and 3. Special libraries. Public libraries are the libraries run by the public to meet the information and document requirement of the public. Similarly, academic libraries are aimed to support the teaching-learning activity in educational institutions like school, college, university and research centers. Special libraries are the libraries catering special group of users or specialize in a subject field or form of documents. The face of these LICs is changing drastically due to the developments in printing and publishing technology, computer and communication technology, storage technology and the like.

Modern LICs are a combination of four major components: viz., 1. Information Sources/Documents; 2. Information Seekers/Users; 3. Information managers/Professionals; and 4. Information Technology/Computers. The shape and form of documents, interest and tastes of users, required skills of Library and Information professionals, and the technology we use are changing day-by-day. Though the aims and objectives of traditional and modern libraries and information centers are same, the components vary greatly.

In modern LICs *Information sources* are printed or non-printed, electronic, digital or online. The print sources include textbooks, reference books, periodicals, conference proceedings, reports, patents, standards, etc. Similarly, the non-print sources include maps, atlases, dissertations and theses, official communications, etc. The electronic sources are in the form of audio/video cassettes, micro-film/fiche, punched cards, etc. The digital resources include information stored in CDs/DVDs, computer hard-disks, etc. The online resources are nothing but the digital resources accessible through online. The effectiveness of the library depends on the utility of the information sources it acquires. The information sources vary from library to library according to the purpose to be served and the category of users served.

Information seekers/Users are the people who visit the library for want of some information. They seek information for some purpose. The purpose may be sometimes educational, informational, recreational or for use in their work. The LICs have to meet the general and specific needs of the information seekers or users. There should be a good mechanism through which the taste, interests, requirements etc. of the users are studied and necessary actions are taken to meet their requirements in desired manner. It is to be noted that there is a growing awareness about information and there is great change in the way people find, use, learn and communicate information. Moreover, the information explosion in the present era necessitates special training to users in searching, locating, retrieving and using correct information from the ocean of information.

Information managers or the *LISc Professionals* are responsible for selection, acquisition, processing, storage, retrieval and dissemination of information or its sources to the information seekers with the support of modern information and communication technologies. They should have adequate knowledge and expertise in library and information works, services, information sources, information technologies, and the management of these components for the attainment of its goal.

Information technology is becoming one of the major components of modern LICs. It is commonly used for information collection, storage, processing, search, retrieval and dissemination. Computers and communication technology is largely used in modern LICs to carry out different activities and services, information storage and retrieval and communication or dissemination of information. It resulted in the development of computerised libraries, digital libraries, virutual libraries, etc. Modern LICs are a combination of these new forms of libraries.

2. CHANGING SCENARIO OF THE LIS PROFESSION IN INDIA

In the early years of *librarianship* (the early name of the profession), the professionals were trained to select, order, acquire, accession, classify, catalogue, and maintain printed source of information and provide lending and reference service. This was continued till the concept of documentation was conceived and practiced in libraries to provide pinpointed services to the specialist users. It resulted in the development of advanced and mechanised information services like indexing and abstracting services, bibliographic service, translation, and reprographic service. In order to train the professionals agencies like DRTC, INSDOC (now renamed as NISCAIR), etc. were developed. It led to a change in focus of libraries from documents to information and emphasise was given to the collection, processing, storage and dissemination of information. Accordingly, the new name was conceived by the profession, **Library and Information Science** (LISc) profession. Though there are remarkable changes in LISc works and services and in the name of the profession, no immediate and remarkable change has come in the focus, library and information works, and services. It is mainly due to the non-inclusion of these changes in the LISc course curriculum followed in the country at that time.

Meantime, there are many applications of theories, practices, tools and techniques etc. from other fields. One of the earliest applications is the principles, theories and techniques of *management* in the management of LICs. It was Ranganathan who applied scientific method in the library field for the better organisation and management of library activities and services. It led to a change in the nomenclature of the profession from librarianship to **Library Science**. Similarly LICs have adopted the theories and principles of *Behavioural Science* (Psychology) very early in the study of users and the stakeholders. *Statistics* is another important subject the LICs use regularly in the evaluation of their activities, services and performance. LISc research makes use of the statistical methods, tools and techniques largely in the tabulation, analysis, and presentation of the research data.

The modern era is known as *Information*

Technology era. In every walks of life computer and its allied technologies is used for one or the other purpose. LICs are one of the major organisations enjoying the fruits of information technology accompanied with its counter part, the *communication technology.* Modern LICs are either partially or fully applied information technology. It uses computers for house keeping operations and services. With the help of communication technology LICs are developing and enjoying the benefits of cooperation through one or the other kinds of networking like LAN, WAN, etc. Now *Internet* is considered as one of the major sources of information for our users. Moreover, LICs are now accessible through internet and Library websites and Digital Libraries are common on Internet. In this LICs are not waiting for their users, instead it goes to the user and serve required information to them at home or at work place.

Today we witness the inflow of electronic and digital media. The LICs are collecting, organising, storing, retrieving and disseminating electronic/digital information on large scale. Modern LICs are shrinking in its physical size and expanding its field of work, information base, users and services. At a time, modern LICs deals with print resources, electronic/ digital resources and maintain digital libraries and library website.

Other concepts of serious concern includes marketing, quality, benchmarking, information flow, information audit, information consolidation and repackaging, intellectual property right, security, content creation, digital divide, and many.

Many changes have already occurred in the traditional profession and many things added. This process is a continuous phenomenon. The LISc professionals in the present era should be competent enough to manage print resources, electronic/digital resources, digital libraries, and library websites. They should also be capable of managing the activities and services of traditional, computerised, or online LICs. According to Mahapatra [2], the LISc profession of the present era should be aimed to: provide training for building up leadership qualities among the LISc profession; develop knowledge on the latest techniques of information storage, transfer and retrieval; help to acquire necessary skills in handling, accessing and use of electronic resources, tools and media; and help to know the latest developments in the Information Technology (IT).

Following skills are required for LISc professionals to work/ manage modern LICs:

1. Skill for identifying and meeting the information needs of the users.
2. Skill for identifying, accessing, organising, interpreting and evaluating information and its sources.
3. Skill for communicating with colleagues, other professionals, management and users.
4. Skill for using information technology in works and services.
5. Skill for managing the resources, technology, staff and users.
6. Skill for teaching and training the staff and the users.
7. Skill for evaluating the performance and quality of works and services.
8. Skill for exploring Internet.
9. Skill for developing and managing digital libraries and library websites.
10. Skill for developing and maintaining quality

Modern LISc education should be aimed to impart the afore said skills to the professionals. Corresponding to the changes in the profession and in the activities and services of LICs, there should be equivalent changes in the professional training provided in LISc schools also. In this context, an attempt is to be made to see how far the present LISc education system in India is capable of developing professionals with necessary skills required for work and manage modern LICs in the country.

3. LIBRARY AND INFORMATION SCIENCE EDUCATION IN INDIA

In India, the first attempt for LISc education was made by Maharaja Sayaji Rao Gaekwad, the ruler of Baroda state, for creating a cadre for the newly established public library system of Baroda state. Accordingly, William Alonson Borden, a disciple of Dewey, established a training course at the Central Library, Baroda in 1911 [3]. Similar to this, the Librarian of the Punjab University, Asa Don Dickinson, another student of Dewey, started the second training course in LISc in Punjab University, Lahore in 1915. This was considered as the second LISc school (the first is Columbia University) in the world started a formal course in LISc [4]. Gradually other universities and library associations in the country started setting up of LISc schools.

In the pre-independence era, there were about six schools in the country offering various kinds of LISc courses. They were: Madras Library Association (1929), University of Madras (1931), Bengal Library Association (1935), Andra University (1935), Banaras Hindu University (1941), and University of Delhi (1947). Madras Library Association was known to start the first

Certificate Course in LISc in India under the leadership of Dr. S.R. Ranganathan. Later it was took over by the Madras University and subsequently converted into a one-year postgraduate Diploma course in 1937. University of Delhi was the first university in India started offering courses leading to M. Phil and Doctorate degrees in LISc [5]. The introduction of one year P.G. Diploma course at University of Madras was served as a model for the development of library science education programmes in the country during the pre and post independence periods until 1950s.

In post-independence period, many universities, colleges, institutes, library associations and libraries came forward to set up LISc schools in the country. In the 1970s, there were about 42 schools which have increased to 167 in 2006 [6].

The courses offered by the universities at various levels are [7]: Certificate in Library & Information Science (CLISc), Diploma in Library & Information Science (DLISc) and Post Diploma in Library & Information Science (PDLISc), Honors in Library and Information Science, BLISc, one year MLISc, 2 year integrated course in MLISc, M.Phil, Ph.D. in Library & information science, Certificate in ICT application in Library (CICTAL), P.G. Diploma in Library Automation and Networking (PGDLAN), etc. Beside these courses, various advanced level short-term training programmes are being offered as a part of continuing education programmes. These courses are run by the institutions/ organizations such as: NISCAIR, New Delhi; SAARC DOC. Centre(SDC), New Delhi; IFLIBNET, Ahmedabd; NASSDOC, New Delhi; DELNET, New Delhi; IIM, Lucknow, SENDOC, Hyderabad, and various Library and information science associations like ILA, IASLIC and universities [8].

At the Bachelor's degree level, LISc courses are conducted by 87 universities/colleges and at Master's degree level, MLISc is offered by 89 universities/ colleges, while Ph.D. in LISc is offered by 52 universities. Eight universities and 12 colleges offer CLISc programmes and six universities and six colleges offer DLISc programmes in the subject [9].

The Aligarh Muslim University offers LISc as a subsidiary subject to Batchelor of Arts course. Similarly, the University of Hyderabad offers Post Graduate Diploma in Library Automation and Networking (PGDLAN). Above to these, some universities in India offer LISc courses on distance mode [10]. The number of LISc schools offering CLISc/ MLISc/M. Phil/ Ph.D level courses in regular and distance mode are in an increasing trend.

LISc is a professional course and offering the course without necessary practical training is against to the professional ethics. Every professional course must contain practical training in the real setup as an important part of the course. Unfortunately, the LISc professional course lacks it even from its inception. The past has made it a professional but theoretical course and so the LISc schools in the country offer this professional course on distance mode. Through that we produce professionals without sufficient knowledge and training in the field and so they will be less competent to manage modern LICs.

4. COURSE CONTENT

In general, the LISc schools offer CLISc, BLISc, MLISc, Mphil and Ph.D level courses. The course content of each of these courses is more or less same in the country. They are discussed below.

4.1 Certificate Course in Library and Information Science (CLISc)

The CLISc/CLIS contains the following topics:

1. Libraries and Society.
2. Library Management.
3. Classification of Books.
4. Cataloguing of Books and Journals
5. Information Sources and Services.

The classes are mainly theoretical, not practical. Practical training is limited to classification and cataloguing. In most of the cases, the classes are handled by less competent faculty/ trained librarian. Normally the CLISc holders are not getting any exposure or training on latest tools and techniques, sources and services. As a result they are not competent enough to manage a library or work in a computerised library or to do any job on digital libraries or library websites. They are supposed to be the supporting staff of professionals working in modern LICs. Unfortunately in Kerala, those who qualify in the CLISc examination are eligible for appointment as the fourth grade librarian of libraries attached to government departments, and educational institutions like schools and colleges. They can manage small public libraries, but they are not competent to manage libraries attached to important institutions like schools, colleges, etc.

4.2 Batchelor of Library and Information Science (BLISc/ BLIS) Course

The course content of BLISc course includes the following topics.

1. Library, Information and Society.
2. Management of LICs.

3. Information Sources and Services.
4. Information Technology (Theory and Practice)
5. Classification of Books (Theory and Practice)
6. Cataloguing of Books and Journals (Theory and Practice)
7. Library records (Tour Diary, Evaluation of Information Sources, Library Catalogue, Bibliography and Fact finding).

The course content of BLISc is not sufficient enough to meet the present requirements of LICs such as computers, networking, digital libraries, Internet, indexing and abstracting, bibliography compilation and advanced information services. However, they can manage small libraries with limited IT applications. In Kerala, one who qualified in BLISc degree examination is eligible for appointment as a librarian in the I, II, III and IV grade libraries and as a junior librarian or a professional assistant in university and special libraries. This is one of the major reasons for the poor performance of the LICs in the state. For meeting the requirements of modern LICs a revision of the course content is must.

4.3 Master of Library and Information Science (MLISc/ MLIS) Course

LISc schools in India offer one year/ two-year integrated MLISc course. The first year of the integrated MLISc course contain more or less the same content of BLISc course. The content of one year/ second year of the integrated MLISc course contains the following aspects:

1. Universe of Knowledge, its development and structure.
2. Information Systems and Services.

3. Information Storage and Retrieval.
4. Research Methodology and Bibliometrics.
5. Information Technology (Theory and Practice).
6. Information Processing (Theory and Practice).
7. Dissertation and Viva Voce.

The Associateship course in Information Science, equivalent to the MLISc course, contains the following areas:

1. Information Society and Information Communication.
2. Sources of Information.
3. Information Processing and Organization.
4. Information Systems and Services.
5. Information Products and Services.
6. Information Technology.
7. Information Systems Management.
8. Elective paper (Research Methodology, Informetrics and collateral areas, Business Information System, Patent Information System, Geological Information System, Medical Information System, Technical Writing, etc.)
9. Dissertation and Viva Voce.

In these courses, the professionals get basic knowledge about the universe of subjects and its formation and organization; local, national and international information systems and its services; collection, storage and retrieval techniques; tools and techniques of collecting, tabulating, analysing and presenting research data; computer hardware and software suitable for libraries, and training in development of database and library website; depth classification using UDC and advanced cataloguing (cataloguing of micro-documents, composite books, cartographic materials, sound recordings, video recordings, maps etc.). The MLISc holders are not getting enough training to manage library networks, content creation, digital libraries, computerized house keeping operations, Internet browsing, www, open sources, metadata, etc. required in advanced LICs.

Those who qualify in the MLISc examination with 55% marks and National Eligibility Test conducted by the UGC are eligible for appointment as assistant librarian in University libraries, librarian in first grade college libraries and information officer/documentation officer in special libraries and lecturer in LISc Schools. Lack of properly trained faculties in teaching and research greatly affect the quality of teaching and research in LISc Schools in the country.

4.4 M. Phil and Ph. D Programme

M. Phil and Ph. D programme is offered in many of the universities, colleges and institutes in India. The duration of M. Phil course is one year. The students have to specialise in one or two topics and have to prepare and submit a dissertation at the end of the course. The students are also trained in teaching. M. Phil courses are supposed to be meant for working professionals to improve their qualifications. Now there is an increased demand for the course in accordance with the change of eligibility for UGC scale from UGC-NET to M. Phil or Ph. D degree. Some of the LISc schools in the country offer M. Phil course on distance mode.

Research is a serious work that leads to the award of Doctor of Philosophy in the subject. Availability of research guides and their knowledge and experience in research decide the quality of the researcher and their findings. Good guidance is the pre-requisite of any good research. The quality of research depends upon the knowledge and experience of the research guide, the research scholar, and the research topic selected. The training on dissertation work attained at the time of post graduation greatly influences the work of a research scholar. A well-guided research scholar of today will be a good research guide of tomorrow. Quality of research in LISc and its application in LICs are yet to be investigated. Satija [11] viewed that the research results are not seriously used to solve the problems of LICs in the country.

5. OBSERVATIONS

Many studies have already been conducted on LISc education in the country. The eminent personalities like Prof. Kaula, Prof. Seetharama, Prof. P.S.G. Kumar etc have made important comments on the present education system in the country. They have also given valuable suggestions for the improvements. They have studied important aspects like method of teaching, course content, faculties, provision of practical training, use of information technology in education, etc.

Prof. Kaula [12], a decade ago, studied the condition of LISc schools in the country offering various courses in LISc and observed that: "more and more institutions and libraries are opening library science courses without having even the minimum facilities for teaching. Even with poor libraries and funds they have started M.L.I.Sc. Programmes. In some universities there are not full time teachers to teach B.L.I.Sc. courses and yet some of them have also started M.L.I.Sc. programme. Open universities have also started [M/]B.Lib. Sc. programmes. Some private colleges have been conducting large number of C. Lib. Sc. programmes with little or practically no facilities for books and libraries. This uncontrolled growth has brought down the standard of the courses. Library associations have also been having large intake of students without accessing the employment opportunities of the products".

Prof. Seetharama [13] had studied the course content of LISc courses and found that: "it is ironical that while the Department of Library Science has changed their names as "Department of Library and Information Science", they have done precious little in reorganising their curriculum. As a matter of fact, these new named departments continue to teach what they have been teaching all these many years". Similarly Arora and Mujoo-Munshi [14] viewed that "while libraries in India are increasingly using services and products of new IT, the library schools in India are slow in restructuring their curriculum in the light of the changes taking place due to potent technological revolution. Fresh Library science graduates find themselves completely bewildered when they happened to be in libraries using computers and other products and the new IT services".

PSG Kumar [15] had commented about the method of teaching followed in LISc schools in India that "Chalk and talk are the only means of communication in almost all the library schools. Educational technology is yet to enter into our library schools". Keeping in mind the importance of practical training in LISc education, Kaula [16] noted that "LIS departments have little or no understanding and cooperation with the central library ... The problem is more psychological than academic ... Much harm has been done to the teaching of library science by the disharmony ....".

In view of the emerging network environment, fundamental shift in the goals of the library, and the changes in information storage and delivery mechanisms, the Curriculum Development Commitee (CDC) had stressed the need for change in LISc course contents, and the knowledge and skills required to function LICs effectively in such environments. The model curriculum designed by the Karisiddappa Committee [17] made maximum efforts to incorporate a considerable number of IT components required for modern LICs. The report provides six core modules and one elective module. The modules are:

1. Foundations of Library & Information Science;
2. Knowledge Organization, Information Processing and Retrieval;
3. Information Sources, Products and Services;
4. Management of Libraries & Information Centers/ Institutions;
5. Information Technology: Basics and Applications;
6. Research Methods and Statistical Techniques; and
7. Electives. (The electives belong to the study of different specialized subjects, e.g., Business Information System, Environmental Information System, Agricultural Information System, etc.)

There are a number of practical papers introduced such as:

1. Knowledge Organization, Information Processing & Retrieval Practice;

2. Information Technology—Basics (practice);
3. Information Sources and Services (practice);
4. Information Retrieval (practice); and
5. Information Technology: Applications (practice).

Though regular assessment of LISc education in the country is going on and reports are coming, much change has not come to the LISc courses, its content, method of teaching, practical training, etc. Moreover, some of the universities in the country have started to offer the LISc course as private study also. Altogether the LISc education system in the country leads to loosing professionalism to the LICs and its professionals. The problem is becoming more serious due to the following:

1. Most of the LISc schools are not well competent to supply properly trained LISc professionals in information technology, computerized library works and services, Internet etc. required for modern LICs.
2. The professionals coming out of the LISc schools do not have necessary communication and administrative skills required to manage modern LICs.
3. The professionals do not get proper training in information technology, computerised information storage and retrieval systems and services and the like needed in advanced LICs.
4. The course contents are inadequate to meet the requirements of modern LICs.
5. Most of the faculties are not well trained and experienced in advanced library and

information works and services, teaching and research.

6. The distance mode of LISc education results in less qualified and trained professionals.
7. The present requirements of LICs are not at all considered in teaching and training of new professionals in LISc schools.
8. Traditional method of teaching is still followed in most of the LISc schools in the country.
9. Lack of proper guidance in dissertation work and the research leads to low quality research in the field.
10. Lack of in-service training makes the course non-professional.

LISc is a fast developing subject and undergo many changes due to the application of computers, communication, and related technologies. The so-called "modern LICs" are transforming to computerised libraries/electronic libraries/digital libraries/virtual libraries. But even today, we are teaching and training the students traditional topics like classification, cataloguing and bibliography compilation. The Special Library Association [18] has rightly said that though the professionals of modern special LICs require good knowledge and training in information sources, information management, information access, information systems and technology, research and information policy, very few LISc schools in the country are providing training and education in these areas. Though the course contains papers on computers and information technologies, adequate training in a library environment is found absent.

6. SUGGESTIONS

Based on the above discussions, the following suggestions are put forward to improve the LISc education in the country:

1. The LISc schools should be equipped with fully qualified and experienced professionals as faculties.
2. The LISc schools should be attached with a good library acting as the laboratory for the students.
3. The distance mode of LISc education should be restricted to working professionals alone.
4. The course content should be revised to meet the requirements of professionals in modern LICs.
5. Practical training, at least for one month in a good library, should be included as part of the CLISc/ BLISc/MLISc course .
6. Self-study reports of various kinds of libraries should be included as part of the course work.
7. IT based teaching and learning system should be introduced.
8. The CLISc holders should not be given the duty of managing LICs of any kind and size.
9. The LISc course should not be offered as private study.
10. Students with good communication skill, management skill, service mind and hard working nature should only be selected for the LISc courses.

7. CONCLUSION

It is to be seriously noted that a reduction in the quality of LISc education will adversely affect the functioning of modern LICs and the profession.

Sufficient knowledge and training should be given to our new professionals in latest library and information management techniques and services. The LISc schools should study and evaluate the performance and quality of the professionals produced by them. They should take necessary steps to revise the course contents to cope up with the requirements of modern libraries. The state and central governments should make necessary initiatives to standardise and update the course content and the syllabus regularly. The UGC should take necessary measures to strengthen the LISc schools to meet the challenges and requirements of LICs. It should appoint a team of experts to study the adequacy of LISc schools to offer different levels of LISc courses and to avoid unnecessary proliferation of incompetent schools in the country. This is must for up-lifting the performance of LISc schools, the LICs in general and the LISc profession in India.

REFERENCES

1. Ranganathan, S.R. (1965). Report of the Library Committee of University Grants Commission. New Delhi: UGC
2. Mahapata,G. (2006). LIS Education in India: Emerging Paradigms, Challenges and Propositions in the Digital Era. Presented at the Asia-Pacific Conference on Library & Information Education & Practice 2006 A-LIEP 2006), Singapore, 3-6, April 2006, p. 3
3. Raina, Roshan Lal (2005). Innovation Continuing Professional Development Programme for LIS Professional conducted by the Library at IIM, Lucknow. *In:* World Library and Information Congress, Library voyages of discovery. Norway: IFLA, p. 2
4. Batta, Bidyarthi and Das, Anup Kumar (2001). Higher Education in Library & Information Science in India. *ILA Bulletin,* 37 , p. 25
5. ibid.
6. Mahapata,G. (2006). LIS Education in India: Emerging Paradigms, Challenges and Propositions in the Digital Era.

Presented at the Asia-Pacific Conference on Library & Information Education & Practice 2006 A-LIEP 2006), Singapore, 3-6, April 2006, p. 3

7. Association of Indian Universities (2004). Handbook on Library and Information Science. 2nd Edition . New Delhi: AIU, p. 99
8. Mahapata,G. (2006). LIS Education in India: Emerging Paradigms, Challenges and Propositions in the Digital Era. Presented at the Asia-Pacific Conference on Library & Information Education & Practice 2006 A-LIEP 2006), Singapore, 3-6, April 2006, p. 3
9. ibid.
10. www.lisgateway.com. (Accessed on 07.08.2007)
11. Satija, M.P. (1999). Doctoral Research in Library and Information Science in India. *Libri,* 49, p. 236
12. Kaula, P.N. (1992). Hundred years of Library and Information Science Education. *In:* Library and Information Science in India /edited by P.S.G. Kumar and C.P. Vashisth. New Delhi: Sterling Publishers, p. 10
13. Seetharama, S. (1987). Knowledge Skill and Role of Future Information Professional Implications of Information Technology. *In:* Education for Special Library and Information Work / edited by S.K. Kapoor. Calcuta: IASLIC, p. 87
14. Arora, J and Mujoo-Munshi, U. (2000). Accepting the Challenge of Information Technology: Reinventing the Library and Information Science Profession in the New Millenium: *In:* Proceedings of SIS Conference, p.11
15. Kumar, P.S.G. Some Issues in Education for Librarianship in India. *In:* Education for Special Library and Information Work / edited by S.K. Kapoor. Calcutta: IASLIC, p. 13
16. Kaula, P.N. (1992). Hundred years of Library and Information Science Education. *In:* Library and Information Science in India / edited by P.S.G. Kumar and C.P. Vashisth. New Delhi: Sterling Publishers, p. 10
17. Karisidappa, C.R.(2004). Library and Information Science Curriculum for Developing Countries. *In:* World Library and Information Congress, Buenos Airs, Argentina, p. 9
18. Special Library Association (1988). Competencies Survey: focus on Special Libraries. *Information Outlook*

2

Knowledge Management

A Paradigm Shift in Organizations

Ajit Agale
Sukeshini Horannavar

ABSTRACT

Organisations need to harness the individual knowledge of their members and apply it in organisational processes to create economic value, combining these individual memories to form a collective organisational knowledge. To get the most value from a company's intellectual assets, Knowledge Management practitioners maintain that knowledge must be shared and serve as the foundation for collaboration. The consulting companies who need to harness the existing knowledge must encourage knowledge management for better performance.

1. INTRODUCTION

The modern world is characterised by dynamic changing markets and continuous technological advances. To cope with these trends, organizations must be more flexible and strengthen their potential to learn as organisations. Thus 'Knowledge' becomes an essential driver in value creation.

Quite understandably, the world is seeing a shift towards knowledge-based organisations that empower the people to get into the continuous learning mode. In such a situation, the management of knowledge is fast becoming a process of creating value from knowledge that is otherwise an intangible asset in the organization's balance sheet. In order to become a learning organization, knowledge must be viewed as the most valuable corporate asset. As knowledge is getting treated as an asset, the need for its management has become more pronounced.

Sharing of knowledge, process assets, and best practices forms the bedrock of knowledge management. Selective knowledge transfer, to intellectual elite, is slowly but surely giving way to a shared vision of knowledge in firms. Such a knowledge warehouse is akin to the firm's digital nervous system. The old adage of 'knowledge is power' has to crumble. It is for us to collectively abolish this myopic archetype and encourage knowledge sharing as a new paradigm towards collective intellectual capital.

Organizations must have the capability of capturing rich experiences and encourage reusability rather than reinventing the wheel every time. In successful companies around the world, knowledge is prudently embedded in products, services, concepts and processes which, in turn, lends a strategic advantage to the business. As a matter of fact, state-of-the-art knowledge inputs are essential for the process of continuous research and innovation in products and services. Therefore, it is hardly surprising that knowledge management is becoming as important as the business itself.

2. KNOWLEDGE MANAGEMENT AND ITS APPROACHES

There is a broad range of thought on Knowledge Management with no unanimous definition current or likely. But still it can be explained as follows:

'Knowledge Management is the art of creating value from the intangible assets of an organization. Knowledge Management tries to facilitate employees' access to knowledge whenever it is required for the effective development of their activities'.

'Knowledge Management is the targeted coordination of knowledge as a factor of production and the management of the organizational environment top support individual knowledge transfer and subsequent creation of collective knowledge. Knowledge Management is therefore not just the management of knowledge itself, but rather the management of organization with a particular focus on knowledge'.

Knowledge Management may be viewed many of the perspectives. Following are the most widely identified approaches to Knowledge Management :

Techno-centric Approach : Focus on technologies, ideally those that enhance knowledge sharing/growth, frequently any technology that does fancy stuff with information.

Organisational Approach : How does the organisation need to be designed to facilitate knowledge processes? Which organisations work best with what processes?

Ecological Approach : Seeing the interaction of people, identity, knowledge and environmental factors as a complex adaptive system.

Combinatory Approach : Combining more than one of the above approaches where possible without contradiction.

A conceptual framework of the Knowledge Management Processes is illustrated in the Figure 1:

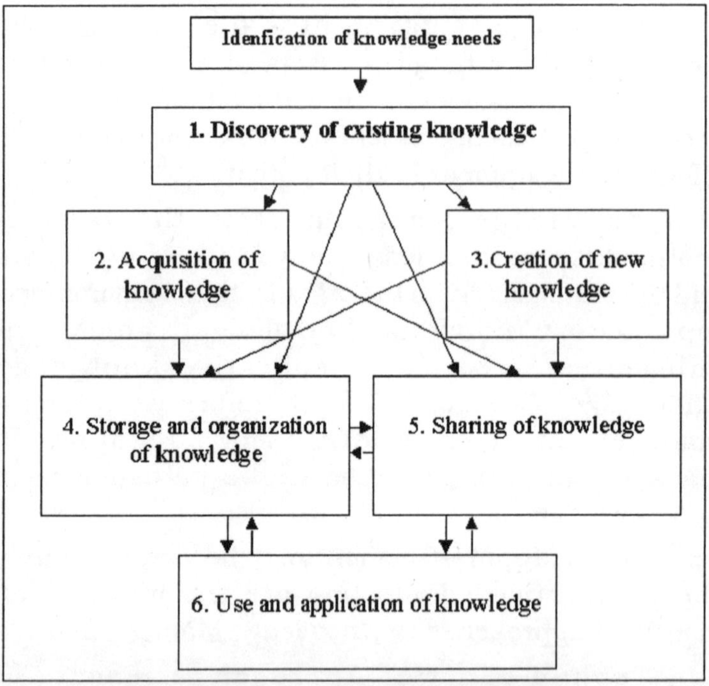

Fig. 1. Knowledge Management Processes

3. ORGANISATIONAL KNOWLEDGE

Organisations need to harness the individual knowledge of their members and apply it in organisational processes to create economic value, combining these individual memories to form a collective Organisational Knowledge Base, which plays a decisive role in the process of Knowledge Management.

This is far more than just a database. It represents

the interaction and communication among the employees.

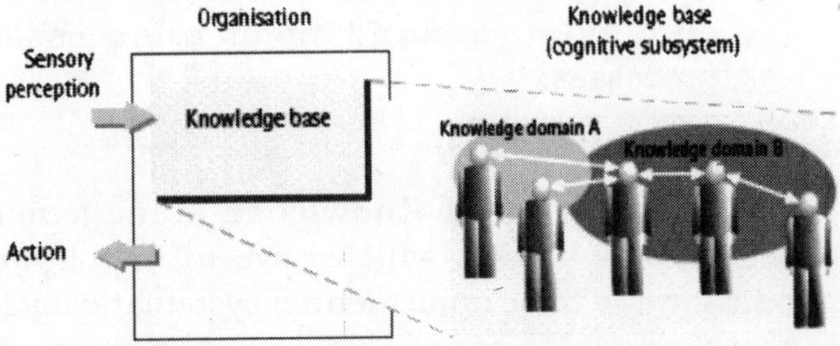

Fig. 2. Organisational Knowledge

4. ORGANISATIONAL KNOWLEDGE MANAGEMENT

In today's information-driven economy, companies uncover the most opportunities — and ultimately derive the most value — from intellectual rather than physical assets. To get the most value from a company's intellectual assets, KM practitioners maintain that knowledge must be shared and serve as the foundation for collaboration. Yet better collaboration is not an end in itself; without an overarching business context, KM is meaningless at best and harmful at worst. Consequently, an effective KM program one should help a company do one or more of the following:

- Foster innovation by encouraging the free flow of ideas
- Improve customer service by streamlining response time
- Boost revenues by getting products and services to market faster
- Enhance employee retention rates by

recognizing the value of employees' knowledge and rewarding them for it

- Streamline operations and reduce costs by eliminating redundant or unnecessary processes.

5. IMPLEMENTATION

Implementation of Knowledge Management involves various phases which have to be followed methodically and to be implemented systematically for the Knowledge Management programme to be successful. Figure 3 is an indicative diagram for the process of Knowledge Management implementation.

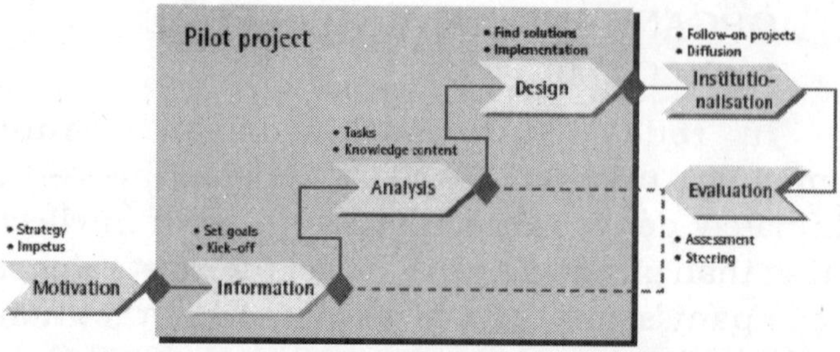

Fig. 3. Knowledge Management Implementation Process

Following are the pre implementation processes that need to be undertaken carefully before proceeding with the actual implementation process of Knowledge Management:

5.1. Knowledge Management Assessment

The aim of Knowledge Management assessment is to measure the benefits to the organisation of any Knowledge Management activities. The basis for this assessment is a selected range of relevant measures derived from the basic model of Knowledge Management. The purpose of assessment is to evaluate the extent to which an individual measure influences the organisation's ability to meet stakeholder goals.

Thus organisation is able to determine the actual contribution a particular Knowledge Management activity makes to meeting stakeholder expectations and at the same time illustrate the real benefits generated by Knowledge Management. The assessment is carried out in seven steps, viz.:

5.1.1. Identify target assessment area

5.1.2. Establish target criteria

5.1.3. Define the ideal situation

5.1.4. Determine factors of influence

5.1.5. Identify drivers

5.1.6. Prioritize fields of action

5.1.7. Set measures

This way knowledge management assessment offers organisations a systematic method of determining the relevance of individual fields of action and setting priorities for Knowledge Management activities.

5.2. Approaches to Introducing Knowledge Management

Two key success factors in the successful implementation of Knowledge Management are willingness on the part of the employees involved and a methodological approach to any of the initiatives. If either of these aspects is ignored, there is an increased risk that the project will not achieve its goals. Willingness comes from those aspects of corporate culture that allow the members of an organisation to act appropriately in a given situation, such as motivation and values. Methodology, on the other hand, highlights the use of particular procedures and concepts knowledge management.

The typical phases under which each

implementation process undergoes in any kind of organization are discussed below:

5.2.1. Initiation Phase

Knowledge Management can be introduced either for historic reasons or to plan for the future, i.e. as a direct consequence of the urgency of the situation or as a strategic management decision. Whatever the reason, everyone should be informed of this decision before any definite steps are taken.

The first definite step towards Knowledge Management often takes the form of a pilot project. A pilot project should ideally be targeted at a particular division or group of employees that is comfortable dealing with change and new challenges. It should also directly everyone who will play a part in or might be affected by any measures introduced. In general, the selection of any key areas for knowledge management should concentrate primarily on knowledge intensive processes critical to company success.

The next stage is to set the goals for the pilot project. These might include:

* Improving knowledge transfer in selected areas
* Improving access to data and knowledge
* Encouraging the use of creative potential
* Activating previously untapped or unused knowledge

Thus setting clear goals and involving everyone concerned are two major success factors in the introduction of knowledge management.

5.2.2. Analysis Phase

The pilot project begins with a kick-off meeting, at the end of which the following points should be clear:

* The expectations of everyone involved in the project and the project goals.
* The project plan, required measures and milestones.

In the analysis phase, selected processes are analyzed with a view to the goals set. Thus the introduction of knowledge management does not simply become the end in itself; it ties in directly with the company's business activities and processes.

This requires a detailed representation and segmentation of the processes involved. The following figure explains the same:

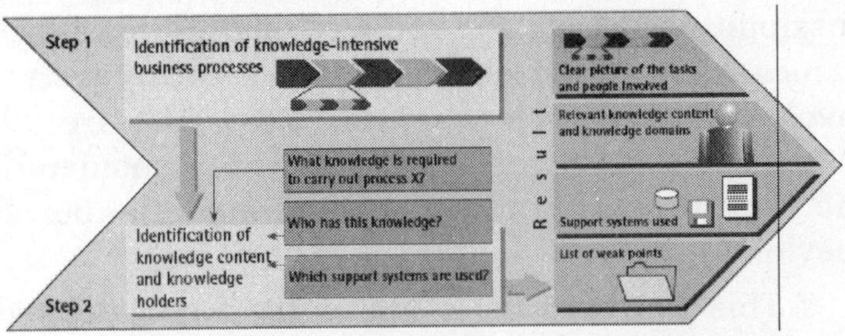

Fig. 4. Steps involved in Analysis Phase

The following questions should be considered in the detailed analysis :

* Which sub-processes are particularly knowledge intensive and/or complex?
* Are there any areas in which knowledge transfer is known to be problematic?
* Which areas of the process are essential for value creation?
* Which knowledge forms the basis of the skills and expertise in this division?

The analysis phase thus provides with:

* A clear picture of the tasks and knowledge holders involved in each individual process.

* A reconstruction of the knowledge base and key knowledge domains.
* Overview of nay tools or support systems used.
* A list of weaknesses.

These results should be presented to all those who are involved in or affected by the knowledge management process.

5.2.3. Design Phase

In the subsequent design phase, the results obtained in the analysis phase can be turned into specific measures. If the weaknesses outnumber the possibilities open to the project team and its defined framework, a joint decision must be made by everyone involved in the project on the areas that are most relevant or urgent. This should take into consideration the work they will involve and the potential benefits they offer.

This weighted list of measures forms the basis for the implementation schedule. The implementation phase should also the inputs from all those who are connected with the knowledge management process. This identification process can be seen as a creative, team based knowledge generation phase (Figure 5).

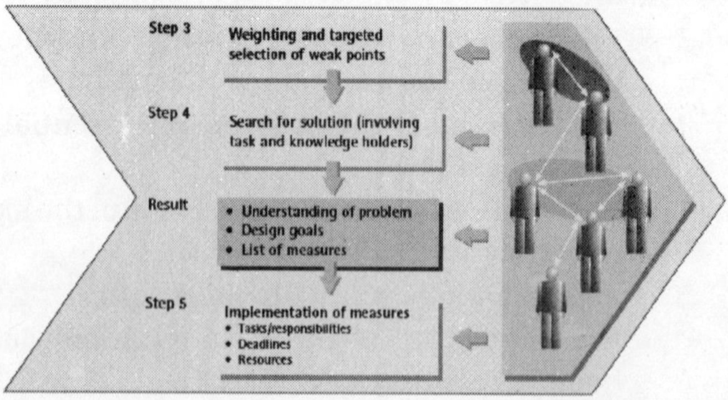

Fig. 5. Steps involved in Design Phase

The design measures can be grouped into three main categories:

* Human
* Organization / Culture
* Support System / Tools

It is common in knowledge management that the only measures ultimately introduced are on support system level.

6. KNOWLEDGE MANAGEMENT IN CONSULTING FIRMS

The implementation of knowledge management in any consulting firm would typically begin with the training of people either through one-to-one mentoring or train a group of people through computer based distance training. But all the companies do not take a uniform approach to managing knowledge. Fig. 6 explains the processes involved in knowledge management in any consulting firm.

The consulting business employs two very different knowledge management strategies. In some companies, the strategy centres on the computer. Knowledge is carefully codified and stored in databases, where it can be accessed and used easily by anyone in the company. This is called the *codification strategy.* In other companies, knowledge is closely tied to the person who developed it and is shared mainly through direct person-to-person contacts. The chief purpose of computers at such companies is to help people communicate knowledge, not to store it. This is called the *personalisation strategy.*

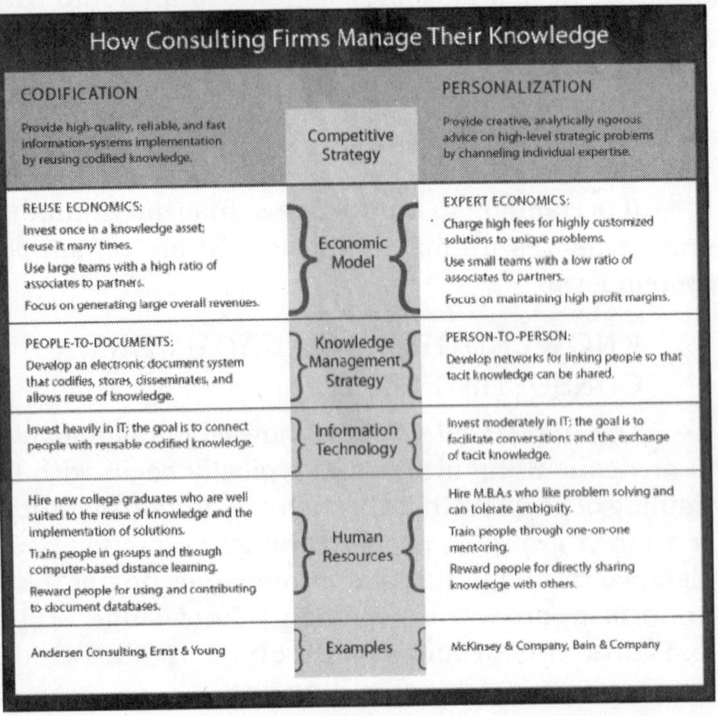

Fig. 6. Knowledge Management in Consulting Firms

Codification Strategy : Knowledge is codified using a "people-to-documents" approach. It is extracted from the person who developed it, made independent of that person, and reused for various purposes.

The codification strategy opens up the possibility of achieving scale in knowledge reuse and thus of growing the business.

Naturally, people-to-documents are not the only way consulting firms share knowledge- they even do have personal one to one interaction. But however the degree of emphasis they place on the codification strategy.

Personalisation Strategy : It focuses on dialogue between individuals, not knowledge objects in a database. Knowledge that has not been codified and/ or couldn't be is transferred in brainstorming sessions and one-on-one conversations. Consultants collectively arrive at deeper insights by going back and forth on problems they need to solve. To make their personalisation strategies work, consulting firms invest heavily in building networks of people. Knowledge is shared not only face-to-face but also over the telephone, by e-mail, and via videoconferences.

A company's knowledge management strategy should reflect its competitive strategy: how it creates value for customers, how that value supports an economic model, and how the company's people deliver on the value and the economics. In short the whole strategy of knowledge management should support the overall development of the organisation.

7. KNOWLEDGE MANAGEMENT - A CASE STUDY

Tata Consultancy Services (TCS) is the world-leading information technology consulting, services, and business process outsourcing organisation that envisioned and pioneered the adoption of the flexible global business practices that today enable companies to operate more efficiently and produce more value. It commenced operations in 1968, when the IT services industry didn't exist as it does today. Now, with a presence in 34 countries across 6 continents, and a comprehensive range of services across diverse industries. Seven of the Fortune Top 10 companies are among our valued customers.

Consulting being the main concern of TCS, it always looks towards making the consulting process more value driven and knowledge oriented. With the advancement of time TCS has realized the importance of knowledge and its utilisation in its development. TCS has implemented knowledge management approach in its various processes.

Following is the summary of the approach followed by TCS in knowledge management implementation:

7.1. Building a Knowledge Base

* Best practices in creating and using a knowledge base for sustainable growth and differentiation of offerings
* How do we create, manage and sustain this knowledge base. What are the best practices in this area?
* Study the process by which offerings like Quartz or NCS became differentiators, and how can this be made a repeatable process?
* How is the knowledge base related to the market on a continuing basis to generate new offerings and differentiators?
* How do we build all corporate knowledge into a 'Corporate Repository' which can be 'mined' in a collaborative fashion by different Industry and Service Practices and by the different Geographies and Business Units to create new assets?

7.2. The Learning Process

* Institutionalising the Learning Process
* How do we learn from past experience (bids to delivery to support)?
* How do we learn from our Stakeholders (Client, Vendor, Partner and Employees)?

* How do we learn from market and academia?
* How do we capture, organize and use learning and relate it to the knowledge base?

7.3. Knowledge, People and Customers

* Relating Knowledge to People and their collective Experience and the Patterns in the Customer Environment
* How do we capture 'experience' (say in a specific domain like Banking, Financial Services and Insurance), make it accessible to others, package it and offer it to the market? What should we be doing differently?
* How should this be used to communicate the value proposition to the customer and to actually ensure that the market respects the experience with an appropriate valuation?
* How do we recognise patterns in the client environment, relate it to our previous knowledge and experience, and adapt to the new situations?
* How do we bring in the right knowledge, experience and learning to improve specific operational areas like the bid process to maximize advantage?

7.4. Knowledge Management Tools at TCS

TCS has brought out various tools to support knowledge management like, eKMS, iCALMS, KnowMax, Support Central etc. **eKMS** (Knowledge Base) is the electronic Knowledge Management System of TCS. It provides access to databases of various analyst firm reports like IDC, Forrester and an in house database of companies' information called Fact Finder. **iCALMS** (Learning Module) is a part of the in house software that allows each of the associate to build their competencies and also to maintain a database of their competencies. These competencies are mapped to the requirement of man power within the organisation and exploited accordingly and help the associates to bring out the best within them by identifying the hidden talents within them. **KnowMax** (Interactive KM Tool) is a recent tool brought out by TCS which is an improved approach towards knowledge management. As it not only gives access to electronic data but also enables communication between the people and also with the system. It also includes a blog where the associates are given access to put on their views and share knowledge.

7.5. Support Central (Interactive KM Tool)

A world-class Business Solutions Platform available from anywhere on the Internet that goes beyond the traditional knowledge management paradigm. It acts as a single, central place to store, find, create, and share valuable corporate knowledge. It also allows connecting to experts behind the knowledge, maintaining transparent processes, and driving operational excellence through complete visibility. We can also Generate reports, dashboards, and charts for business metrics, quality control, and compliance.

8. CONCLUSION

Knowledge Management will no doubt bring success to the organisation provided it is implemented properly. Following a proper methodology and adhering to it will definitely result in fruitful implementation of knowledge management. The strategies involved in the implementation may differ but the ultimate goal is to achieve efficiency. As the organisations these days are more leaned towards IT and are comfortable using the automated systems the codification strategy would be easy to adopt. The firms like TCS who are involved not only in consulting but also into IT development can enhance the use as well as development of customised tools for knowledge sharing which in turn contribute the overall development of the organisation.

REFERENCES

1. Morten T Hansen, Nitin Nohria and Thomas Tierney (1999). What's Your Strategy for Managing Knowledge?, *Harvard Business Review,* March-April,
2. Wikipedia.
3. http://www.wm-forum.org/
4. http://www.bmlconsulting.com/
5. Davenport, T. H. and Prusak, L. (1998). "Working Knowledge". Boston: Harvard Business School Press
6. Koenig, Micheal, E. D. (2003). Knowledge Management, user Education and Librarianship, *Library Review,* 52 (1)
7. Rowley Jennifer, (2003). Knowledge Management: the New Librarianship? *Library Management,* 24 (8/9)
8. https://supportcentral.tcs.com/products/sup_products.asp?prod_id=21
9. http://www.tcs.com/

3
Are Library and Information Professionals Still Significant?

A.Amudhavalli

ABSTRACT

The Internet age has brought about many changes in the way people looks for and access information. This brings us to the question whether libraries–and consequently, librarians–are still important in this day and age. This question is something, which every one of us ought to ponder over seriously as most of us are quite indifferent over this issue This question is something, which every one of us ought to ponder over seriously as most of us are quite indifferent over this issue. Society is not ready to abandon the library, and it probably won't ever be. Libraries can adapt to social and technological changes, but they can't be replaced. While libraries are distinct from the Internet, librarians are the most suited professionals to guide scholars and citizens toward a better understanding of how to find valuable information online.

1. INTRODUCTION

The Internet age has brought about many changes in the way people looks for and access information. While information was previously limited to those who had physical access to publications (books, journals, serials, magazines), now you can access almost anything at the comfort of your own home. This doesn't only include written material; with Broadband you can access rich media at amazing speeds.

This brings us to the question whether libraries– and consequently, librarians–are still important in this day and age. It might be tempting to relegate libraries and librarians as old school and passé along with the steam-powered locomotive and the manual typewriter. After all, you have a whole world of Knowledge waiting to be accessed online. And with social media, it gets even better, since Knowledge starts to become a collective from numerous sources and not only from a few sources.

This question is something, which every one of us ought to ponder over seriously as most of us are quite indifferent over this issue. With all remarks over the air, observations and self-realisation, it is no doubt that our survival itself is a big question these days. Library & Information Professionals (LIPs) are also called as 'endangered species'. Are we really so????? If yes, who is responsible for such a status and situation?? It is not that Internet alone is the sole cause for this threatening trend. And there is no single answer for this issue. In this paper, I wish to analyse and think aloud frankly the varied causal factors for this declining dimension of our profession and look up for certain pragmatic solutions. As a senior professional, I've heard, managed, and shared views on information professionals and can speak with some authority on what they did right or wrong – not from an academic or scientific standpoint, but from a practical "how to save your job and status" point of view.

Here are some issues to be taken care of as well as some ideas on how to create value and bring attention to it.

2. TECHNOLOGY PHOBIA

The emergence of IT environment has despite its merits has its own negative implications on the role and responsibilities of the LIPs. In developing countries like India, it is even today an untouchable toy for many particularly senior LIPs. They are comfortable with manual systems and they also carry the fear of loss of positions and placements. It is either attitudinal problem or competence from the junior professionals. Yet, a majority of the LIPs – both practitioners and preachers - are to overcome this fear and ignorance and fare well with confidence and commitment.

3. INTERNET'S OFFERS

Many predict that the digital age will wipe library bookshelves clean, and permanently end the centuries-old era of libraries. Technology's baffling prowess and progress even has the prediction of the institution's demise. Not that everything is available in the web. Even if available, it is abundant and overload is there, it costs more time and money. The end users need to be guided to browse and search effectively for right information. It should be realised that the Internet is not the end for all and it only supplements a library collection and supports the library system.

4. INTERNET IS NOT 'THE END'

Almost everything is available online–from bomb recipes to patents to photos of wardrobe malfunctions.

But not all; a good majority of publications are still only in hard format. That's why Google came up with Book Search–to index material that's only found on paper, though even Google Book Search isn't perfect. Just like museums, who could preserve our human heritage? We can't just expect to eliminate physical libraries and replace them with virtual ones. There is a vast amount of content available online, but you can only do so much to search through these to find what you're looking for. Reading a novel online is definitely different from reading it on paper. Reading a book is a sensual experience in itself–smelling the paper, feeling the texture and weight, hearing pages leaf by, and actually seeing the lines of ink (some even taste their books. Wow!). So I would agree that pitting the Internet against libraries is just plain silly. The net and libraries should be complements. Both are resources–mediums for finding information.

5. PROFESSIONAL ETHICS

Unlike any other profession, I am sad to state that it is ours that lacks good will, understanding, cooperation and sharing attitudes to each other. Under such circumstances, it is perhaps not surprising that union membership among LIPs is split into different organisations along professional and paraprofessional lines. This is particularly true in academic libraries. It is clear that professionals are being buffeted by strong winds of change and the need for a collective voice is obvious. This suggests that unions will have to be one and not too many with competitive and commercial spirits.

6. PROFESSIONAL RECOGNITION

Library staff in most of the organisations is organised as part of the administrative, clerical or service staff. This is in under sharp criticism, which affects the professional's status, pay structure, opportunities, positions, institutional and societal respect and recognition. In sharp contrast to governmental policies and decisions, private and corporate sectors are much better that their service environment is more competitive and satisfactory. None of the professional bodes either at national or state levels are bothered to address and seek salvation. No individual can succeed in seeking policy measures but a collective effort and unity alone can solve. All these have led to lack of motivation, professional ambitions and growth and ultimately frustration.

7. COCOONING

Some of us believe it's best to stay inconspicuous, so we hunker down at the desk waiting for our phone to ring with an information request. Because it's easy to occupy yourself reading reports and surfing the web, we're convinced to be busy. A better use of our time is looking for ways to weave oneself into the fabric of operational departments by aggressively promoting services and then providing responsive results (not excuses). Another idea? How about providing information on a regular basis without being asked? This does not suggest you become a clipping service. Instead, find out what our users would like to see periodically, then start providing it in an easy to digest format. A good way to do this is to spot patterns in ad hoc requests and proactively provide that information on a regular basis. Eventually, our customers will become addicted and you become less dispensable.

8. FEAR OF CRITICISM

The irrefutable law of the corporate jungle is that 'right info is not available at right time'. And who usually takes the blunt end of the stick for this behaviour? It's we, LIPs, of course, so get used to it. The heat comes with the job and should never be a reason to not provide pertinent information. If we're consistently responsive with quality work, our value will be understood and appreciated in spite of the inevitable critical outbursts.

9. WORKPLACE

LIPs are now being asked to make radical changes to the way they work. That includes: eliminating hierarchy, working in teams, considering and meeting client needs, learning to communicate with information technologists, implementing business practices such as long range and yearly planning and being accountable for implementing those plans, and changing long instilled work practices and organisational structures. The five characteristics are key to professional success: the ability to Guide in the face of an uncertain future, Collaborate, Prioritise and maintain agility and flexibility in the face of changing goals, Empower, Understand the core capabilities of one's organisation, work group and colleagues.

10. INFORMATION DELIVERY

Librarians are not just about books. We serve as guides–gateways if you must–to finding the right sources of information. Librarians are, after all, trained in managing vast resources of information. Perhaps we also make for excellent moderators and guides to finding the right stuff online. We, therefore, must be the ones who cross over into the Internet to make information more easily accessible. Instead of eliminating the need for librarians, technology is reinforcing their validity. There are many great ways of delivering and maintaining information inexpensively.

11. HUMANISTIC APPROACH

In the issue of access many people because of lack of technology, or socio-economic status will not have access to electronic information of the future. Thus creating the problem of the 'information haves and have-nots' and information rich/information poor. Future library and information professionals should be equipped in skills related to how to deal with people's needs and technological usage in order to maintain the librarians' principle of equal access to the public. The information superhighway promises vast riches of information, but it also threatens to widen the gulf between the "information rich" and "information poor". Information professionals of the future should also continue to promote effective human relations through information to individuals, groups, organisations, and different people. As more and more societies will be dominated by the use of technology, library students must have the education and skills of working with different people of diverse background and be sensitive to their needs. Furthermore, they also need to understand other societies outside of their own, as Tyulina (1983) reminds us "We live in a time when significant efforts are made by different countries, nations, and peoples toward better understanding of each other, the knowledge that mutual understanding is the most important condition for maintaining peace in the world." she continues to say that "As technology acts as a cultural eraser, librarianship serves an increasingly important role, bringing together the records of the best achievement of humanity and the individual human being, thus helping to establish better understanding among people. In this respect our profession may be considered one of the "peace-keeping tools."

12. PLACEMENTS

In another one decade about 80% of the LIPs would have retired from service and replacements are hardly ever experienced. It is felt that even many large institutions are happy with the 'contract service' rather than regular postings. It does not sound well or a good indicator of professional progress. I am sure that we senior professionals are solely responsible for this trend. It is felt that regular postings lead to personnel management problems and human relations related issues. And this suits the top management in terms of financial commitments. Most of the positions are vacant and simply referred to as 'no suitable candidate is found'. If any appointment is made, it is because of either political pressure or corruption at some level, leading to neglect of right and qualified LIP.

13. LIS SCHOOLS & CURRICULA

When looking at the future of Library and Information Science education the primary question before us is, how will library schools prepare themselves to meet those new challenges? In order to meet these challenges it is necessary that library schools should look into their external and internal environments. Library educators of the future must have a good understanding of the coming situation of the 21st century and beyond. Their students need to be equipped with knowledge and skills of technology and its usefulness to society as a whole. One of the things that library educators can do is to provide the foundation so that new professionals of the 21st century can keep their knowledge and understanding of integrating technology and other forms of information process (1) to serve their clientele (2) to make decisions or solve problems. Maximum preparation for the information professionals offers a degree of vision and the broadest resource base for technological adaptability, growth, creativity, productivity, professional and high performance. These are the attributes information professional will need to survive and thrive amid the rapid and foreseeable changes of the twenty first century. Library schools must develop a strategy of redefining, re-examining, rethinking, redesigning, and restructuring many aspects of library and information science education. Information professionals of tomorrow desire a world class education in library and information science, but they must also keep pace in the profession through continuing education for a rapidly changing world.

As we move toward the 21st century concerted effort by library educators must be made to educate library and information professionals of the future who will be able to deal with the "information age" to assist the public in finding solutions to their problems. Cooperation from employers and professional association are very important to the education of the information professional of the 21st century. The challenges the coming decade will bring is tremendous. Therefore, library and information science schools should meet these challenges by adopting strategic planning methods and moving from reactive to proactive way of looking at the library profession to accommodate the new organisational and social forms. As Martin Dillon (1995) put it "if we are to move into this brave new world prepared for the many changes that will occur, library schools by whatever name must take a strong leadership role."

14. THE FUTURE

Information professionals of the future need to

have the spirit of the pioneer. They need to be willing to accept that we cannot predict what people are going to be doing, how they are going to be doing it, or with whom. Information professionals need to be both flexible and agile – just being flexible is not enough. They need to be empowered to decide and to act. They need to be able to translate planning and decision-making into actions. Certainly, not everyone yet understands how to take this step. Translation and implementation skills are really needed – to get people to understand how, when you have made a decision or developed a plan, you take it and actually make it work. Staff need to be empowered to learn. A part of our compensation programme assesses demonstrated competencies in applying new skills and new knowledge to our organization's endeavors.

If we do create the kind of workforce that I have defined, we will be able to assume leadership roles within our institution and within our communities at the national and international levels. This is our time. This is the information professional's time, more than any other. The role of the information professional is at the heart of all of these critical activities - technology development, technology applications, content development, new ways of thinking about things, new ways of doing work, new ways of collaborating. We have to be there, and we have to be prepared to stake a claim to our leadership roles within our institutions and beyond.

How organisations are run continues to evolve. They used to be run by their inventors. Next, the business and financial people came in. We now have lawyers getting involved due to legal issues and regulatory issues. But the time has come for the information professional to take a role as leader and guide. Information management is a vital part of everything our organisations do. I see a future that increasingly brings people together with knowledge resources of various kinds and in various formats, breaking down all barriers of space and time. They will come together to collaborate on short or long-term projects, moving in and out of this collaboration space over time. These activities take place under the umbrella of the "Knowledge Community." Information professionals, with our abilities and understandings, will be critical to the development and results of these knowledge communities. Our institutions need us as guides on this exciting expedition into an information-centric 21st century.

15. CONCLUSION

Society is not ready to abandon the library, and it probably won't ever be. Libraries can adapt to social and technological changes, but they can't be replaced. While libraries are distinct from the Internet, librarians are the most suited professionals to guide scholars and citizens toward a better understanding of how to find valuable information on online. Indeed, a lot of information is online. But a lot is still on paper. Instead of regarding libraries as obsolete, state and federal governments should increase funding for improved staffing and technology. Rather than lope blindly through the digital age, guided only by the corporate interests of web economics, society should foster a culture of guides and guideposts. Information structure has its flaws, as some would believe, and therefore libraries and librarians are still important as gatekeepers of information. Today, more than ever, libraries and librarians are extremely important for the preservation and improvement of our culture.

REFERENCES

1. Blake, Virgil L.P. (1989). Ethics and Intellectual Freedom in the Education of Library and Information Science Professionals, *The Bookmark*, Fall, pp. 28-31.

2. Buckland, Michael K. (1986). Education for Librarianship in this Century, *Library Trends,* Spring, pp.777-788.

3. Dillon, Martin. (1995). Core Librarianship in an Electronic World. *In: The Samual Lazerow Lecture Series,* The School of Library and Information Studies: Texas Woman's University, pp. 1-27

4. Lemke, Antje B. (1987). Alternative Specialties in Library Education, *Journal of Education for Librarianship,* 78 (January), pp. 285-291.

5. Malinconico, S. Michael (1992). What Librarians need to know to Survive in an Age of Technology, *Education for Library and Information Science.* 45(3), pp. 226-240.

6. Suprenant, Thomas T. (1989). The Challenge of Technology: an Opening Discussion, *The Bookmark,* (Fall), pp.13-15.

7. Turock, Betty J. (1995). "Equity on the Information Superhighway". Library Advocacy Now. ALA.

8. Tyulina, Natalia (1983). Foreword. *In:* World librarianship: a Comparative study / edited by Richard Krzys and Gaston Litton New York: Marcel Dekker, pp.v-vi.

4

Traditional Knowledge Organisation Systems in the Electronic Environment

Lalitha Aswath

ABSTRACT

This paper discusses about the organisation of information in the traditional environment versus electronic environment. It highlights the relevance of information storage and retrieval in the web environment and its merits, with a warning that technology is only a tool to harness and not an end by itself.

1. INTRODUCTION

Organisation is the essence of human society. Since the beginning, human beings have shown an innate need to organise (1). The need to organise large amount of information and knowledge created by them has led to the development of classification schemes and other organisational tools both in natural sciences and other fields too. Organising information and knowledge is an old need of libraries too. When modern science and technology began to emerge in the 17th century, many thinkers like Francis Bacon pondered ways to organise growing bodies of knowledge.

2. ORGANISATION OF INFORMATION IN TRADITIONAL ENVIRONMENT

Since the end of the 19th century, librarians have developed formal systems for organization of knowledge to manage their large collection of books. As libraries grew in size, the need for systems to organise those growing collections had become a compelling practical issue. The largest library in the world, the Library of Congress in Washington, DC developed a system to index its documents by subject (the Library of Congress Subject Headings) and to shelve them by disciplines (the Library of Congress Classification).

Melvil Dewey, librarian at the Amherst College, devised a system using only ten digits (Dewey Decimal Classification -DDC). Though more than one century old, DDC is still the most widely used system to classify books world over and continuously being updated.

Rapid changes in the generation of information and access to information led to the changes in information organisation and dissemination. From the first edition of DDC in 1876 when knowledge was expanding at a fast rate to the present where Internet allows information generation, packaging and access in digital formats, classification systems have shown a progressive trend towards information organisation and access. Though there is a change in the nature of information resources, the need to express its content, description of its format, facilitate its access to enable its use remains constant (2).

Beginning of the 1930's Indian Mathematician and Librarian S.R.Ranganathan introduced the idea of decomposing a subject into different facets. Each facet belongs to a general category – Personality, Matter, Energy, Space and Time (PMEST). S.R.Ranganathan and his successors in the Classification Research Group (CRG) explored in depth the most helpful ways to sort faceted subjects and developed a coherent theory with advanced principles, including:

* How to sort main classes?
* How to sort facets within each class?
* How to sort subjects within the same facet?
* How to express sorting by an efficient notation...?

This results in a very scientific way of organising subjects and knowledge.

Library classification schemes have four main purposes:

1. To order the fields of knowledge in a systematic way.
2. To bring related items together in a helpful sequence.
3. To provide orderly access to the shelves either for browsing or via the catalogs
4. To provide an exact location for an item on the shelf. (3)

Library is a store of information packages i.e. recorded information such as books, articles, videos, electronic documents, etc. Books or conventional forms of packages represent a small percentage of the documents used by people in everyday work/life today, and computer files, databases, internal communications, notes of various kinds, and many other forms of communication, forms the major percentage. Library classification schemes bring order and control to the collection so that an information package can be retrieved according to a particular aspect of its character. And a successful classification scheme is one that saves the time of the user by creating an order convenient to the user.

3. ORGANISATION OF INFORMATION IN THE E-ENVIRONMENT

Internet is also a store of information resources, not necessarily published and without a systematic order. Lynch claims that the Internet is merely a huge amount of disorganised data, a 'chaotic repository for the collective output of the world's digital printing process '. (4) Here search engines provide access and retrieval points for Internet resources, but do not allow the users to navigate using subject categorisation, since each search engine has its own vocabulary and organisational schema, access and results are different. The traditional library classification has the advantage of creating cohesion across diverse information packages by establishing a shared conceptual context.

Classification schemes have been built on General Classification Theory, which is based on four basic principles:

1. Every thing, object etc., has to have a different and unambiguous description of its unique qualities.
2. Principles involving similarities and differences must be used in creating classes.
3. Hierarchies and relational methods which will bring order in grouping fundamental categories and to identify fundamental differences clearly.
4. A final system providing a logical progression from general to particular. (5)

This resulted in schedules of classes, divisions and sections that move from general to specific. Once the relationships between the classes, sub-classes, divisions and sections are established, library classification system assign notation to each. Notation is used to assign call numbers to individual information packages, the call numbers assigned works as a collocation device. For a library this means the information packages are ordered according to call number. The call number assigned to an information package also works as a location device. "Ultimately, in a physical world, each object must rest in its place – both absolutely and, in a classified collection". (Dillon &Jul p204)

There is a change in the nature of information resources. Traditional resources like 'Books', on closely-related subjects can be assigned such call numbers, making it possible to place them near each other on library shelves/racks, and making it easier for information seekers to find books on those topics when looking at those shelves/ racks. This is very useful, but it doesn't solve all the problems of locating information on a subject.

The assignment of an exact location allows for easier retrieval and reshelving. However, the current practice of assigning a single location for an information package is limited. If the subject of information package falls into two different classes, it must be located physically in a single place by class.

3.1. Relevance to Web Environment

Internet resources do not require a physical location in stacks and are freed from the need for a linear arrangement. A resource can be stored in a place remote from the place of access. Physical location is not necessary because the resources can be grouped "On-the-fly" as a result of searching or browsing, regardless of their actual storage place. (6) Subject classification can be taken a step further, without the need for linear arrangement. Instead of making a choice between two classes, multidimensional classification can be contemplated.

Another problem cited is that Internet resources are not stored in a physical setting, rather they are stored in cyber space and their location may change. URL provide the address for the place of the resource on the Internet. The longevity of an average URL can be measured in weeks. Library classification again offers a solution. Changes in location are similar to the reclassification of the resources in a library. Repeatable metadata elements would allow for multiple Internet addresses. (7)

In traditional environment, information search on any topic begins with encyclopedic literature, but today probably any information search begins with a quick Google search. So why should any body care so much for specialised classification schemes recommended by library professionals? Many people think that Library Science belongs to a obsolete world of dark rooms filled with shelves- which has nothing to do with the real needs of contemporary life. Different professionals like Librarians, Computer scientists, and managers who have once lived in separate communities and used their own terminologies and often unaware that they are addressing problems that looked different but were in fact substantially similar and coined metaphors like digital libraries, virtual libraries and virtual reference desks, domains for subject fields, topic maps for facet analysis and ontology for classification systems etc., All this is nothing but combining the modern technology with traditional library techniques.

Experts in faceted classification theory in the 1950s were cognizant of the coming computer revolution and guessed the importance of computers in future knowledge organization and complement to classification theory, but not an alternative.

In fact, the important difference lies in the physical forms in which documents are recorded and the technological means to access them. But documents, no matter whether they are web sites, computer files, books, manuscripts, engraved stones, etc., still have content. And if one wants to find them when needed, one has to analyse the subjects they contain.

At the same time, new technologies have provided us with new forms of indexing and searching. Full-text search makes all words in document searchable. That was simply not possible with printed documents. We can view this as an additional form of semantic indexing — the simplest and most basic possible form.

However, a single word taken out of a text can be misleading without its context. So searches of words in full texts don't solve all problems of retrieval. That is why selected keywords, abstracts, subject headings, thesauri, and classification schemes are necessary. Advances in full-text search are themselves helping to bridge that divide.

It is evident that the world of books can still teach useful lessons in the digital environment. Sometimes the experience of the Library Science community is even more useful in the computer environment than in the world of paper documents. In fact, computers exist to manage and process labeled data, so they are the perfect match to knowledge-organisation systems.

Further, computers can make the work of indexers faster by suggesting to them a list of possible categories, to which the document belongs to on the basis of the words it contains. But this can be often misleading. Human indexers are still needed to judge the actual relevance of the suggested classes and to apply principles of good indexing, but their work is made lighter by the help of the machine.

Ranganathan was aware of the possibilities. Indeed, in the last edition of his book (8) he wrote:

World War II ushered in the Electronic Age into the world. The Computer is one of the versatile forms in which Electronics can help mankind. We must accept the computer. We must derive all the benefits it is capable of giving us...... Apart from this, an important question is, can classificationists and classifiers abdicate their function and depend on the computer in the rendering of library service to the satisfaction of all? They cannot. Because, classification involves judgement — judgement of the subject of the document in all its facets and arrays manifest in it. This cannot be done by the statistical analysis of the words in documents, that is, what a computer does.

It has been misconceived that automatic computer procedures make human indexing unnecessary, and the value of traditional indexing techniques is limited to an elitist and isolated library environment and has nothing to do with the new chaos of electronic documents. Clearly, to obtain both powerful and effective organisation of large amounts of information in any form, we need a synthesis between library classification perspectives and computer-based indexing and retrieval.

Organisation of Internet resources may seem overwhelming. There are millions and millions of sites already existing on the Internet and the number is growing daily. The number of sites may look relatively small when compared to the over 43 million bibliographic records of OCLC's *world cat database.*

If Internet is to thrive as a new means of information storage and communication, something like library classification will be needed to organise and retrieve. Classification schemes are used to provide systematic order, bring related items together, provide access through browsing and provide an exact location for each information package. Library classification adds value to Internet resources. They supply a shared context and create cohesion across diverse information technologies through established systems. The notation device, combined with online technology, allows browsing of an entire collection regardless of format. As long as the need to express content, description of the format, facilitating access and enabling use remains constant the need for classification remains. Of course, the one force that has received greatest attention is 'Technology ', because it is the most obvious force. Historically the introduction of new technology - electricity to type writer and the duplicating machine to computer has resulted in major change in organisation any item/s. But it should be remembered that technology is a 'Tool' and it is the people, their attitude, their acceptance of change is of primary concern. Technology simply enables it.

REFERENCES

1. Taylor, Arlene G. (1999). "The Organization of information. Englewood". Colorado: Libraries Unlimited.
2. Dillon, Martin and Jul, Erik (1996). Cataloguing Internet Resources: The Convergence of Libraries and Internet Resources. *Cataloguing and Classification Quarterly,* 22 (3/4), pp. 197-238

3. Dittman, Helena and Jane Hardy (2000). "Learn Library of Congress Classification". Lanham, Maryland: Scarecrow Press.
4. Lynch, Cliffiord (1997). Searching the Internet. *Scientific American,* 276 (3), pp.49-56.
5. Richmond, Phyllis (1990). General Theory Classification. *In:* Classification of Library Materials / edited by Betty G. Bengston and Janet S. Hill. New York: Neal-Schuman Publishers, pp. 16-26.
6. Younger, Jennifer A (1997). Resource Description in the Digital Age. *Library Trends,* 45 (3), pp. 462-487.
7. Weinberg, Bella Hass (1998). Improved Internet access: Guidance from Research on Indexing and Classification. *American Society for Information Science,* 25 (2), pp.26-29.
8. Ranganathan, S.R. (1967). Prolegomena to Library Classification. Bangalore: Sarada Ranganathan Endowment for Library Science, Chapter XA.

5

The Impact of Knowledge Management on Organisational Development

Nagappa V. Bakkannanavar
Anju Govindani

ABSTRACT

This paper deals with the concepts, need, objectives, features, components, requisites, initiatives, impact of Knowledge Management on organisational development, value proposition in organisations, librarians role, future, etc.

1. INTRODUCTION

The concepts of knowledge and management are old, the former means to understand the facts or skills that one gained through learning or experience while the latter is the act or skill of directing and organizing the work. However quite recently they have been put together for conceptualising an organisation as an integrated knowledge system. Man has gained skill through experience and implementing such skill by directing and organising leads to knowledge proliferation in multifaceted and multidimensional directions. For accessing such newly emerged knowledge, it is necessary to have Knowledge Management (KM).

Increasingly organisations world over are realising that today knowledge is the real key to success. It is simply too valuable a resource to be left alone. In an era of discontinuous change, increased business complexity and specialisation, the life cycle of knowledge is getting shorter and shorter every day. Many of the skills and knowledge gained in the past are considered outdated today. Some of the yesterday's best practices are today's worst practices. In order to maintain competitive edge in such a dynamically changing environment, organisations need to keep their knowledge on a cutting edge, deploy it, leverage it in operations and spread it quickly across the organisation. Today it is imperative to devise a comprehensive knowledge strategy to translate Business Strategy into a success.

This concept has very wide applicability in all types of organisation. It believes in human-centric approach to find solutions to all the problems in an organisation with the perspective of improving working results year after year to an appreciable extent. It is an incontrovertible fact that the human forces undoubtedly the biggest asset in any industry / Organisation, and its intuitive and tacit knowledge should be harnessed in productive ways with a view to reaping the gains at a later stage. Knowledge is power and the reservoir of knowledge that resides in employees is very important for all-round growth of any organisation. A mechanism should be in place by which knowledge that lay buried not only in core professionals but also in every employee, irrespective of their cadre, is managed efficiently and leveraged into organisational assets in the long run that can be easily accessed by individuals at any point of time.

2. CONCEPTS & DEFINITIONS OF KM

The term Knowledge Management (KM) was first applied in the profit-seeking enterprises to improve the operations to gain competitive advantage and make profits. Now, knowledge management can also be applied to non-profit–making institutions such as government bodies and statutory bodies as well by exploring present and future roles in the transformation of individuals, communities, government and societies at large.

It can also be used to LICs simultaneously for communicating knowledge between different levels of management and who are directly involve improving work processes as well as in service sectors. KM stimulates and manages an environment in which knowledge is created, shared and used for the benefit of the organization, its people, and its customer or users. KM has gained significance with the advent and application of IT. KM enables sharing of information by the people by overcoming the limitations of geographical boundaries.

KM is seen as a logical extension society in that its purpose is to cope with explosion of information and capitalize on increased knowledge in workplace. One of the earliest examples of KM can be seen in the stone age days when people sat around a fire in the evening and shared their experiences of hunting and gathering food. Simply put KM is all about capturing knowledge from where it is available, and disseminating to where it is required.

KM has been borrowed from the corporate world which was used as a strategy to seek as well as capture the knowledge residing in people's heads and consciousness to help the environment. Corporate knowledge is at present well accepted as a decisive factor in major enterprises in advanced countries, nowadays followed by developing countries in their companies as well for achieving better results by manipulating the know-how, increasing the effectiveness and efficiency of human resources, employing limited inputs and others.

KM is the systematic process of creating, maintaining and nurturing an organisation to make the best use of its individual and collective knowledge to achieve the corporate mission, broadly viewed as sustainable competitive advantage or achieving high performance. The goal is for an organization to become aware of its knowledge, individually and collectively, and to shape itself so that it makes the most efficient use of the knowledge it has or can obtain. By management we don't mean control in the sense of strong authority and direction. This style of management fails with knowledge because no one can control another person's mind-where the knowledge is. Instead, managers must first set examples through leadership, management and personal behaviour. Then they must strive to create and nurture a culture and an infrastructure that stimulate workers to create, use, and share their knowledge and that also supports their freedom to act effectively over a broad range of situations. When an organisation lives in a turbulent, unpredictable, and challenging world, it must also be a learning organisation, capable of handling change, uncertainty and complexity. That is, the culture and infrastructure must be such that individuals and groups of individuals can and will continuously questioning their beliefs in order to create and apply their new knowledge to achieve desired goals and objectives.

KM is a conscious strategy of getting the right knowledge to the right people at the right time and helping people share and put information into action in ways that strive to improve organisational performance (American Productivity Centre, 1999). Therefore, KM is nothing but cupping knowledge. It should be shared among the employees who are working at different levels in the organisation in the most convenient way to get things done by others for enhancing and improving operations to gain competitive advantages and increase profits. KM can also help to evaluate the overall performance of the organization not at present but in the future.

Searching and retrieval facility, data ware housing and the proliferation of intranets has revolutionised that ability of organisation to find, accumulate, organise and access information and knowledge. It is an organisational wide effort for capturing and synthesizing information from which knowledge can be created, stored and shared. The objective is to enable the human resource to work together more effectively and respond to customer needs quickly.

KM has been defined as, "Management of Organisational knowledge for creating business value and generating competitive advantage. It consists of processing, sharing, using and storing knowledge". Another definition runs as, "KM is the explicit and systematic management of vital knowledge and its associated processes of creating, gathering, organising, diffusion, use and exploitation. IT requires turning personal knowledge into corporate knowledge that can be widely shared throughout an organisation and appropriately applied." "KM involves blending a company's internal and external information and turning it into actionable knowledge via a technology platform".

3. NEED FOR KM

The success of business in an increasingly competitive market place depends critically on the quality of knowledge, which those organisations apply to their key business processes. The factors, which make KM and in inevitable business process, are

* Market places are increasingly competitive and the rate of innovation is rising
* Reductions in staffing create a need to replace informal knowledge with formal methods
* Competitive pressure reduces the size of workforce that holds valuable business knowledge
* The amount of time available to experience and acquire knowledge has diminished
* Early retirements and increasing mobility of the workforce lead to loss of knowledge
* There is a need to manage increasing complexity as small operating companies are trans-national sourcing operations
* Changes in strategic direction may result in the loss of knowledge in a specific area
* Products and services are increasingly complex, endowing them with a significant information component
* The need for life long learning is an inescapable reality
* The market places increasingly competitive and the rate of innovation is rising, so that

knowledge must evolve and we assimilated at an ever faster rate

* Corporations are organising their business to be focused on creating customer value. Staff functions are being reduced, as are management structures. There is need to replace the informal KM of the staff function with formal methods in customer aligned business processes
* Competitive pressures are reducing the size of the work force, which holds this knowledge
* Knowledge takes time to experience and acquire. Employees have less and less time for this
* There are trends for employees to retire earlier and for increasing mobility, leading to loss of knowledge
* There is a need to manage increasing complexity as small operating company's re-trans-national sourcing operations
* A change in strategic direction may result in the loss of knowledge in a specific area. A subsequent reversal in policy may then lead to a renewed requirement for this knowledge, but the employees with that knowledge may no longer be there.

4. OBJECTIVES OF KM

The broad objectives of KM are:

1. To leverage internal and external expertise to build and apply industry leading skills
2. To develop and exploit intangible assets including brands, technology and know-how

The primary objective of KM is to provide right

knowledge at the right time to the right person. This would enable individuals to make appropriate and informed choice, based on relevant information pieced together through intelligent systems.

4. FEATURES OF KM

The following are the important features of KM:

1. KM should not be thought of all about people only but of technology also, and therefore human resources department and the technology department should drive KM together
2. KM is to implement the concept of sharing information and expertise, by which employees not only share their knowledge but also make it available to the entire organization
3. Knowledge is a very different kind of asset to other assets such as property and equipment. And at the same time peoples are always reluctant to change. It is observed that for many workers and managers, knowledge has become the source of authority. Therefore they may not like to share knowledge. This will be the stumbling block to introduce KM in any organization
4. The KM is to change the culture from "Knowledge is power" to "Knowledge sharing is power"
5. KM is the subject that accepts intellectual capital as the main management assets
6. KM provides an environment and opportunities of learning while doing.

5. COMPONENTS OF KM

KM basically involves the following three components:

1. People create share and use knowledge
2. Processes acquire, create, organise, share and transfer knowledge
3. Technology the enabler and facilitator to store and provide access to KM

Thus, KM can be visualised as a three legged stool, where the stool would cease to be functional even if one or more legs are not developed and shaped. While technology and processes are important to KM, it is people who determine its success.

6. REQUISITES FOR KM

The requisites for Knowledge Management can be summarized as:

1. Build a strong data structure
2. Change in the organisational structure
3. Create skilled workforce
4. Tools and Techniques
5. Develop a new atmosphere
6. Bridge the gap between practice and preaching
7. Average seminars/ workshops at regular intervals
8. Top management support
9. Good communication and information sharing
10. Assessment of knowledge requirements for new jobs
11. Better HRM policies for proper identification

and reward of knowledge workers

12. Adoption of effective KM solutions

KM initiatives would be centered on the three things of the Organization:

1. Knowledge of the Organisation : Knowledge of the Organisation is available in people, files and networks. But the centre is the people. As per Prof Nonaka, the knowledge states are: (a.) Tacit to Tacit- A socialisation process learning by observations and imitation, (b.) Tacit to Explicit- Externalisation that refers to finding ways to structure and record knowledge for the purpose of sharing, (c.) Explicit to Explicit- Combination a form of synthesis of recorded knowledge to derive new knowledge, and (d.) Explicit to Tacit- Internalisation that achieve s a coherent structure and insight. The Socialisation, Externalisation, Combination and Internalisation (SECI) together give a subjective structure of knowledge management for any organisation.

2. Technology : This necessarily means network support among others. In reference to weightless economy, an issue promoted by KM, the main rule is, "The Law of Connexion", that states that; "the network economy is fed by the deep resonance of two stellar bangs: the collapsing microcosm of chips. The era of computers is over. That of communication between computers is opening".

3. Culture Change : KM is based on sharing of knowledge. This culture is required to be brought in the organisation for KM initiatives. By sharing knowledge all the three components of the organisation, namely individual, team and organisation become gainful. By the sharing of knowledge the best idea and best solutions are arrived at; and ultimately every component gains by it.

7. TOOLS OF KM

Tools make it easier to implement KM processes and functions but they do not take the place of them. Tools help a knowledge manager deliver the right information at the right time, but don't tell him/her what to collect, how to collect it, or how to get people to use it. Tools can also be the catalyst to help transform how people work by giving them new ways to collaborate or access content. But they are not a substitute for the thinking, analysis or, management that must drive and direct the change. At present, there are numerous tools available to facilitate KM and most organisations have implemented several of these. Key types of knowledge-related tools that are currently available in the marketplace are given below :

Tools

E-Mail/ Messaging	*Content Management*
Conferencing/ Chat	Document Management
Workflow	CRM
Groupware	Data Mining
Collaboration	Data Warehousing
Web Publishing	Imaging and OCR
Portals	Knowledge Mapping
Indexing	Knowledge Auditing
Search and Retrieval	Expertise Networking
Category Builders	Training
Taxonomy Builders	Intelligent Agents
Push	Capturing/ Codifying
Publish and Subscribe	XML

8. IMPORTANCE OF KM TO ORGANISATIONS

8.1. Enable e-Government

a. Provide an IT-enabled information base to

enable citizens and customers to access information and services they need.

b. Establish a network of knowledgeable govt. employees who can add value to citizen or customer's requests.

8.2. Increase Productivity

(a) Reduce costs, risks, learning curves and start-up time.

(b) Contribute to bottom line/ mission goals.

8.3. Share Best Practices/ Processes

(a) Share best known practices across the enterprise.

(b) Learn from failed efforts.

(c) Provide platform for knowledge re-use and innovation.

(d) Establish benchmark for internal and external performance-individuals and teams.

(e) Acclimate new employees to "the ways we do things around here".

8.4. Provide Leadership and Decision Making

(a) Provide the right information in a context that aids decision making.

(b) Integrate new information into decision processes by sharing and collaborating with players and stakeholders in decision processes.

(c) Use information and knowledge to align organisational actions with missions and visions.

8.5. Increase Customer Satisfaction

a. Focus on knowledge of customer needs to

drive the organisations' efforts.

b. Improve customer outcomes and experiences with services rendered.

8.6. Create Competitive Advantage/ Market Differentiation

a. To achieve knowledge superiority over adversaries or competitors.

b. As a business proposition, product or service.

c. Change the value proposition from delivering goods and services to delivering knowledge and expertise about those goods and services.

d. Focuses collective organisational intellect on customer needs

e. To meet business/ mission goals.

8.7. Foster Innovation

a. Provide an infrastructure for electronic and social networking to develop new products or services.

b. Foster and provide access to rich pools of ideas so others can capitalize on them.

8.8. Foster Collaboration

a. Increase collaboration opportunities enrich the exchange of tacit and explicit knowledge between people.

8.9. Encourage and Use learning

a. Facilitate and accelerate learning- create opportunities for individuals and groups to put new knowledge to use.

b. Leverage Organisational knowledge- brings the right information to the right people in an understandable context that addresses new challenges.

c. Value individual learning by rewarding it and leveraging it to the enterprise level.

8.10. Foster Social Capital

a. Increase the transfer of individual knowledge to the organisation

b. Foster across organisational boundaries, time, and space.

c. Link people who have the requisite tacit and explicit knowledge with those who need it to do their jobs.

8.11. Attract and Retain Human Capital

a. People are our primary asset and are crucial to maintaining organisational expertise.

b. Capture and leverage what people know, know-how and know-what.

c. Promote career growth.

8.12. Create and use structural capital

a. Convert intellectual capital to structural capital

b. Focus strategic thinking on capitalizing on knowledge vs. focusing on the budget.

8.13. The Challenges of KM Implementation

An organization, which has decided to implement KM, will have to take up various challenges. These are

1. Employee Participation : Employees view information as power and as such avoid sharing it with others. Organisations usually ignore the people and cultural issues, and this result into major problems that occur in KM. KM is not only a change, but also a paradigm shift. To ensure employee participation, management should try and create an environment, where an individual knowledge is valued and rewarded, establishing a culture that recognises tacit knowledge, and encourages employee to share it. One way companies can motivate the employees to participate in KM is, by creating an incentive programme. However, there is a danger that employees will participate solely to earn incentives, without any regard for the quality, or relevance of the information they contribute.

2. Not All Information is Knowledge : It is necessary to lookout the information overload. Quantity rarely equals quality, and in case of KM, this is more so. Indeed, the purpose of KM programme is to identify and disseminate relevant knowledge from a sea of information.

3. KM not Static : As with many physical assets, the value of knowledge can erode over time. Since knowledge can get stale fast, the content in a KM programme should be constantly updated, amended and deleted. The relevance of knowledge at any given time changes, like the skills of employees. Therefore, there is no end to a KM programme. Like product development, marketing and R & D, KM is a constantly evolving business practice.

4. Not allowing Technology to Dictate KM : It is often confused that the KM is a technology-based concept. Companies that implement a centralised database system, electronic message board, web portal or any other collaborative tool, should do so to facilitate their own business goals, and not for a KM programme. However, the KM is technology independent, but at the same time, it is often facilitated by IT. The systems developed for business purpose can be used for KM. While technology can support KM, it is not the starting point of a KM programme. An Organisation has to make

KM decisions based on people, knowledge and business objectives. The technology will come last, only as a tool.

5. HRM Policies : The HRM policies give more weightage to seniority than merit in the promotion process, and also there is no separate placement policy for knowledge workers. These policies are hindrance in the way of effective knowledge Management.

10. IMPACT OF KM ON ORGANISATIONAL DEVELOPMENT

According to Peter, "The successful companies, in the KM terms are the ones that have looked at the business processes rather than seeing the solution revolving rounds the company intranet". The main reasons for using KM techniques are to be competitive. Through Globalisation, there are a lot more competitors coming into markets quickly. Therefore, you need to do more in order to appear different. Another layer of knowledge is how to integrate things in the organisations so that this process makes the organisation look different. KM is not dumping data on the intranet, but for sharing of knowledge and information.

KM is relevant, when the market is dynamic, uncertainty dominates, technologies proliferate, and competitors multiply, resulting in products and services becoming obsolete RAPIDLY. Innovation in products and services is essential for survival. Hence, successful organisations are characterised by their ability to create new knowledge consistently, disseminate it quickly, and embody it in their new products and services. Successful management of organisational knowledge is essential for creating business value and generating competitive advantage. Flexible organisations with a focus to learn more new things and manage to adapt to new cultures having the knowledge as primary driver, have emerged as market leaders. Continuous strife in business have helped the leaders to acquire, retain and use knowledge to serve the customers better and blend them to be competitive by using technology and engaging knowledge employees.

Organisations are categorised into two categories, based on when, where and how they use KM to derive benefits for the organisation from the expanding opportunities of the markets.

1. It is the organisation, which realises the need to cope with competitors and stand as a valid player in the competitive and open markets through the core knowledge to play in it.
2. The organisation which realises the potentials of the markets and positions itself to exploit them to its advantage through risk taking ability coupled with innovative knowledge of today obtained through insight, which shall become the core knowledge of tomorrow.

Now, it is clear that one who adapts to market and applies the innovative knowledge of today with insight is the creator of core knowledge of tomorrow. Therefore, it is the KM that makes an organisation as a trendsetter or leader or competitor or participator or straggler in the market and the environment. Hence, the sustainability of an organization depends on how well it is involved in KM and its lifecycle is altered by none other than KM. Every leader knows this to be true, yet few have continued systematic methods for KM processes. A new organisational form is emerging in the companies that run on knowledge and new positions like Chief Learning Officer has come in place. Management caters to the critical issues of organisational adaptation, survival and competence in face of increasingly discontinuous change. In an organisation, an effective KM system helps employees to seek support in decision-making processes by obtaining answers from knowledge base. KM system is facilitating the present and future employees with various levels of access rights for individual to access the knowledge base, created and updated through individual or organis ational know-how with the help of technology. KM system, basically aids employees through collection of information from different sources, i.e. internal and external, such as documents, databases, etc., and by capturing and storing it in knowledge base through continuous updating process, for ongoing use.

KM is the systematic process of finding, selecting, organising, distilling and presenting information in a way that improves an employee's comprehension in the specific area of interest. It helps an organisation to gain insight and understanding from its own experience. KM addresses business problems particular to a business-whether it is creating and delivering innovative products or services or managing and enhancing relationships with customers, partners and suppliers. KM initiative includes leader with a business vision, knowledge employee to share and appropriate technology to capture.

11. VALUE PROPOSITION OF KM IN ORGANISATION

1. Better Customer Knowledge: KM techniques focus on capturing knowledge about customers, understanding their needs and preferences, and integrating them with business processes enabling increased sales and revenue, as also customer satisfaction and retention.

2. Better Knowledge about Products : Information and Knowledge about the product behaviour, and deficiencies can enable organisation to bring about suitable modifications and enhancements, in time, to tailor them to customer needs.

3. Better Knowledge of Processes : Knowledge gaps in the area of laid down processes and procedures many a times also hinder customer service. If not addressed adequately and quickly, resulting delays can translate into a loss of business. The KM framework provides a vibrant and throbbing arena for getting requisite information in least time, as also enable continuous improvements, leading to better decisions and better customer service.

4. Better Knowledge of People : Tacit knowledge residing in people's heads, and gained through experience is often more valuable than that encapsulated in databases. On account of no formal methods of recording this tacit knowledge of people, it remains a personal domain. Organisations are often not aware of their own knowledge storehouses. KM enables the tracking and recording of the skills and experience of the employees, which needs to be continuously tapped for much larger business benefits. It also enables organisation to know who are the experts in different fields.

5. Better Market Intelligence : External environments- regulatory, corporate and consumer-driven, is no longer as stable, as they were even a decade back. This creates a volatile business environment. Updated and continuous information of this environment provides an organisation the most vital input for staying ahead in the highly competitive world. New products and services must come out of a centralised knowledge pool of a stable, reliable and intelligent knowledge base.

6. Sharing of Best Practices : Knowledge management provides a business critical platform for continuous sharing of thoughts, ideas and innovations. Providing effective knowledge about past projects, initiatives, failures, successes, and efforts readily available and accessible, can make significant contribution towards better and correct decisions and avoiding costly mistakes. KM helps avoid unnecessary work duplication, expansive re-invention and repeated mistakes.

7. Better Customer Service : By developing learning networks and learning from past situations, organisations can improve their customer efficiency and satisfaction, thereby accelerating business growth.

8. Prevention of Knowledge Walkouts : When employees leave organisations for various reasons, there is substantial knowledge-loss in these organizations. The collaboration techniques of KM enable sharing of tacit knowledge residing in the head of employees, which can be put to use even after the employee has left. Thus, KM serves organisations from knowledge walkouts and also increases productivity.

The KM techniques enable the organisations to exploit the above value propositions to their full extent, thereby resulting in achieving the business goals and objectives. All things being equal, better knowledge and its efficient management would be the key differentiator for becoming the first among equals.

12. MAJOR ROLE OF THE LIBRARIANS

Tools of KM consists 70% of services and 30% of Technologies. Librarians provide these 70% services.

This indicates the role of Librarians as Knowledge Manager. Where their functions are:

* Providing services to the user community
* Sharing of information and understanding of user needs
* Analysing documents, classifying and sorting them for easy retrieval
* Building the index etc.

From an organisational perspective, there is much merit in encouraging an adaptable learning environment and in focusing on identifying and gathering organisational intelligence in a strategic manner. There is also value to the organisation in encouraging the effective transfer of expertise, know-how and knowledge. These ideas might be summarized as a "Knowledge Awareness Strategy". The application of knowledge strategies means the capturing of all types of knowledge and all types of information available including tacit and explicit knowledge residing in people's heads and consciousness, and information residing in production, research, marketing as well as many other information sources. Today, all organisations are trying to build an infrastructures which enables people to share explicit knowledge- be through meeting, discussion groups, documents, E-mails, seminars, and project files. There is considerable potential for library professional to become more involved and take more directive roles in KM initiatives. These Professional are beginning to broaden their horizons, change their attitude to obtain the opportunities of KM initiatives in the organisations. As more and more organisations adopt the use of knowledge management methods and practices, the need for trained and qualified knowledge management professionals will continue to grow.

Of course, the basic role of the library professional in an organisation is unchanged. The organisation will expect the library professional to acquire and organise information, make it available for use, disseminate it and, ultimately, dispose of information resources in all media and formats. A knowledge awareness perspective in the organisation calls for the library professional to be more systematic in tracking existing organisational informational strengths and this will probably lead to developing new information resources relating to the available in-house expertise. Library professional can adopt a more strategic organisational view of their work by monitoring what is really happening in the organisation through "Management by walking about". He/She can spend a third of his/her time walking around the organisation, talking to people about what they were doing, gathering information on what was going on in different departments. However, to engage them fully requires that the librarian or information manager find a new focus within the organisation-ideally, if information profession has to play its role and make impact. In such organisations, they should be located in the chief executive's office. They should form part of a team devoted to acquiring external information of value to organisational strategy and establishing systems to ensure that the knowledge held in people's minds can be tapped when it is needed. Merely to leap into the "KM" balloon without being in a position to deliver, will simply mean being first out of the balloon when ballast is jettisoned.

To succeed in a KM environment every library professional should:

1. Apply their own skill and experience confidently, in unfavorable and critical

situations to tackle the problems.

2. Realise the goals and objectives of their organisation carefully, its strategies, its challenges, its products and services, where knowledge and information can add value.
3. Update the existing skills and experience of the information professionals for capturing individual knowledge and information available in the organisation and sharing it with others for getting better results than before.
4. Create knowledge culture within the organisation to achieve the objectives successfully in competitive environment.

The information professionals' roles need redefinition to deal with both formal and informal knowledge within the organisation. They apply their knowledge to create value for the organisation and are responsible for managing the creation, capture, synthesis, sharing and application of the collective intelligence of the organisation. They will manage the process to ensure that business needs are served, develop high-level knowledge management strategies, and create a knowledge management infrastructure. Turning information into solutions, information professionals piece information together and reflect on their experience, generate insight, and use this insight to solve problems.

For this the information professional needs to have a good overall understanding of the business and organisation, and creativity in gathering information and creating synergy from the use of information. They also need to proactively anticipate and respond to changes in the environment, be lifelong learners, exhibit self-learning capabilities, and demonstrate self-control and problem-solving skills. Finally they must promote a culture of sharing information and knowledge, and be knowledgeable and competent in adapting applications of new technologies in their organization. Information professionals are already educated and trained to exhibit a number of important skills like IT skills, information skills, communication skills, leadership and management skills, analytical skills, and personal characteristics. With the addition of an appropriate mix of these skills, they are poised to take on the expanded role of knowledge work and play a key role in the emerging information and knowledge-intensive organisation.

13. FUTURE OF KM

As uncertainty and complexity increase in the future and decisions become more challenging, individual, team and organisational learning, coupled with a strong knowledge management program, offers the best capability an organisation can have to change, adapt, and influence its environment in a way that maximises its performance over time. Within the organisation, focused, flexible and friendly communities will help knowledge workers continually learn and change. By combining the strengths of organisational learning and knowledge management, smart organisations will create cultures, structures, and leadership styles that enable them to scan, perceive, anticipate, and take effective action on new, ambiguous, unexpected and complex threats and opportunities. Achieving such an ideal is as challenging as it is productive.

The emphasis of knowledge exchange is shifting. Although corporate information exchange used to be limited to just personal use or peer-to-peer sharing within departments, it is fast becoming a more free-flowing global process. In the near future, we will see KM practices becoming the foundation of the changing business landscape. Business leaders will shape the company culture to be more conducive to KM, and technology will help employees more easily re-use information in a world of escalating connectivity.

The capacity to turn knowing into knowledge and knowledge into productivity and innovation will be the hallmark of the successful enterprise in the Twenty-First Century. The industrial revolution is giving way to the knowledge revolution. The stage is set, the players are moving into place, and those who see the new vision are writing the script. In many ways this will be a quiet revolution- no gunfire, no loud machines, no armies of workers marching into the cities. Managing an organisation in the knowledge era will become synonymous with managing all forms of knowledge. The rules of the game will evolve- the principles of good management will become synonymous with the principles of KM.

The future world where knowledge shared becomes power and the entire organisation behaves as an intelligent, self-selecting, self-adapting system continually integrating and processing incoming data and information to determines its actions, is clearly idealistic- but not beyond the possible. The ultimate challenge of the future is to liberate and amplify the knowledge and creativity of all organisational members. For in them alone lives the source and power of intelligence and wisdom, which will enable the rise of the Knowledge Organization.

14. CONCLUSION

KM is gradually taking hold in the business world as the key component to unlocking the enterprise's intellectual capital. Company recognises, more than ever, the business is about value. In today's knowledge economy, it is not just basic transactions that determine corporate value. Intangible asset growth, such as successful test results for a software programme or a new medication, creates market value. Supporting, promoting and valuing the intellectual and human capital that produce profitability are the primary business challenges of this decade. More and more companies are meeting the new challenges by learning how to fuel the knowledge engine that powers twenty-first century business with shared information, experience and know-how.

Today, knowledge is the business asset of any progressive organisation. All things being equal, it is the smarter, intelligent and learning organisations that get ahead. The implementation of knowledge management helps the information flows in the organization and in implementing organisation-learning practices. KM is not about just managing or organizing books or journals, searching the Internet for users or arranging for the circulation of materials. Each of these can of course, be an isolated part of KM. The focus and thrust of KM, however, is in putting the accumulated knowledge to use. Knowledge resides in people, and is manifested through their actions. Such Knowledge is tacit knowledge. Knowledge is also explicit, and is recorded as information. Readers can learn and effectively use explicit knowledge though library resources.

In today's competitive business environment, many organisations are struggling to meet or keep up with the demands put upon them by their customers, competitors, investors, and regulators. With the globalisation of business, no organisation is immune to this pressure. Organisations that excel at leveraging their know-how in a systematic way will create and sustain a competitive advantage that will exceed the current and future demands placed upon them.

KM will create sustainable competitive advantage for organisations if approached in the appropriate manner. KM is not a single programme or series of programmes or projects, but the synthesis of core business processes that should permeate every aspect of organisation. Ultimately knowledge management is not about managing knowledge but nurturing people with knowledge. KM is not just a database or software, it is system that captures and collects, organised unorganised, documented and undocumented knowledge of the organisation, and scientifically processes it for further retrieval, sharing and reuse to handle the management of the organisation with the help of the networked system of the organisation.

REFERENCES

1. http://www.skyrme.com/insights/22km.htm
2. Davidson, Carl (2003). Knowledge Management. New Delhi: Vision Books, p. 11
3. Holsapple, C.W. (2003). Hand Book on Knowledge Management, New Delhi: Springer, p. 407.
4. Raman, A Thothathri (2003). Knowledge Management: A Resource Book, New Delhi: Excel Books, pp. 113 & 122.
5. Suliman, Al-Hawamdeh. (2003). Knowledge Management: Cultivating Knowledge Professionals. Oxford: Chandos Publishing, pp. 20 & 173.
6. Warier, E. Sudhir (2003). Knowledge Management. New Delhi: Vikas Publishing, pp. 58 & 72.

6

Knowledge Management

G.S. Birdar
R.R. Naik

ABSTRACT

Knowledge Management systems are constrained by their overly rational, static and a contextual view of knowledge. Effectiveness of such systems is constrained by the rapid and discontinuous change that characterises new organisational environments. The prevailing Knowledge Management paradigm limits itself by its emphasis on convergence and consensus-oriented processing of information. Strategy experts have underscored that the focus of organisational knowledge management should shift from 'prediction of future' [That cannot be computed] to 'anticipation of surprise.' Such systems may be enabled by leveraging the divergent interpretations of information based upon the meaning-making capability of human beings.

1. INTRODUCTION

The current conceptualisation of Information Technology (IT) enabled knowledge management suffers from fallibility in imposing the traditional information-processing model on the strategic needs of contemporary organisations. The traditional knowledge management model emphasises convergence and compliance to achieve free-specified organisation goals. The knowledge management systems were modeled on the same paradigm to ensure adherence to organisational routines built into information technology. Optimisation-based routinisation of organisational goals with the objective of realizing greater efficiencies was suitable for an era marked by relatively stable and predictable environment. *"To conceive of knowledge as collection of information seems to rob the concept of all of its life... Knowledge resides in the user and not in the collection. It is how the user reacts to a collection of information that matters."*- Churchman (1971 p.10). Present colloquium is about the various issues and challenges in management of Information Resources. The management of the most important resource that is Knowledge. As T.S.Elliot has said in his poem "*Choruses from the Rock*" *Where is the Wisdom we have lost in Knowledge where is the Knowledge we have lost in Information*" Information Resource Management is all about recognising the value of Information resource. Here main problem lies in handling /managing the various information resources, specially the resources which provide tacit knowledge. Tacit knowledge is that knowledge which can't be communicated in words, i.e., the Knowledge that is retained in the mind of human.

In this scenario, Knowledge Management appears to be a facet of Information Resource Management. Because, in the present competitive era every organisation/industry is trying to tap the knowledge, which human resources of the organisation and organisation itself possess. It is a difficult task as it is impossible to document tacit knowledge. But here one has to take into account the subtle difference between Information and Knowledge. Knowledge is a form of Information, which can exist only within an individuals' mind. It being subjective, cannot be directly transferred or communicated from one person to another, but must be converted into Information first. Information is then regarded as the objective and therefore communicable and recordable form of Knowledge.

Knowledge Management has structural and functional basis in the Information Management or Information Resource Management. The main difference is the high degree of dynamic activity involved in the Knowledge Management. According to Aslib the scope and definitions and activities under the denotation of Information Resource Management is totally encompassed by Knowledge Management, which is the latest context in the Information arena and a nature extension of the ideas of Information Resource Management. Both the Knowledge Management and Information Resource Management involve similar processes such as acquisition, creation, renewal, archival, and dissemination.

2. KNOWLEDGE MANAGEMENT

In simple terms Knowledge Management means, management of Knowledge. Knowledge management enables the creation, communication and application of Knowledge of all kinds to achieve goals. (Tiwana, 2000) Knowledge Management in general tries to organize and make available important know-how, wherever and whenever it's needed. This includes processes, procedures, patents, reference work, formulas, best practices, forecasts and fixes. Technologically, intranets, groupware, data warehouses, networks, bulletin boards, videoconferencing are key tools for storing and distributing this intelligence. (Maglitta, 1996).

Knowledge management incorporates intelligent searching, categorisation and accessing of data from disparate data bases, E- mail and files (Willet & Copeland, 1998). Knowledge Management can be defined as "the art of creating value of an organization's intangible assets". [Intangible assets are: Human centered assets, Intellectual Property assets, Infrastructure assets, and Market assets.] Knowledge Management provides access to experience, knowledge, and expertise that create new capabilities, enable superior performance, encourage innovation, and leverages existing information and knowledge assets of the organisation, facilitates information and knowledge dissemination across boundaries and integrates the information and knowledge into day-to-day business process.

3. COMPONENTS OF KNOWLEDGE MANAGEMENT

The following are the components of Knowledge Management:

* People management – recognition of skills of people
* Process management – links into the identification and deployment of practices may be associated with Business Process Reengineering.
* Information Management

4. KNOWLEDGE RESOURCES

Organisations have numerous kinds of knowledge resources. The Intellectual and Knowledge based assets fall into one of two categories: explicit or tacit. Explicit Knowledge is that what we can express to others. It is formal and systematic. For this it can be easily communicated and shared, in product specifications or a computer program.

Michael Polanyi pointed out that we know more than we can tell or explain to others. Tacit Knowledge is that knowledge which comprises the rest of explicit knowledge i.e., which we cannot communicate in words or symbols. Tacit knowledge is highly personal. It is hard to formalise and therefore it is difficult to communicate. Tacit knowledge transferred by tradition and shared experience, through for example apprenticeship or job training.

5. KEY ELEMENTS OF KNOWLEDGE MANAGEMENT

Implementation of Knowledge Management requires:

* High-level commitment to change.
* Human Resource of organisation.
* To and fro communication in the hierarchical structure of management.
* Understanding among the staff.
* Keeping track of the process of workflow in the organization.

The Knowledge Management system should be able to provide information relevant to the ongoing projects at the right time and in the right context.

6. PURPOSES OF KNOWLEDGE MANAGEMENT

* It is to gain significant returns out of the data and information we produce and the way in which we produce it.

* Along with collection of new materials, selection for inclusion in database, inputting data, indexing, searching and retrieval and delivering the out put to the end user;

Some additional tasks like data cleaning or deletion of redundant records from the database and checking for the systems security. Creating links with external sources and updating any manual of procedures specific to the operations going on in the organisation. From this knowledge, Librarians can build a web front and can allow user to access the information in a quick and easy way.

7. PROCESS OF KNOWLEDGE MANAGEMENT

Davenport explains that knowledge management process is about acquisition, creation, packaging, and application or reuse of knowledge. Some examples of each of these types of knowledge management process are:

* Knowledge Acquisition: finding existing knowledge, understanding requirements, searching among multiple sources.
* Knowledge Creation: research activities, creative processes in advertising, writing books or articles, making movies, and so on.
* Packaging: publishing, editing, design work.
* Applying or using existing knowledge: auditing, medical diagnosis;
* Reuse of knowledge for new purpose: leveraging knowledge product development processes, software development.

8. LIBRARIANS AS KNOWLEDGE MANAGERS

Tools of Knowledge Management consists 70% of

services and 30% of Technologies. Librarians provide these 70% services. This indicates the role of Librarians as Knowledge Manager. Where their functions are:

* Providing services to the user community
* Sharing of information and understanding of user needs.
* Analysing documents, classifying and sorting them for easy retrieval.
* Building the index etc.

9. CHALLENGES OF KNOWLEDGE MANAGEMENT

i. Intellectual Capital : managing of tacit knowledge is not easy. Because, we don't know what is in human mind. It is not possible to document tacit knowledge.

ii. Culture : Because of narrow mindedness or insecurity majority of people don't want to share their knowledge; some people don't want to interfere they want to stay neutral and they are away from knowledge sharing.

iii. Obsolescence : There are types of information which gets obsolete as soon as it is generated, e.g., Stock market information. Because of these types of ever changing information it is difficult to give this information quickly to capable user.

iv. Overloading : Knowledge gets accumulated. If obsolete information is not removed it leads overload. And it is difficult to identify which is useful from this information.

v. Technology : Due to rapid changes in technology it is difficult to communicate the knowledge to the user because, technology helps Knowledge

Management to a large extent. Technology is tool for Knowledge Management.

vi.Structure : Structure of Knowledge management should show overall economy.

Whether to follow centralised or decentralised system.

10. ISSUES

i. Knowledge maps : This involves building an actual map of special databases, which points towards the resource required data.

ii. Acquisition : Acquisition along with external sources should also be extended to internal sources of knowledge. The librarian works with the knowledge team to survey the various in house documents to identify and digitise, like standards, reports, and reports of technical discussions.

iii. Categorizing : The knowledge which is located inside or outside has to be represented in a way which is suitable for access or transfer on the basis of controlled vocabulary in a hierarchy.

iv. Narratives : Extracting and diffusing the success stories and technical anecdotes from resource persons.

v. Managing databases

vi. Capturing tacit knowledge (Singh, 2001)

11. CONCLUSION

To conclude I would like to say that Knowledge Management is not managing or organising books or journals, searching the Internet for clients or arranging the circulation of materials. However, each of the activities can in some way be part of the Knowledge Management spectrum and process. Knowledge

Management is about enhancing the use of organisational knowledge through sound practices of Knowledge Management and Organisational learning. Thus Knowledge Management is a combination of Information Management, Communication and Human Resources.

The information–processing model is apparent in the knowledge management practice of a major US-based global communications company :"What's important is to find use full knowledge, bottle it, and pass it around".(Stewart & Kauffman,1995).*"There is great big river of data out there. Rather than building dams to try and bottle it all up in to discrete little entities, we just give people canoes and compasses...."*

REFERENCES

1. Bawden, David (2001). The Shifting Terminologies of Information. *Aslib Proceedings,* 53 (3), March, pp. 93 - 98.
2. Binwal, J.C (2001). Knowledge Management. *IASLIC Bulletin,* 46 (2), pp. 65 - 78.
3. Devika. P. Madalli (Ed). (2002). Information Resource Management. DRTC Workshop 13-15, March. Bangalore: DRTC
4. Haravu, L.J. (2002). Lectures on Knowledge Management: Paradigm, Challenges and Opportunities. Bangalore: Sarada Ranganathan Endowment for Library Science
5. Kim, Seonghee. The Role of Knowledge Professionals for Knowledge Management *In:* Libraries in the Information Society / edited by V. Ershova, Tatiana and E. Hohlov, Yuri. IFLA Publications 102- K.G. Saur.
6. Singh,Pramod Kumar (2001). Knowledge Management Application in Libraries and Information Centres. DRTC Project-2, 1999-2001.
7. Tiwana, Amrit (2000). The Knowledge Management Tool kit: practical techniques for building a Knowledge Management system. Prentice Hall
8. http://www.brint.com/interview/maeil.htm

9. Yates-Mercer, Yates and Bawden, David (2002). Managing the Paradox: the Valuation of Knowledge and Knowledge Management. *Journal of Information Science*, 28 (1), pp. 19-29

7

Total Quality Management in Library & Information Centres

V. Chandrakumar

ABSTRACT

The evolution of Quality Management and can be traced back to the days of the Industrial Revolution. Total Quality Management (TQM) is the integration of all efforts of the organisation towards customer satisfaction at economical levels and consists of enunciating, initiating, developing and maintaining the Quality of: People, Processes and Products. This paper discusses the significance of TQM, benefits, barriers, tools & techniques and concludes with the potential challenges.

1. INTRODUCTION

All organisations, big or small, have the four common elements: Purpose, People, Processes and Products. Purpose – this is what drives the organisation. It could consist of one or more of the following: Vision and Mission, Commercial considerations and Societal objectives. People - it is the people at various levels who convert the vision of an organisation into reality. People operate at various levels: Conceptual, Directional, and Functional. Processes - these are the means available to "people" to convert thought into action. They could be: Intellectual, Technological and Financial. Products - these are the end result of efforts put in by the people in an organisation. They could be: Concepts, Physical entities and Services

The evolution of Quality Management and can be traced back to the days of the Industrial Revolution. Initially all "production" was limited in scale, and complexity. The responsibility of ensuring the quality of the product was vested with the producer. With workers beginning to become more conscious of their rights and privileges, the trade union movement began to gather strength. It therefore became imperative for "Management" to learn how to relate with representatives of trade unions, giving rise to the need of "Industrial Relations".

The latter half of the Twentieth Century saw a paradigm shift in the approach of enterprises towards Quality. While Inspection merely separated products into "acceptable" and "not acceptable", Quality control looked at reasons for rejection, and Quality Assurance provided evidence that Quality was indeed being controlled.

2. MOVE TOWARDS TOTAL QUALITY MANAGEMENT

Total Quality Management (TQM) is the integration of all efforts of the organisation towards customer satisfaction at economical levels and consists of enunciating, initiating, developing and maintaining the Quality of:

* People
* Processes

* Products

Total means that everyone in the organisation is involved in the final product or service to the customer. Quality means delighting the customer by continually meeting and improving upon agreed requirements Management recognises that TQM will not happen by accident. It is a "managed" process involving people, systems, tools, techniques. TQM is "a system of continuous improvement employing participative management and centered on the needs of customers" (Jurow & Barnard, 1993).

3. KEY ELEMENTS OF TQM

* Utilise performance management as a key strategy in achieving business objectives
* Define performance management processes in terms of values, culture and strategic vision
* Provide training to subordinates in terms of knowledge, skills and attitudes required to implement the processes in a professional manner
* Monitor and evaluate their implementation, and keep them on track

4. WHY TQM?

The following are the some of the reasons for why TQM is necessary to any organisations whether profit oriented or non-profit oriented organisation like libraries:

* Increasing competition
* Demanding customer
* Reduction of wastes inherent in the system
* Change perceptions of stakeholders
* Empower employees

* Mere survival

5. BENEFITS OF TQM

While applying TQM in any organisations, the organisation will reap the following benefits:

* Greatly improved product or service
* Major decrease in wasted resources
* Massive leap in productivity
* Sustained competitive advantage
* Increased market share
* Enhanced Returns on Investment
* Motivated work force

6. BARRIERS TO TQM

Some of the barriers are may exist for implementing the TQM in organisations. These are:

* Lack of management commitment
* Lack of vision and planning
* Satisfaction with a Quick fix
* Bureaucratic approach
* Noninvolvement of participants
* Lack of measurable

7. TQM TOOLS AND TECHNIQUES

Application of tools and techniques of TQM is important in organisation. Six pillars of TQM are: Leadership, Customer delight, Employee Empowerment, Process Approach, Application of Tools and Continuous Improvement. Top management should have Leadership quality. The stated role of top management i.e., manager is:

* setting purpose
* providing direction

* facilitating the work environment
* coaching
* supporting
* Counseling

A clear purpose statement or vision of what it is and where it is going and a set of principles and values, which define its relationships with its customers, suppliers and employees, but more importantly, each member of the organisation must know the vision, mission and values, Internalise them, Consciously apply them and If possible, participate in evolving, reviewing or modifying them. Customer delight is the second pillar of the TQM. Leadership is all about commitment. Empowerment of employees involves:

* Converting employees into leaders
* Allowing them to challenge the way things are done
* Providing them resources to realise their suggestions
* Recognising their achievements and success
* Encouraging them to work closely with others

The Fourth Pillar is Process approach - any business is the result of many individual processes performed in a logical manner. The central element of a process is an activity. Application of tools – The fifth pillar - The problems of an organisation need to be solved. This can be done by an individual responsible for the process and his/her immediate superior. However, in large organisations, there are many processes involved. Solutions can therefore require the contribution of, or affect a wide group of people. The output of a team can be more effective than the sum total of individuals working together. The essence of problem solving is Team work. Numerous tool kits are available to put an institution into TQM, one among is Six Sigma. Six Sigma is a proven methodology that:

* Delights customers
* Generates profits
* Keeps owners and workers inspired
* Seeks to identify and eliminate defects
* Focuses on outputs
* Critical to customers

Based on his work with Japanese managers and others, (Deming 1986; Walton, 1986) outlined 14 steps that managers in any type of organisation can take to implement a Total Quality Management programme.

* Create constancy of purpose for improvement of product and service. Constancy of purpose requires innovation, investment in research and education, continuous improvement of product and service, maintenance of equipment, furniture and fixtures, and new aids to production.
* Adopt the new philosophy. Management must undergo a transformation and begin to believe in quality products and services.
* Cease dependence on mass inspection. Inspect products and services only enough to be able to identify ways to improve the process.
* End the practice of awarding business on price tag alone. The lowest priced goods are not always the highest quality; choose a supplier based on its record of improvement and then make a long-term commitment to it.
* Improve constantly and forever the system of product and service. Improvement is not a one-time effort; management is responsible for leading

the organisation into the practice of continual improvement in quality and productivity.

* Institute training and retraining. Workers need to know how to do their jobs correctly even if they need to learn new skills.
* Institute leadership. Leadership is the job of management. Managers have the responsibility to discover the barriers that prevent staff from taking pride in what they do. The staff will know what those barriers are.
* Drive out fear. People often fear reprisal if they "make waves" at work. Managers need to create an environment where workers can express concerns with confidence.
* Break down barriers between staff areas. Managers should promote teamwork by helping staff in different areas/departments work together. Fostering interrelationships among departments encourages higher quality decision-making.
* Eliminate slogans, exhortations, and targets for the workforce. Using slogans alone, without an investigation into the processes of the workplace, can be offensive to workers because they imply that a better job could be done. Managers need to learn real ways of motivating people in their organisations.
* Eliminate numerical quotas. Quotas impede quality more than any other working condition; they leave no room for improvement. Workers need the flexibility to give customers the level of service they need.
* Remove barriers to pride of workmanship. Give workers respect and feedback about how they are doing their jobs.

* Institute a vigorous programme of education and retraining. With continuous improvement, job descriptions will change. As a result, employees need to be educated and retrained so they will be successful at new job responsibilities.
* Take action to accomplish the transformation. Management must work as a team to carry out the above stated 13 steps.

8. TQM IN LIBRARIES

TQM is now practiced in business as well as in government, the military, education, and in non-profit organizations including libraries (Jurow & Barnard, 1993). The practice of Quality Management in Library & Information Science sector existed since the evolution of the subject itself, but the terminology used for these varied widely. Performance indicators; performance evaluation; evaluation of reference sources using check-list of criteria; Evaluation of Information Retrieval systems using Precision and Recall ratios; Cost-Benefit and Cost- Effectiveness studies; user surveys electing opinions on library services - all these studies make part and parcel of Quality Studies using different mechanisms of assessment and methodologies. Quality studies in LIS sector are mostly isolated and are made on different aspects of library management, services, user-studies, etc. The evidence produced by the few TQM cases in the LIS sector indicates that TQM is a highly relevant management theory for information sector (Saroja and Sujatha).

Library should focus on providing the best services possible, and be willing to change to serve its customers. To determine if changes need to be made, a library administrator might ask the following questions:

* What are our niche markets?
* What do the customers come in for?
* How can I look at the efficiency of my library?
* How do we serve the current customers that exist today?

Sirkin suggests some ways a library might use the principles of TQM to enhance library services. These are:

* Create service brochures and information kits
* Conduct a user survey about library services
* Improve signage
* Change hours of operation
* Provide a more convenient material return
* Simplify checkout of materials
* Use flexibility in staff assignments
* Cooperate with local government
* Ask vendors to give product demonstrations
* Give new staff a thorough orientation
* Create interdepartmental library advisory groups
* Improve the physical layout of the library
* Track complaints
* Develop an active outreach programme
* Open satellite offices
* Publicise new or changed services
* Develop user and staff training materials
* Target services to specific groups
* Offer electronic document delivery
* Follow the mission statement
* Serve with a smile

8.1. Purpose

The main functions of any library or information centre is information / resource acquisition, organisation and dissemination. The said functions should be based on Vision and Mission statement of the parent institution (*Libraries or information centres are considered as subordinate body)* and societal objectives. For example, clearly defined policies for collection development; processing; stacking, lending, weeding out of books will help to achieve total quality control to certain extent.

8.2. People

In a library, people working at various levels who are that one convert the vision of an organisation into reality. As far as the library and information centre is concern the people are staff of different levels and categories. The possible groups include top level managers (librarian / information officer / director), middle level managers (assistant librarian / information assistant), skilled employee, and unskilled employee.

8.3. Process

These are the means available to "people" to convert thought into action. The intellectual processes could be acquisition of information material / resources, classification, cataloguing or metadata harvesting, delivering various technical services, etc. The technological processes include design and creation of databases, portal, preparation for automated personalised services such as Current Awareness Services, Selective Dissemination of Information, etc. Preparation of information products for Marketing, planning, drafting and maintaining of budget and balance sheet, etc. are the some financial processes.

8.4. Product

These are the end result of efforts put in by the people in an organisation. They could be: Concepts, Physical entities and Services. Decide the services required to meet the changing needs of the clientele. New conceptual ideas can be evolved based on system which can be added to the discipline. The physical entities such as information consolidation and repackaged products such bibliographies, indexing and abstracting periodicals, bulletins, etc., are the out puts. The new services can be introduced using available resources with help of Information and Communication Technology. Evaluation of services in terms of accuracy of information, relevance to the purpose and cost of providing service is necessary.

9. POTENTIAL CHALLENGES

While TQM clearly has positive aspects, implementing it can have potential challenges as well. Jurow and Barnard (1993) identify four barriers to the adoption of TQM in libraries: (1) vocabulary: objections to terms such as "total," "quality," and "management" which imply that high standards are not already being met; (2) commitment: TQM takes several years to implement and requires a long-term commitment by library managers; (3) process: our culture tends to be impatient and we try to solve problems quickly, contrary to TQM's careful process analysis; and (4) professionalisation: professional staff can be resistant to turning over their practices and services to what they perceive as the "uninformed whims of the customer." Sirkin (1993) also notes that it is not possible to satisfy everyone's demands; choices will need to be made.

10. SUMMARY

Libraries are ideal places to implement TQM. They are service organisations dedicated to their customers, the patrons. By formulating a strategic plan, and following it with a commitment to continuous quality improvement, library managers can transform and improve their organisations. Riggs (1992) summarises the notable principles of TQM: (1) manage by fact: make library decisions after careful analysis of data gathered with tools such as checksheets, histograms, and Pareto charts; (2) eliminate rework: library work is often labor intensive—simplify it and make sure it is done properly the first time; (3) respect people and ideas: staff are the library's most valuable resources, and they should be encouraged to point out problems without fear of management; and (4) empower people: trust library staff to act responsibly and give them the appropriate authority to make decisions that can improve the quality of work they do.

* Quality Assurance of Library and Information System should be part of the Quality Assurance of parent institution's TQM project;
* Need to develop standards / norms for assessing quality of information services with particular reference to libraries and information centres;
* Need to evolve methodologies and mechanisms for improvement of quality information services;
* More funds to be allocated for studying the quality of information services on project basis;
* Training of staff members in providing quality information services.

Finally, remember that TQM is not a "quick fix." It needs to be implemented gradually over period of time.

REFERENCES

1. Jurow, S. and Barnard, S. B. (Eds.) (1993). Integrating Total Quality Management in a Library Setting. Binghamton, NY: Haworth Press.
2. Jurow, S. & Barnard, S. B. (1993). Introduction: TQM Fundamentals and Overview of Contents. *Journal of Library Administration,* 18(1/2), pp. 1-13.
3. Riggs, D. E. (1992). TQM: Quality Improvement in New Clothes. *College and Research Libraries,* 53(6), pp. 481-483. (EJ 454 720)
4. Riggs, D. E. (1993). Managing Quality: TQM in Libraries. *Library Administration & Management,* 7(2), pp. 73-78.
5. Saroja, G. and Sujatha, G. Application of Total Quality Management to Library and Information Services in Indian Open Universities. Available at http://www.col.org/forum/PCFpapers/saroja.pdf. (Accessed on 1st August, 2007)
6. Sirkin, A. F. (1993). Customer Service: Another side of TQM. *Journal of Library Administration,* 18(1/2), pp. 71-83
7. Total Quality Management in Libraries [videorecording]. (1995). Towson, MD: American Library Association.
8. Walton, M. (1986). The Deming Management Method. New York, NY: Perigee.

8

Knowledge Management in Digital Information System: Recent Challenges & Solutions

Subarna Kumar Das

ABSTRACT

Knowledge management is emerging as a key concern of organisations, particularly those who have already redesigned their business processes and embedded a total quality approach into their practices. Knowledge management may mean management of knowledge, both explicit and tacit knowledge. Knowledge Management provides access to experience, knowledge and expertise that create new capabilities, enable superior performance, encourage innovation, and enhance customer value. Present paper attempt to highlights the growth and development of knowledge management in the changing context of digital environment as well as current and common challenges in knowledge management and its probable solution.

1. BACKGROUND AND MEANING

Knowledge Management is an upcoming field of

management, which focuses on maximising business performance by making the most of the synergy between people, processes and technology. Knowledge management is all about establishing the link between an organisation's obvious and implied intellectuals property and positive business outcome. In practice, however, it involves an organisation recognising and mapping its intellectual assets, creating knowledge for competitive advantage, making large amounts of business information available, and allocating the best practices and technology that facilitates all of the above, including groupware and intranet [1]. Knowledge management is not easy to define precisely or simply. It is a complex domain, like management itself. However, there are noteworthy connections between knowledge management and many popular management practices and strategies, including best practices, change management, benchmarking and risk of business process reengineering. Most recent business strategies accept and recognise that information and management, to mention a few. Largely, the business community also sees knowledge management as an accepted extension knowledge are its assets, and policies, strategies and tools are needed in order to manage those assets [2]. The need to manage knowledge cannot be denied, but not many have acted upon that need. Wherever knowledge management is being implemented, it may stretch from technology-oriented methods of gaining access to, managing and delivering information, to substantial efforts at changing the organisational culture [11]. Four steps in getting started in knowledge management are described by Boynton:

1. Making knowledge visible
2. Building knowledge intensity

3. Developing a knowledge culture
4. Building knowledge infrastructure

Knowledge Management (KM) caters to the critical issues of organisational adaptation, survival and competence in face of increasingly discontinuous environmental change....essentially, it embodies organisational process that seek synergistic combination of data and information processing capacity of information processing capacity of information technologies, and the creative and innovative capacity of human beings[7]

KM promotes an integrated approach to identifying, capturing, retrieving, sharing, and evaluating an enterprises information asset [8]. These information assets may include databases, documents, policies, procedures, as well as the un-captured tacit expertise and experience stored in individual's heads." [9]

KM may simply be defined as doing what is needed to get the most out of knowledge resources. In general, KM Focuses on organising and making available important knowledge. KM is also related to the concept of intellectual capital

2. THE CONCEPT OF KNOWLEDGE

Data can be viewed as information- by utilising new ways to channel raw data into meaningful information. That information, in turn, can then become the knowledge that leads to wisdom. Consider this observation made by Neil Fleming as a basis for thought relating to the following diagram :

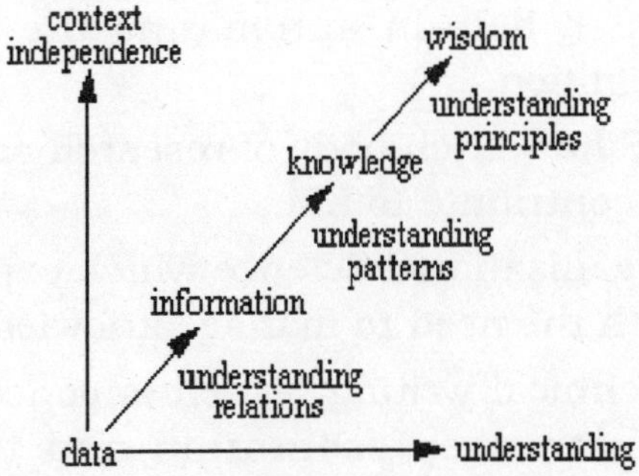

* collection of data is not information
* A collection of information is not knowledge.
* A collection of knowledge is not wisdom.
* A collection of wisdom is not truth.

The idea is that information, knowledge, and wisdom are more than simply collections. Rather, the whole represents more than the sum of its parts and has a synergy of its own. We begin with data, which is just a meaningless point in space and time, without reference to either space or time. It is like an event out of context, a letter out of context, a word out of context. The key concept here being "out of context." And, since it is out of context, it is without a meaningful relation to anything else.

3. GROWTH AND DEVELOPMENT

KM has emerged today as a multidisciplinary subject. As a discipline, it draws from a broad spectrum of disciplines and technologies such as follows:

1. Cognitive Science, which provides insight into learning and knowing that ultimately helps in improving the tool and technique for gathering and transferring knowledge.

2. Artificial Intelligence and Expert Systems which help in automating the process of cognition.
3. LIS has a rich body of research and practice to contribute to KM.
4. Organisational Science which explicitly deal with the need to manage knowledge.
5. Technical writing, which is concerned with effective representation and transfer of knowledge.
6. Decision Support System which provides insights to knowledge in the performance of cognitive tasks.
7. Computer supported collaboration work (Groupware) which has immense potentialities for KM.
8. Relational and Object Databases, which provide useful ideas to represent and manage knowledge resources.
9. Simulation which is becoming a component of KM for learning and creation of knowledge.
10. Other technologies, which include hypertext, web technology, full-text search and retrieval, performance support systems, object-oriented information modeling, help desk technology, electronic publishing technology, multimedia technology, etc.

4. KM IN DIGITAL ENVIRONMENT

* Service areas are increasingly competitive and the rate of innovation is rising.
* Reductions in staffing create a need to replace informal knowledge with formal methods.

* Competitive pressures reduce the size of the workforce that holds valuable business knowledge.
* Early retirements and increasing mobility of the work force lead to loss of knowledge.
* Changes in strategic direction may result in the loss of knowledge in a specific area.
* Most of our work is information based.
* Organisations compete on the basis of knowledge.
* Products and services are increasingly complex endowing them with a significant information component.
* The amount of time available to experience and acquire knowledge has diminished.
* Competitive marketplace.
* Accelerating rate of innovations that need to be assimilated at an even faster rate.
* Increasing mobility among employees leading to loss of knowledge.
* Competitive pressure leading to reduction in the size of the workforce holding special and static knowledge.
* Majority of employees have less and less time to acquire knowledge. On the other hand, knowledge acquiring is a process needing and more time.
* Sometimes a company may take decision to change in strategic direction. It may result in loss of knowledge in a specific area. May be after a lapse of certain period, the company reverses its policy and feels the need of the lost knowledge, Meanwhile, it may happen

that the employees with that knowledge have left the organisation.

5. COMMON CHALLENGES

Most of the challenges in knowledge management primarily stem from the types of knowledge reuse situations and purposes. Knowledge workers may produce knowledge that they themselves re-use while working. However, each knowledge re-use situation is unique in terms of requirements and context. Whenever these differences between the knowledge re-use situations are ignored, the organisation faces various challenges in implementing its knowledge management practices. Some of the common challenges resulting due to this and other factors are listed below:

DATA ACCURACY : Valuable raw data generated by a particular group within an organisation may need to be validated before being transformed into normalised or consistent content.

DATA INTERPRETATION : Information derived by one group may need to be mapped to a standard context in order to be meaningful to someone else in the organisation.

DATA RELEVANCY : The quality and value of knowledge depend on relevance. Knowledge that lacks relevance simply adds complexity, cost, and risk to an organisation without any compensating benefits. If the data does not support or truly answer the question being asked by the user, it requires the appropriate meta data (data about data) to be held in the knowledge management solution.

ABILITY OF THE DATA TO SUPPORT/DENY HYPOTHESES : The organisation could cleanse the system of very old files, thus diluting its own knowledge management initiative. Alternatively, it could set up another team to cleanse the database of redundant files, thus increasing its costs substantially. Apart from these, the real challenge for an organisation could be to monitor various departments and ensure that they take responsibility for keeping their repositories clean of redundant files.

LEGITIMACY : In the print-only world, there has been a complex but well-defined system of content validation and description that involves librarians, referees, reviewers and publishers. After going through the various defined processes, its selection gave that material a legitimacy that students and scholars came to depend upon. Furthermore, technological advances and collaborative efforts have allowed the costs of this process to be reduced through shared electronic cataloging (e.g. OCLC) and through the purchase or licensing of abstracting and indexing electronic databases. Librarians recognised ages ago that the only scalable and affordable approach to such processes was to take advantage of leveraged and shared resources.

ELECTRONIC INFORMATION RESOURCES : The rise of electronic information resources freely accessible through the Internet has distrupted this relatively efficient system in a number of ways. There is no clear and defined role for libraries with regard to the selection, preservation and provision of access in regard to the digital resources accessible through the net. Additionally, students and faculty have a need to learn how to evaluate these new information resources, and it is far more difficult to do so on the Web than it has been in a traditional library. With a traditional library, the very fact that a book or a journal was held by a library represented a conscious set of decisions about the validity of the information, and implied a filtering process that suggested a reasonable level of legitimacy. This is not true when one surfs the Web.

LACK OF SCALABILITY : Another problem is that of scale, as some libraries, academic departments, and even individual scholars are creating their own collections of web sites, selecting and describing network resources they find useful and credible. In some cases these resources are even added to centralised databases, but the combination of the growth of the web, and the lack of scalability of these individual, highly labour intensive approaches do not make such efforts a viable or affordable means of addressing this important challenge. There is some hope on the horizon in dealing with some of these issues, as there are some newly emerging, shared (and hence leveraged) cataloging resources such as OCLC's Cooperative Online Resource Catalogue (CORC) Project, and the subject gateways being established by the ROADS Project in the UK.

REALITY : Currently, scholars trying to thoroughly research an area have to go to a library to do the traditional search process and then do an electronic search of the web and other electronic resources. This also implies that these people doing this searching have the ability to discern the quality, authenticity and validity of the information that they find on the web. Of greatest concern, is that a student might go just to the Web, either assuming that the information available there is complete and accurate, or assuming that the Web alone provides an adequate search. There is plenty of reason to believe that students today and in the future will fall into this trap, because their preferred method of working is to do everything online. While everything possible should be done to educate students and others that each of these two different approaches has its own respective merits, it is unrealistic to think that such educational efforts will be successful with the vast majority of students who have grown up with the Web.

SEARCH ENGINES : Another problem with the Web today is the nature of the various search engines such as Yahoo! and AltaVista. While such services offer far wider coverage than any traditional cataloging approach can possibly match, they do so with far less quality, filtering and a very different, often less powerful, level of description. A search using one of these search engines may yield half million or more hits. These search engines are also tainted by a bias in the selection process rooted in their commercial advertising relationships, rather than solely on the search parameters.

EVALUATION : There is no clear and defined role for libraries with regard to the selection, preservation and provision of access in regards to the digital resources accessible through the net [13]. Besides, Academic information seekers should have a need to learn how to evaluate these new information resources, and it is far more difficult to do so on the web than it has been in a traditional library.

USE OF INFORMATION : Most of the users do not use or know how to use their advanced features and the more sophisticated search algorithms embedded in these highly used applications[14]. Consequently, they search virtually the entire web.

CHOICE OF ONLINE : A student might go just to the web, either assuming that the information available there is complete and accurate, or assuming that the web alone provides an adequate search. There is a plenty of reason to believe that users today and in the future will fall into trap, because they preferred method is everything they want to do through online[15].

6. CONCLUSION

Knowledge has become important productive factor for the modern digital information system. The society will inevitably require intensified management of knowledge. How to manage knowledge will become an important subject facing libraries in near future. Knowledge Management in Libraries should be focused on effective research and development of knowledge, creation of knowledge bases, exchange and sharing of knowledge between library staff including its users, training of library staff, speeding up explicit processing of the implicit knowledge and realising of its sharing. Economic environment and information environment is changing quickly today. Since Knowledge management has become a powerful tool for promoting innovation and realising reengineering the various walks of life, it occupies very outstanding position in the creation of the knowledge innovation systems of a country. Hence it is very essential to focus on Knowledge Management systems in Libraries by which the timely information service can be provided to the online user society.

REFERENCES

1. Malhotra, Y. (1997). Knowledge Management in Inquiring Organizations. *Proceedings of the Americas Conference in Information Systems,* pp. 293-295.
2. Malhotra, Y. (1998). Role of Social Influence, Self Determination and Quality of Use in Information Technology Acceptance and Utilization: A Theoretical Framework and Empirical Field Study. Unpublished Ph.D. thesis, Katz Graduate School of Business, University of Pittsburgh
3. Malhotra, Y. (2000). Knowledge Management and New Organization Forms: A Framework for Business Model Innovation. *Information Resources Management Journal,* 13 (1)

4. Malhotra, Y. (Ed.) (2000). Knowledge Management and Virtual Organizations. Hershey: PA, Idea Group Publishing
5. Malhotra, Y. (2001). Expert Systems for Knowledge Management: Crossing the Chasm Between Information Processing and Sense Making. *Expert Systems With Applications,* 20 (1)
6. Malhotra, Y. (Ed.). (2001). Knowledge Management and Business Model Innovation. Hershey: PA, Idea Group Publishing
7. Malhotra, Y. (2002). Is Knowledge Management Really an Oxymoron? Unraveling the Role of Organizational Controls in Knowledge Management. *In:* Knowledge Mapping and Management. Hershey / edited by D. White. PA Idea Group Publishing, pp. 1-13
8. Malhotra, Y. (2006). Information Ecology and Knowledge Management: Toward Knowledge Ecology for Hyper turbulent Organizational Environments. *In:* UNESCO Encyclopedia of Life Support Systems (EOLSS) / edited by D.L. Kiel, Paris, France: EOLSS Publishers,
9. Prusak, L. Where Did Knowledge Management Come From? *IBM Systems Journal,* 4
10. Knowledge Management in the Information Age. *Oracle Magazine,* May, 1998
11. Sreekumar,M.G et al (Eds). (2006). Digital Libraries In Knowledge Management. New Delhi. ESS ESS Publishers
12. www.media-access.com/whatishtml
13. www.aiai.ed.ac.uk
14. www.sveiby.com.au
15. www.computerworld.com
16. Binwal, J.C. (2001). Knowledge Management. *IASLIC Bulletin, 46* (2)

9

Dynamics of Information Technology & Future Librarianship

Anil Kumar Dhiman

ABSTRACT

The information age now is set for a viewing of four extraordinary discontinuities, i.e., time and space, mind and body, real and virtual, and humans and technology. No one can provide a picture of the future. The images being formed will change constantly as new information allows the reader to increase his or her understanding and intuitive connection to issues that are confounding, upsetting, and mind-bending. As the twenty-first century progresses, information users will be changing in ways that parallel our own changes, but to hear we will have to understand a new language and to minimise the filters and ideologies that language imposes on our understanding.

1. INTRODUCTION

Information technology has brought crucial changes in the pattern of generating and acquiring knowledge. Earlier, the books were the only media of imparting education and knowledge; later came the audiovisual methods and aids, but the emergence of computers and computer-aided technology has completely changed the scenario. The last decade witnessed more development, which resulted in the emergence of digital technology. The digital technology that is the combination of Internet, digital resources and the satellite system etc. is more prevalent nowadays. Today's libraries are experiencing rapid changes in their approach to information access and provision due to the convergence of the information and communication technology.

Then the question arises, we should know the direction in which libraries are moving. Movement toward higher, life-enhancing values represents an increase in value-added services. Movement toward lower, thing-enhancing values represents a decrease in value-added services. This indicates that movement from information toward digits will create a lower value-added service for information users.

2. CHANGES IN THE RECENT PAST

As we know that we are moving across the information society, where there is a paradigm shift in traditional libraries and the modern libraries. Information Technology has gone under several changes since its invention, particularly in electronic and digital era. Starting from the formation of clay tablets in Babylonian civilisation, it has traveled for its evolution through paper age, punched cards up to electronic media, particularly the computers. The important features that have affected the quality of information are accuracy, comprehensiveness, freshness and time. Information Technology can be used in Library and Information Science profession to:

* support functions associated with technical processing and circulation work.
* support information storage, retrieval and dissemination systems.
* support management of information services in libraries; and
* promote library extension services.

Though IT has different fields that affected the life of human being as well as the information era, the most important technologies which are being utilised for library and information science activities are: Internet, Digital Products, Multimedia and the Networking. Besides, the concept of Open Access Movement and the Digital Libraries are also coming as the emerging fields in libraries.

2.1. Internet

Internet is a network of interconnected worldwide webs of different types of organisations like universities, business, defense and science organisations etc. It has emerged not only as an important search device of the research and development community but also of political activists, farmers, librarians, journalists, scientists and many others. Internet users in multi-user domains (MUDs) frequently think of their experiences in cyberspace as real. Internet example taken from Turkle's Life on the Screen, which is cited by Martell reveals the reality. An eleven-year-old girl who uses computers regularly and belongs to a chat group in an MUD has built a room she calls a condo. It is beautifully furnished. She has created magical jewelry and makeup for her dressing table. When she visits the condo, she invites her cyber friends to join her there, she chats, orders a virtual pizza, and flirts. So, when people can play at having different genders and different lives, it is not surprising that for some this play has become as real as what we conventionally think of as their lives, although for them this is no longer a valid distinction.

Internet has lot of information in the form of webs. It is just like encyclopedia; whatever we want to know that is available on net. If any body knows the exact web address of particular site, he can go directly on that site and can access the information. If we do not know the exact address, there are the search engines to help to the users. Using search engines, many sites are open as and when we type and enter our query through search engines. Relevant sites may be accessed after refining the search on the net.

2.2. Digital Products

CD-ROMs and DVDs are the most common digital products to store the information and knowledge. CD-ROM or compact disc-read only memory is a sliver plated disc of 1.2 mm thickness and 12 cm diameter, which can store 700 megabytes of data that is equal to the data of around 500 floppies or 3,00,000 typed pages. Since, it stores large amount of structured data-bibliographic, full-text, and image types, it has brought about a revolution in the information world. The databases, which do not need to be updated quite frequently, and retrospective databases are most suitable for CD-ROMs. Today, a large number of organisations around the world are publishing scientific data, bibliographic and full text information on CD-ROMs rather than other media.

It is noteworthy to mention that now-a-days, writable and rewritable CDs are also available, on which we can write the data once or more than one times. Today's with more capacity, Digital Versatile Disks or the DVDs are also coming with 4.7 to 8.5 gaga bytes capacity, which can store much data in comparison to CDs.

2.3. Multimedia

Multimedia are the technologies that facilitate the integration of two or more types of media such as text, graphics, sound, voice, motion video, or animation into a computer-based application. It is the collection of multi-sensory presentation technologies combined through a common user interface into an information delivery system. The presentation data types can include text, images, graphics, audio, animation and video. The user interface is a computer - based system that might consist of CD-ROM disks or DVDs and customised graphical display hardware for data compression, decompression, acceleration and translation. It allows the user to browse and navigate quickly any type of complex information and is immensely helpful in education process and learning. It can be used either as a single stand-alone system or multi-user system for information dissemination.

2.4. Networking

Networking is the network of two or more than two computers, which are interlinked together for data communication. Depending upon the distance covered in networking, the networks may be of two types viz., Local Area Network or LAN and Wide area network or WAN. LAN is a digital communication facility, carrying data at high speed among a large number of information processors directly interconnected within a building or in adjacent buildings. While in WAN, the computers are situated at a very long distance and are interconnected either with the help of satellite links or leased lines. Moreover, today's wireless networks are also coming in existence.

Computers networks play increasingly an important role in the libraries. Information services like references services, current awareness service, selective dissemination of information, computer assisted learning, user education are feasible with the help of computers besides, the housekeeping operation like circulation and serial control etc. Various Library and Information Networks like, Information and Library Network (INFLIBNET), Developing Library Network (DELNET), Biotechnology Information System (BTIS), Scientific and Industrial Research Network (SIRNET), Calcutta Library Network (CALIBNET), Madras Library Network (MALIBNET), Bombay Library Network (BONET), Mysore Library Network (MYLIBNET), Pune Library Network (PUNENET), and the Ahmedabad Library Network (ADINET) etc. could be able to survive because of networking.

2.5. Open Access Movement

Open Access Movements are catching up the world over. Open-access (OA) literature is digital, online, free of charge, and free of most copyright and licensing restrictions. It is all about democratising the scientific intellectual capital, which often draws its energy from publicly or privately funded research. It is not against proprietary or peer reviewed scholarly journals.

It is just self-archiving the articles the author has published in (peer-reviewed) non-OA journals. It has nothing to do with changing peer review. Self-archiving is a way of supplementing non-OA journal access with an OA version for those would-be users whose institutions cannot afford the non-OA journal. Today there are more than 400 such interoperable institutional archives providing access to the full texts of many thousands of research papers. Besides, there are also open access journals for which readers and their libraries do not have to pay a subscription. More than 1,700 journals - including a few hundreds from developing countries are now OA journals.

Open Access Archives (OAAs) are part of the world-wide initiative, facilitated by common technical standards and open source software, to publish scholarly literature, composed of peer-reviewed journal articles and conference papers as well as technical reports, theses and working papers, on the Internet and make it available to readers free of charge and free of unnecessary licensing restrictions. These are the "electronic repositories of submitted material that may include already-published articles (post-prints), pre-published articles (pre-prints), theses, manuals, teaching material or any other material that the authors or their institutes wish to make publicly available without financial or technical barrier. Such archives may be based on an institute's output, or may be discipline-based or regionally-based.

The number of OAJs and OAAs is slowly growing. There are several online services assisting Internet users to locate these resources. Among them following two services are prominent:

* *Directory of Open Access Repositories (OpenDOAR)* – OpenDOAR aims to support the rapidly emerging movement towards Open Access to research information. It is classifying/listing archives holding research papers, conference papers, theses and other academic materials that are available as open access.

* *Directory of Open Access Journals (DOAJ)* - DOAJ aims to increase the visibility and ease of use of Open Access (OA) scientific and scholarly journals thereby promoting their increased usage and impact and it indexes OA journals from around the world.

2.6. Digital Libraries

Digital libraries as cited by Dhiman and Rani, are the organisations that provide the resources, including the specialised staff, to select, structure, offer intellectual access to, interpret, distribute, preserve the integrity of and ensure the persistence over time of collection of digital works so that they are readily and economically available for use by a defined community or set of communities. The digital libraries do enable the seamless integration of the scholarly electronic information, help in creating and maintaining local digital content, and strengthen the mechanisms and the capacity of the library's information systems and services. These libraries increase the portability, efficiency of access, flexibility, availability and preservation of digital objects.

Libraries today face the unprecedented challenge of managing an array of content spread across a host of publication types and in a rapidly proliferating mix of formats. There are a host of problems the enthusiastic library fraternity face in their digital library development endeavours starting from the copyright issues, technology complexities, infrastructure threats, diverse publication types, multiplicity of digital object formats and above all the publishers' stringent policies and monopoly. It is therefore essential that the libraries adopt necessary strategies towards developing digital libraries from the lessons learnt. It is imperative on the part of the information professional to have a componentised and a multi-system approach to knowledge technologies and information management. Seamless aggregation and meticulous integration of diverse data streams is the most appropriate strategy to be adopted and applied.

3. HUMANS AND TECHNOLOGY

It is assumed that humans are meaningfully free from the technologies surrounding them. Elsewhere, it is commonly accepted that humans are inseparable from these technologies. The discontinuity between humans and technology is of overwhelming interest. It is believed that the unwillingness of humans to recognise their underlying relationship to technology creates a discontinuity of significant proportions. Thus, traditional attitudes about the humans and technology relationship must end.

3.1. Cyborg

The cyborg is a condensed image both imagination and material reality. The union of cyberspace and the human organism has been most dramatically articulated by Haraway in Cyborg Manifesto. Her language is uncompromising. By the late twentieth century, our time, a mythic time, we are all chimeras, theorised and fabricated hybrids of machine and organism; in short, we are cyborgs. We are inside of what we make, and it's inside of us. Haraway's world is one of tangled networks part human, part machine; complex hybrids of meat and metal that relegates old-fashioned concepts like natural and artificial to the archives. Haraway was excited about the future, optimistic. She foresaw a more equitable world as male-dominated institutions are replaced by those with universal, diverse values. Casimir also saw a new identity, that of the borg, arising in a postmodern culture, a world of reframing dichotomies a world of discontinuity and of contextualised truth and meaning, a new metaphysics, and a new hierarchy.

Cyberspace is frequently framed in a context similar to the one used to depict ventures into space moon shots and planetary explorations. The cyberspace and the technologies surrounding them constitute the central phase in a post-industrial rite of passage between organically human and cyber-psychically digital life-forms as reconfigured through computer software systems.

3.2. Beyond Artificial Intelligence

The possibility of intelligence emerging directly from computers rather than being programmed by humans is startling. Humans will create artificial intelligence. Artificial intelligence will create a new form of intelligence. This development might qualify as a new stage of evolution

4. FUTURE LIBRARIANSHIP

Arunachalam points out the advent of the Internet brought with it hitherto unheard of possibilities for human creativity, information access, and global communication. Access to technology at affordable costs as well as free and open access to invaluable content spread across the world is the two important components of public access. Community owned Internet kiosks or telecenters can do wonders in combating the digital divide or lack of technology in developing countries. Telecentres are now empowering communities in the use of the Internet like education, health, micro-enterprises, and so on. They are different from cybercafés, which are mainly run with a profit motive and generally have limited focus. Internet alone has emerged as a big change in the field of libraries and information centers providing information to its users. In the changing environment of information technology, libraries will have to modify their mission in order to survive. Librarians will have to be diligent and thoughtful in all that they now propose to do in future. Suman has pointed out the following transformative actions might be seen in the forthcoming libraries due to adoption of information technologies.

* The future libraries have to be user-friendly as more library systems evolve. The metadata and the data-mining concepts will be of highest influence. Technological infrastructure needs to be developed in libraries to be more efficient and able to access the information in all types of media.
* The future libraries will combine the best of print and digital resources. Libraries have to employ multiple instructional strategies such as technology-based formats, learning communities, residencies, experimental / service learning, learning with peers, and individual learning. The relative roles of electronic communication and non-electronic communication such as print, sound-recordings, film and video etc. have to be defined clearly. Print on paper will be the pre-eminent medium for the communication of cumulative knowledge.
* The future collection development is unclear but five technologies viz., search engines capabilities, web TV, push technologies, electronic commerce and connected CD and DVD use are going to play important role in

near future.

* Libraries will have to transform their own roles and units to make significant contributions to the transformation of their parent institutions. The proposed changes will give libraries an opportunity to restructure their organization around partnerships with other professionals and the institutions. This will also help to develop new learning environments.
* Libraries will have to evolve as a gateway/ portal to digital information, regardless of their location. Libraries must formulate effective acquisition and licensing policies in relation to digital information and ensure that their users can access all the information that they need for their research. However, this transformation will require strong leadership, risk taking and a revolutionary vision.

Besides, librarians and the information specialists will need to review what is available in the area of digital information and then accordingly adjust acquisitions to demand.

5. SUGGESTIONS

It is clear that nowadays, IT / Internet technologies are dominating the field of libraries and Library Science. These technologies in the library resource enrichment and resource sharing clearly reveal the strength and potentialities of these technologies in future libraries. Libraries are scattered across the country, have a highly strategic role to play in the development, particularly in science and technology scenario and more specifically, the scientific productivity of the researchers, scientists and faculty members. This implies that there should be a proper coordination and integration and thereby pooling the resources of all the libraries scattered and distributed across the country, which can be achieved only with the help of IT/ Internet technologies.

The following points are suggested for developing library services and the library's proficiencies in future as under:

* A National Library Board is to be created by the Government towards advising and framing a National Policy on advanced and IT enabled nation-wide public library services.
* A National Policy for the introduction and application of IT in the special libraries must be formulated and implemented by the Government in coordination with the National Library Board.
* Induction of IT / Internet and related - technologies and creation of necessary infrastructure are highly essential. It should be given top priority in the libraries and information centers to meet the challenges of technology push as well as the user demands.
* Digital libraries enable the creation of local content, strengthen the mechanisms and capacity of the library's information systems and services. They increase the portability, efficiency of access, flexibility, availability and preservation of content. As such, the libraries should make the best use of open source digital library software and create local digital libraries, which are interoperable and international in standards.
* Open Access Archives or Institutional Repositories play substantial role in pooling the intellectual capital of an organisation. Numerous

open source software are available for creating them and libraries should install, configure and customise institutional repositories and publish them on the Internet.

* With the Internet Information Infrastructure (III) in place, libraries should emphasise and take initiatives on consortium. In this model the participating libraries have several added advantages such as homogeneity of participating libraries, library specific preferences and customisation, special voice on the resources allocation and subscriptions, user-feedback based resource fine-tuning, elevated level of sense of belongingness leading to increased productivity and sustainability etc.

* Library's web site or the library portal helps the libraries in the seamless content integration and content aggregation activities. It plays a dual role of giving it a world wide visibility and acts as its virtual front office. Libraries must make the best use of this user behaviour proactively in promoting information resources and services.

* Libraries should explore and make the best use of virtual libraries which provide invaluable information on almost every discipline.

* Library networks have a pivotal role in enhancing resource sharing and in enriching the resources in libraries. They need to embrace technology proactively and come up with innovative ideas and systems for the benefit of the members. Besides, the existing library networks can be made more meaningful and relevant by value adding their resources and services such as web based union catalogues of their predominant resources, online journal gateways, access to full-

text databases, E-Reference works etc. E-Books are also to be offered by library networks along with e-journals.

6. CONCLUSION

Information technologies had revolutionised the entire scenario of libraries. Allen Kent has rightly said "*the success and survival of libraries will much depend on how much and to what extent the libraries cooperate with each other in future*". It is good news that many consortia like, INDEST for IITs and IIMs, CSIR Library Consortium and UGC-INFONET for university libraries have been functioning well in the IT environment.

There exists a considerable Digital Divide - the gap between the IT / information rich libraries and the IT / information poor libraries, which is widening at an alarming rate. Lack of proper information and infrastructure planning, serious lapse in the timely adoption of proper strategies to face the changing technologies and environment, lack of management encouragement/support and above all the scarcity of funds go together to constitute the situation. IT / Internet technologies are the best technologies to tackle the Digital Divide.

Besides, the Human Resources available in the library / information center will also play central and crucial role in the successful shaping and sourcing of cutting edge IT infrastructure and state-of-art information resources/services. As such there should be a proper policy on the human resources and its promotional opportunities in the libraries. In addition, the library staff should be properly educated and trained to reap the full benefits offered by IT / Internet technologies.

REFERENCES

1. Arunachalam, S. (2005). Public Access to the Internet. *In:* Word Matters: Multicultural perspectives on information societies / edited by Alain Ambrosi et al. C&F Editions, WSIS, Tunis.
2. Casimir, V. (1997). Data and Dicks Deckard: Cyborg as Problematic Signifier. *Extrapolation.* 38 (4), p. 278.
3. Chan, L et al. (2005). Improving Access to Research Literature in Developing Countries: Challenges and Opportunities Provided by Open Access [Paper presented at the World Library and Information Congress Oslo, 14-18 August 2005] [Online]. Available at http://www.ifla.org/IV/ifla71/papers/150e-Chan.pdf.
4. Dhiman, A.K. (2003). Basics of Information Technology for Librarians and Information Scientists. 2 Vols. New Delhi: Ess Ess Publications
5. Dhiman, A.K. and Rani, Yashoda. (2006). Library Consortia: Some Problematic Issues. *Indian Journal of Information, Library & Society,* 19 (1-2), pp. 16-31.
6. Dhiman, A.K. and Rani, Yashoda. (2007). Resource Sharing, Networking and Library & Information Science Networks. New Delhi: Ess Ess Publications
7. Haraway, D. (1991). Cyborg Manifesto: Science, Technology, and Socialist-Feminism in the Late Twentieth Century. *In:* Donna Haraway, Simians, Cyborgs, and Women: the Reinvention of Nature. New York: Routledge
8. Martell, C. (2000). The Disembodied Librarian in the Digital Age. *College and Research Libraries.* January, pp.10-28.
9. Sreekumar M.G. and Sunitha, T. (2005). Seamless Aggregation and Integration of Diverse Datastreams: Essential Strategies for Building Practical Digital Libraries and Electronic Information Systems. *International Information and Library Review.* 37, pp. 383-393.
10. Sreekumar, M.G. (2006). Information Management Strategies for Sustainable National Development. WSIS Follow - Up Conference on Access to Information and Knowledge for Development. Presented at the Workshop on Building African Capacity to Implement the outcomes of the World Summit on the Information Society (WSIS) in the Sphere of Libraries and Access to Information and Knowledge.
11. Suman, A. (2006). Libraries- Perspective and Prospects. *DESIDOC Bulletin of Information Technology.* 26 (3), pp. 3-7.

10

Representation of Institutional Knowledge on Institutional Websites : A Case Study of University of California's eScholarship Repository

Hamsa Kalyani
T D Kemparaju
T B Rajashekhar

ABSTRACT

Research, teaching and learning are key processes in an academic institutions leading to creation and advancement of knowledge. Traditionally scholars have been mainly interested in quick dissemination of their research results in terms of sharing these with their peers informally or through formal publishing. Today academic institutions find the need to capture and organise this knowledge at the institutional level for re-use and fulfill knowledge management needs with help of enabling technologies provided by Internet and web technologies. This paper discusses the use of Internet and web technologies by University of California (UC) to preserve organise and disseminate its intellectual knowledge. The paper discusses in some detail the various components and features of California Digital Library's eScholarship Repository and its significance in today's networked world.

1. INTRODUCTION

Internet and World Wide Web (WWW) provide alternative means of creating, preserving and disseminating scholarly information. Faculty and students of academic institutions are using digital technologies for production as well as use and dissemination of information at their personal level. The universities now face the challenge of developing financially sustainable models for managing scholarly content. University of California has been among the first to adopt digital technologies for developing and providing access to its institutional research content.

2. eSCHOLARSHIP PROGRAMME

The University of California (UC) has 10 campuses with about 1600 faculty and researchers. It is one of the largest research institutions in the world and UC Berkeley is ranked 4th in the world, based on academic and research performance including Nobel prize and articles in respected journals. One of initiatives of UC was establishment California Digital Library (CDL) in 1997. This was primarily responsible for hosting MELVYL, the UC union bibliographic catalog and was the coordinator of licensing arrangements for UC campuses. In July 2000, the Escholarship programme was set up by CDL in order to create an infrastructure to support the comprehensive management of scholarly information from creation to dissemination and long-term access and preservation. Two important reasons led to the development of Escholarship programme. One being the slow process of commercial publishing and the other being inability of commercial publishers to establish methods to archive this information and ensure that this will be readily available for future scholars. UC spent $27 million last year on licensed content. The exponential growth in serial pricing and development of new technologies for scholarly publishing are also reasons for the development of this programme.

During the evolution of this programme, efforts were made by the librarians to find out how faculty used new technologies in their teaching and research. It resulted in CDL supporting 12 different projects in various disciplines. This was found to be unsustainable on long term basis. Therefore many repository software were tested for managing scholarly content. Eprints software developed at Southampton University, UK, was initially used to build the institutional repository. This involved getting individual faculty to deposit materials that they wanted to disseminate or publish. Later Bepress's Edikit software was found to be suitable as it could not only handle peer-reviewed publications but also allowed different units and departments to take editorial and administrative responsibility for the content deposited by them rather than individual faculty.

eScholarship programme launched eScholarship Repository in April 2002. The repository offers UC faculty a central online location for depositing scholarly output. The repository enables UC research units, centers or departments to deposit any faculty research or scholarly output they deem appropriate. The full range of scholarly output includes pre-publication materials, journals, peer-reviewed series, monographs, post prints and seminar series. Epublishing software used is Edikit from Bepress (Berkeley Electronic Press), now sold by Proquest as Digital Commons. The software system allows authors and editors to manage the entire process from submission through peer-review to the final online publication from their desktops. Escholarship repository is open access initiative (OAI) complaint. The UC units can join the eScholarship Repository by forming a sponsoring unit to decide appropriate content and ensure that standards are maintained.

3. eSCHOLARSHIP COMPONENTS

EScholarship has essentially three core components, the Escholarship Editions, Escholarship Publications and Escholarship Repository.

3.1. eScholarship Editions

eScholarship in partnership with UC Press has made 1846 monographs and digital texts available online free using XML format and with Java based infrastructure to all faculty, students and staff of UC community. Out of these 1846 books 519 are available free for the public. Table of contents (TOC) is provided. Books can be viewed from TOC chapterwise. Books are also searchable by keyword, author, title and subject. Full-text searching and internal links to footnote and index references is provided. Statistics such as the number of books in each subject is also provided.

3.2. eScholarship Publications

escholarship programme includes different types of publications like experimental interactive publications, journals, peer-reviewed series and monographs.

3.2.1. Interactive Publications

Electronic Cultural Atlas Initiative ePublications series (ECAI) provides stable, long-term access to peer-reviewed, map-based digital scholarship in history and the humanities. The TimeMap software is used for publishing interactive publications. ECAI publications include a text component, a web-based map and fully interactive downloadable map. Each publication includes images, maps and pdf files along with ISBN. The first series (launched in September 2002) is titled *A Sasanian Seal Collection in Context*.

3.2.2. Journals and Peer-Reviewed Series

In addition to capturing intellectual output of its research community, academic institutions have initiated number open access journals thus providing an alternative to conventional publishing model. In 2003, UC launched an infrastructure within the framework of Escholarship repository to publish peer-reviewed journals and series.

Dermatology Online journal, the first digital journal, which includes articles from 1995 to present, was the first to migrate into this repository. The journal was created to explore the educational potential of distributed hypermedia served via the World Wide Web. The journal is attempting to serve the dual role of providing a good source of relevant information and trying to improve the way in which information is transferred and accessed. There is one general search feature and there is a link to information about authors. This site also includes RXDERM discussion archives.

There are twelve open access journals in the repository. The first peer-reviewed journal that was introduced into the repository is *San Francisco Estuary and Watershed Science*. The other peer-reviewed journals include *Interactions: UCLA Journal of Education and Information Studies*; *Opolis: An International Journal of Suburban and Metropolitan Studies*; *Structure and Dynamics: eJournal of Anthropological and Related Sciences*; *Transit and California Agriculture.* More recently Escholarship hosted *Comitatus: A Journal of Medieval and Renaissance Studies* from its first volume in 1970. This is now a peer-reviewed journal also available in print version for a subscription.

The non-peer-reviewed journals include *Journal of Learning through the Arts* (2005-); *Nutrition Bytes* (1995-), *Nutrition Noteworthy(1998-)* and *Places: A Forum of Environmental Design(1983-).* This section also includes the series of monographs published in the areas of Entomology, Geological Sciences, Linguistics and Zoology.

There is another interesting peer-reviewed publications programme entitled Global, Area, and International Archive (GAIA). This is an initiative of the division of International and Area Studies, UC, Berkeley, in partnership with the UC Press, the CDL, and international research programs across the UC. The GAIA digital collection follows a two-tier system within the Escholarship Repository. The first tier consisting of working papers deposited by UC International and Area Studies affiliated units and forms a part of the Escholarship programme. The second tier consists of those working papers that have undergone the process of peer-review based on recommendations made by scholars. The collection includes articles, books and research series. The collection (as 28.2.07) includes 6 articles, 5 edited volumes and 11 research series published previously by IAS. The publications include title, author or editor, year, ISBN, suggested citation, peer-review information, abstract and contents by chapter. The programme is open to contributions of scholars across the world and hence provides an opportunity for researchers outside UC to share their research work on a global platform.

3.2.3. Seminar Series

This is a more recent addition to Escholarship Repository. The seminar series can be hosted by UC department, unit. There are 16 in this series so far. Research and scholarly output included here has been selected and deposited by UC academic department and research units. A *Seminar Series* features the full-text versions of papers and supplementary materials from graduate seminars, lecture series, and colloquia sponsored by UC faculty. The *Seminar Series* also includes the schedule, the list of speakers and lecture topics.

3.2.4. Post prints

The post prints service was launched on 23 February 2005. This service allows one to deposit articles published by UC faculty in societies, universities or commercial publishers in the Escholarship Repository. The post prints have to be deposited by individual authors. UC faculty either retains appropriate copyright or obtains permission from their publishers to deposit previously published articles into the repository. The post prints range from 1981-2006. There are more than 1100 post prints. The post prints are fully searchable and available free of charge.

3.3. Scholarship Repository

The repository provides an alternative to commercial publishing or self-archiving. The repository has amassed quality content since its inception with 15,834 papers as on 28.2.07. The repository is being used extensively recording 4,738,328 full-text downloads to date.

4. FEATURES AND SERVICES

A typical record of the repository includes title, downloadable PDF version, size, date of upload, abstract, suggested citation (full reference including web address). The repository provides browse and search features. The browsing feature includes browsing research and scholarship by campus; research unit, center or department; journals and peer-reviewed series; seminar series; and post prints. Within each research unit browsing by year and searching by author is possible. The papers are listed chronologically. The search option includes searching for words in the full-text across all documents in the repository as well as searching for works by an author. Statistics such as full-text downloads so far and full-text downloads in the previous week are always indicated on the website. Information such as top ten downloads, paper of the day, top ten recent papers and top ten all time papers are provided. Value added services such as *tell a colleague* about a particular paper and promotional practices such as an email message to faculty stating how many users have accessed their papers are useful. The *My account* feature allows one to create a user profile and the users will get email notification of newly posted materials tailored to their interest. Users can even set the frequency with which email alerts should be sent to them.

The benefits to content providers include the following:

* The repository software is easy to use and

makes publication and dissemination quick and efficient.

* The repository promises permanence of materials by providing persistent access.
* The administrative time is saved as the software automatically creates PDFs from MS Word or RTF files. It creates and updates links, generates title pages for papers and creates a citation.
* The repository accepts associated content such as datasets, spreadsheets, power point presentations and other non-textual materials like sound and video files and executables.
* However this has to be accompanied by textual commentary if they are not a part of an article.
* Non-peer-reviewed papers may be revised or even removed upon request of the author but a citation will remain with a note about withdrawal. Multiple versions of the paper may be posted for any period of time.
* Peer-reviewed series carries a label that acts as a link to a description of the peer-reviewed process employed for that unit's submission. Papers cannot be removed after they are posted.
* The repository provides increased visibility for the researcher, department as well as institution.

5. CONCLUSION

The UC eScholarship initiative is intended to be a long-term collaborative effort among faculty and librarians. The repository provides a platform for publishing peer-reviewed as well as non-peer-reviewed content. While the infrastructure supports different types of documents and formats, the ability of the system to index these documents automatically as well as with keywords and vocabulary provided by the contributors in order to facilitate fast searching and relevance ranking of results is the challenge ahead. EScholarship repository provides a model for all academic institutions to emulate.

REFERENCES

1. Candee, Catherine (2004). Fat Cat Publishers Breaking the System. *Syllabus Magazine.* May
2. Huwe, Terence (2002). Social Sciences E-Prints Come of Age: The California Digital Library's Working Paper Repository. *Online.* September/October
3. Soehner, Catherine B (2002). The eScholarship Repository: A University of California Response to the Scholarly Communication Crisis. *Science & Technology Libraries,* 22 (3/4), pp. 29-37.

11

Libraries & Librarians in Knowledge Management in the Twenty First Century

Asis Kumar Hazra
Samir Chattopadhyay

ABSTRACT

Knowledge Management (KM) has emerged as a key concern of organisations. It involves the identification and analysis of available and required knowledge, and the subsequent planning and control of action to develop knowledge assets so as to fulfill organisational objectives. As a learning organisation, libraries should provide a strong leadership in knowledge management and librarian has to recast his/ her role as a knowledge professional. KM in libraries is to promote relationship in and between library and user, to strengthen knowledge internetworking and to quicken knowledge flow. This paper briefly describes the concept of data, information and knowledge and difference between information and knowledge. Concept of tacit and explicit knowledge, Knowledge Management and its components and the necessary factors for developing a KM system are being briefly discussed. The paper deals with what libraries can do to improve their knowledge management in all of the key areas of library services. Lastly it highlights some skill and competencies of librarian for knowledge management in libraries.

1. INTRODUCTION

Knowledge Management (KM) is the hottest topic of the day. KM is concerned with the developing organisations in such a manner as to derive knowledge from information. Doing this requires people, process and technology. It is not just a better to index, store and retrieve information; it is fundamental change in the nature of how people work with information to derive knowledge from information. Knowledge exits in the minds of people, not technology. Technology can capture information, but it can not convert information into knowledge. Only human being can convert information into knowledge when read and assimilated after retrieval. Useful technologies for this phase of the knowledge of the KM process include statistical analysis, software, data mining tools and decision support system, artificial intelligence, and visualization tools.

According to Boynton four steps in getting started in KM are:

* Making knowledge visible
* Building knowledge intensity
* Developing a knowledge culture
* Building knowledge infrastructure

These four steps are interdependent in that embarking on one without the others will hinder the acceptance and success of knowledge management as a major organisational focus. Some well-run organisations have been doing these four steps for many years, while others are beginning to recognise their importance and the extent to which they need to be integrated with how work gets done. KM is not owned by any one group in an organisation, nor by any profession or industry. But if librarians and information specialist want to be key persons in the emerging KM phenomenon, they need to understand the multiple perspective of other person. KM in libraries is to promote relationship in and between library and user, to strengthen knowledge internetworking and to quicken knowledge flow.

2. DATA, INFORMATION AND KNOWLEDGE

Knowledge is neither data nor information but it is related to both. It is still important to emphasise that data, information and knowledge are not interchangeable concept. According to Les Alberthal "Data can be viewed as an abundant, vital and necessary resource". With enough preparation, we would be able to tap into that reservoir—and ride the wave—by utilising new ways to channel raw data into meaningful information. That information, in turn, can then become the knowledge".

In brief Data, Information and Knowledge are:

* **Data:** Scattered, unrelated facts, writings, numbers, or symbols.
* **Information:** Selected, organised and analysed data.
* **Knowledge:** Information combined with user's ability and experience that is used to solve a problem or to create new knowledge.

2.1. Difference between Information and Knowledge

* Information is visible but Knowledge is invisible
* Information is independent from action and decision but knowledge is closely related to action and decision.
* Information is different in format after processing whereas knowledge is different in thought after processing.
* Information is physical product but knowledge is spiritual product
* Information is independent from existing environment but knowledge is identified with existing environment.
* Information is easily transferable, and duplicable, whereas knowledge is transferable through learning, but not duplicable.

3. EXPLICIT AND TACIT KNOWLEDGE

Explicit knowledge is expressed in words and numbers and shared in the form of data, scientific formulae, specifications, manuals, and the like. This kind of knowledge can be readily transmitted better individuals formally and systematically. *Tacit knowledge* is highly personal and hard to formalise, making it difficult to communicate or share with others. Tacit knowledge is deeply rooted in an individual's actions and experiences as well as in his/her ideals, values, and emotions. Tacitness may be considered as a variable, the degree of tacitness being a function of the extent to which the knowledge is or can be codified and abstracted. Knowledge may dynamically shifts between tacit and explicit over time although some knowledge always will remain tacit. Nonaka identifies four basic pattern for creating knowledge in any organisation which is given below:

* From Tacit to Tacit. When one individual shares tacit knowledge with another in face-to-face contact.
* From Explicit to Explicit. When an individual combines discrete pieces of explicit knowledge into a new whole, such as a finance manager collecting and synthesising information and opinions from different parts of the organisation then putting this into a financial report.
* From Tacit to Explicit. This extends the organisation's knowledge base by codifying experience, insight, or judgment into a form which can be reused by others.
* From Explicit to Tacit. When staff begin to internalise new or shared explicit knowledge and then use it to broaden, extend, and rethink their own tacit knowledge.

4. CONCEPT OF KM

KM is a discipline that promotes an integrated approach to identifying, managing and sharing all of an organisation's knowledge assets including unarticulated expertise and experience resident in individual workers. In other words, KM is taking advantage of what we know. KM involves the identification and analysis of available and required knowledge, and the subsequent planning and control of actions to develop knowledge assets so as to fulfill organisational objectives. KM is not about managing or organising books or journals, searching the inherent for clients or arranging for the circulation of materials.

However, each of these activities can in some way be part of the knowledge management spectrum and processes. KM is about enhancing the use of organisational knowledge through sound practices of KM and organisational learning. Thus, KM is a combination of information Management, Communications, and Human Resources .

According to Davenport, KM is about the following:

* Knowledge Acquisition: finding existing knowledge, understanding requirements, searching among multiple sources.
* Knowledge Creation: research activities, creative processes in advertising, writing books or articles, making movies, and so on.
* Packaging: publishing, editing, design work
* Applying or using existing knowledge : auditing, medical diagnosis;
* Reuse of knowledge for new purpose: leveraging knowledge in product development processes, software development.

5. COMPONENTS OF KM

Rudy Ruggles, leading KM thinker/practitioners, has identified the following items as integral components of KM:

* Generating new knowledge;
* Accessing valuable knowledge from outside sources;
* Using accessible knowledge in decision making;
* Embedding knowledge in processes, products, and/or services;

* Representing knowledge in documents, databases, and software;
* Facilitating knowledge growth through culture and incentives;
* Transferring existing knowledge into other parts of the organisation;
* Measuring the value of knowledge assets and/or impact of KM.

6. FACTORS FOR DEVELOPING KM

In developing a KM system, it is necessary to take into account the following factors:

* KM does not come cheap;
* Effective KM requires hybrid solutions using people and technology;
* KM is highly political, has socio-culture and human implications;
* KM requires development of knowledge managers;
* KM benefits more from maps than models, more from markets than from hierarchies;
* Sharing of knowledge may be perceived as an 'unnatural act';
* KM entails improving knowledge-based work process and providing knowledge-based products and services;
* Accessing knowledge is only the beginning;
* KM is never-ending continuous process;
* KM requires a knowledge contract.

7. LIBRARIES & KM

Libraries in the 21st century need to be as a learning and knowledge center for their users as well as the intellectual commons for their respective communities. As a learning organisation, libraries should provide a strong leadership in KM. The most important mission of public, academic, and research libraries is to expand the access of knowledge for their users. Charged by this mission, libraries should aim their knowledge management goal high. The following are some examples of what libraries can do to improve their KM in all of the key areas of library services.

7.1. Knowledge Resources Management

In Knowledge Economy Society (KES), there is exponential growth in human knowledge in a variety of formats, so libraries need to develop their resources access and sharing strategies from printed to electronic and digital resources in concert with their objective and charges. Restricted by limited funding, technology, staff, and space, libraries must carefully analyse the needs of their users and seek to develop cooperative acquisition plans to meet these needs. An integrated Online Public Access Catalogue (OPAC) with both internal and external resources as well as printed and other formats of knowledge should be developed and maintained. Useful websites and knowledge sources should be regularly searched and selected from the Internet and included in OPACs by hard links. A system for the reviewing and updating of these resources should be performed.

7.2. Resources Sharing & Networking

Libraries should developed a well organise resource sharing and networking environment. It will greatly expand by the rapid development of computer, telecommunication, networking, and digital technologies. The successes of resource sharing and networking are largely depend on the result of the full cooperation and participation of all member libraries without selfishness. Large and major libraries must take the lead in such an endeavour. Supports in policies and funding from the government or parent organisations are also critically important. All libraries, regardless of size and specialties, have been benefited by library cooperation and resources sharing.

7.3. Information Technology Development

Knowledge acquisition is the beginning of KM in libraries. The application of information technologies enlarges the scope of knowledge acquisition, raises knowledge acquisition speed and reduces knowledge acquisition cost. It is impossible to accomplish such important tasks by using human brains only in the modern society in which the knowledge changes day by day. It will be possible to link closely knowledge sources and knowledge workers by computer networks, thus constructing knowledge networks in libraries based on realisation of single-point information. The priority of information technologies in the field of knowledge storage not only finds expression in quantity, but also in retrieval, sorting and security of the knowledge. Information technology is also indispensable in the application and exchange of knowledge and other fields. It functions as a source and tool for knowledge innovation.

7.4. User Services

The most important goal of KM is to provide users with a variety of quality services in order to improve the communication, use and creation of knowledge As much as possible these services should be according to the needs and requirements of each user. Information about each user can be obtained by analysing the records of user registration, surveys, circulation and interlibrary loans, frequently asked reference questions, and the use of e-journal and digital resources, etc. User satisfaction and needs should be collected through periodic users' surveys. The findings should be used for the planning and redesign of library services. It is very important, however, that user's privacy should always be protected. Some of the manual services such as current awareness service and selective dissemination of information, which libraries have been providing, can now be done automatically by employing the Information Technology with great efficiency and convenience.

7.5. Human Resource Management

Human Resource Management (HRM) is the core of KM in Libraries. The most important resource in the Knowledge Economy Society (KES) is the talents who grasp knowledge. The talent competition has become the focus of market competition in the KES. In the KES, the libraries will attach importance to vocational training and lifelong education of library staffs to raise their scientific knowledge level and ability of acquiring and innovating knowledge. They also will and fully respect the human value, guide and bring into play wisdom potentialities of library staffs, take developing knowledge resources in the brains of library staffs as an important way for rising work efficiency. An all-round improvement of library staff's quality and positioning of the human value will become important objectives of KM in libraries. Libraries should also encourage the transfer of knowledge and experience from experienced staff to new staff members. A mentoring system should be in place to help newcomers to learn from experienced library staff. Informal seminars and discussion sessions where staff can interact and exchange their views and other specific experience and knowledge should be scheduled at regular intervals and at convenient times. Libraries should pay attention to favourable working conditions and environment, which will contribute to better staff retention.

8. LIBRARIAN & KM

The following are some skills and competencies required for a librarian for KM in libraries:

* Having the knowledge and skill to manage large collections of knowledge resource of various types include their electronic version;
* Organisng and codifying information sources and making these accessible to others;
* Sharing and exchange of information by understanding the user need;
* Ability to designing and implementing information system;
* Processing , analysing and storing the document for easy retrieval;
* Knowledge of Information and Communication Technologies (ICTs) and their application in libraries;
* Extend interaction and collaboration, and ability to effectively teach end user, individual and groups;
* Having knowledge of digital library concept such as:
    - Managing the digital libraries;
    - Organising digital knowledge and information;
    - Disseminating digital information from the computer-held digital information;

- — Providing digital reference services and electronic information services;
- — Providing knowledge mining from the emerging knowledge warehouses;
- — Handling the task of massive digitisation, digital storage process, and digital presentation;
- — Providing universal access and retrieval of digital knowledge, ultimately access to all;
- — Cataloguing and classification of digital documents and digital knowledge;

* Being active and open to the changing environment;

* Analysing total library activities or system thinking;

* Being a strong promoter of diversity in the workplace;

* Ability to establishing trusting and respectful relationship with customer and staff;

* Developing the skills of continuous learning from lessons learned or best practices;

* Efficiently and effectively communicating with the colleagues and customers;

* Awareness of all possible sources where one can have access to information.

Librarian should also be aware of:

* Legal and Ethical issues;

* Confidentiality; Security, encryption;

* Hacking; virus;

* Cyber crimes; cyber-terrorism;

* IPR issues, copyright, cyber laws.

9. CONCLUSION

Libraries have grown with in the social, cultural, scientific and technological environments, modern libraries are not merely storehouses of knowledge and information but are also live and active institution involved in the vital service to the society. KM will inject new blood into the library culture. Some common activities that will take place in knowledge management initiatives are creation of knowledge teams, sharing of best practices, development of knowledge databases, creation of knowledge centres, collaborative technologies i.e. use of intranets or groupware for rapid information access and intellectual capital teams - to identify and audit intangible assets such as knowledge. For a library professional, understanding KM- the concept, IT practice tool and strategies is important for designing development of information system, products and services in the library and to apply KM efficiently and effectively. KM will introduced to help a library of what ever nature to create, share and use knowledge effectively because it pays off in fewer mistakes, less redundancy, quicker problem solving, better decision making, reduced research and development cost, increased worker independence, enhanced customer relations, and improved services to customers.

REFERENCES

1. Abram, Stephen. Knowledge Management: Is this the Answer? Available at http://www.informart.ca/sla/km/abram,
2. Bellinger, Gene. Knowledge Management—Emerging Perspectives. Available at http://www.systems-thinking.org/kmgmt/kmgmt.htm
3. Broadbent, Marianne. Phenomenon of Knowledge Management: What does it mean to the Information Profession? Available at http://www.sla.org/pubs/serial/io/

1998/may98/broadben.html

4. Davenport, Thomas H. The Future of Knowledge Management. Available at http://www.cio.com/archive010196-davenpor-content.html
5. Definition of Knowledge Management. Available at http:/www.brint.com/peterold.htm
6. Definition of Knowledge Management. Available at http:/www.tdan.com/i008fe03.htm
7. MLIS Course Materials, MLI-101 (2005). New Delhi: Indira Gandhi National Open University.
8. Joshi, Meenakshi (2002). Is Knowledge Management same as Information Resource Management? *In:* Workshop on Information Resource Management, DRTC, Bangalore, 13th -15th March. Available at https://drtc.isibang.ac.in/handle/1849/107
9. Kim, Seonghee (1999). The Roles of Knowledge Professionals for Knowledge Management. *In:* 65th IFLA Council and General Conference Bangkok, Thailand, August 20-28, 1999. Available at http://www.ifla.org/IV/ifla65/papers/042-115e.htm
10. Kumar, S. Shravan (2002). Librarian as Knowledge Managers. Workshop on Information Resource Management, DRTC, Bangalore, March 13-15. Available at https://drtc.isibang.ac.in/handle/1 849/106
11. Lee, Hwa-Wei. Knowledge Management and the Role of Libraries. Washington, DC: Asian Division, Library of Congress. Available at http://www.white-clouds.com/iclc.cliej/cll91ee.htm
12. Shanghong, Tang (2000). Knowledge Management in Libraries in the 21st Century. *In:* 66th IFLA Council and General Conference, Jerusalem. Available at http://www.ifla.org/IV/ifla66/paper/057-11e.htm
13. Sreenivasulu, V. The Role of Digital Librarian in the Management of Digital Information System. Available at http://eprints.relis.org/archive/00004227/01/role-DL-DIS.pdf
14. http://en.wikipedia.org/wiki/Knowledge_management
15. What is Knowledge Management? Available at http://www2.sims.berkeley.edu/courses/isl3/sq9/projectsweb site/about km.html

12
Role of Libraries in Knowledge Management

S. Humayoon Kabir

ABSTRACT

Defines and explain the concepts 'knowledge' and 'knowledge Management'. An overview of KM and the role of libraries and librarians in its implementation are discussed. Skills required for librarians to be successful in KM enumerated. Suggests that librarians should be in charge of KM in their organisation in order to leverage the intellectual assets and to facilitate knowledge creation.

1. INTRODUCTION

We live in a world that is changing day by day. Change advances peoples intellect and also moves organisations. For change to be effective, peoples must change and thereby organisations. The key to change and growth is awareness, sharing ideas and coming up with new and innovative ways of staying ahead of competition. It involves learning, innovating and adopting behaviour designed to improve quality and performance. In the twenty first century knowledge is widely recognised as the single most important factor in creating superior performance for the individual as well as the organisation. Knowledge is a form of information which can exist only within an individual's mind. It cannot be directly transferred or communicated from one person to another because it is subjective in nature. But transfer is possible if it is converted into information first. Information is then regarded as the objective and therefore communicable and recorded form of knowledge.

Knowledge Management (KM) is a concept that has developed over the past decade or so and it has generated a great interest in management thinking first. Further this new emerging field was popularised by the business world as it is seen that over the past several years many organisations have striven to increase their effectiveness. The focus of KM is organisational knowledge and treated as a valuable asset to a company or an organisation. It is regarded as creating values from knowledge, information and people. Organisations with large knowledgeable assets have led the effort, including big businesses such as IBM, Microsoft, Hewlet Packard etc. As Lew Platt, Chief Knowledge Officer of Hewlet Packard says "If Hewlet Packard knew what Hewlet Packard knows, we would be three times more profitable". In the corporate sector managing knowledge is considered key to achieving breakthrough competitive advantage. After the business people, the academics showed unprecedented interest in the knowledge management field and started conducting research on it. Now the applications of KM have spread to all types of organisations including government agencies, research & development departments and academic institutions.

When we trace the appearance of the term, KM

has entered the lexicon in recent years only. The web of science (all three citation indexes) studied by T.D.Wilson shows that the term KM did not occur in literature until 1986. There were only a few occurrences from 1986 to 1996. However there is an exponential growth of the topic from 1997 till date which shows the interest in this particular subject field.

2. KM & LIBRARIES

As everybody knows that there is unprecedented growth of information and knowledge and that is having a profound impact not only on business organisations but also the libraries. This has made Knowledge Management (KM) more important in libraries. KM is a facet of Information Resource Management (IRM) because in the present competitive era every organisation/industry is trying to tap knowledge, which human resources of the organisation and organisation itself possess. It is a difficult task as it is impossible to document tacit knowledge. It is to be noted that the scope, definition and activities under IRM is totally encompassed by KM. Therefore KM and IRM involves similar processes such as acquisition, creation, renewal, archival and dissemination. Let us see what libraries can do to improve their KM in library activities.

2.1. Knowledge Resource Management

Libraries need to develop their resources access and sharing strategies from printed to electronic and digital resources. Since there is limited funding, technology, staff, space etc. libraries should conduct user studies and develop co-operative acquisition programmes. An integrated OPAC (Online Public Access Catalogue) with both internal and external resources should be developed. Useful websites and knowledge sources from the Internet, which are needed for the user community should be regularly searched and selected by the library staff and should be included in the OPAC by hard links which is highly helpful to the clientele. Libraries in addition to explicit knowledge should develop means to organisations. Each and every library should have its own website and it should serve as a portal for all explicit and tacit knowledge from inside and outside the organisation. Using the Dublin Core metadata, web information should be captured through co-operative efforts. New methods such as data mining, text mining, content management, search engines, increasing programmes, natural language searching, linguistic analyses, semantic networks, knowledge extraction, concept yellow pages should be employed.

2.2. Resource Sharing and Networking

Due to the rapid development of computer, telecommunication, networking, and digital technologies during the last fifty years resource sharing and networking expanded a lot. Libraries should become member of several consortia then only they may be able to co-operatively capture digital resources of all types and make them easily searchable by users. Funding from the government or parent institutions are important here. Experience over the past years indicates that libraries, regardless of its size and speciality, have been benefited by resource sharing and networking.

2.3. Information Technology (IT) Development

IT should be used as an enabler to facilitate the implementation of KM. In this regard the chief librarian should be considered as the Chief Knowledge Officer (CKO) of the entire organisation. The CKO should work co-operatively with the Chief Information Officer,

Planning Department, the computer centre/ department, finance department and develop a KM system. This system needs computer and technology infrastructure, Intranet, extranet, internet etc. Upgrading and strengthening the above including the software programs facilitate capture, analysis, organise, storage, and sharing of all internal and external information resources. This helps in effective knowledge exchange among the users, faculty, research scholars, subject specialists and other resource persons, publishers, government agencies, businesses and industries.

2.4. User Services

In the business world customer oriented approach already came into being. Unlike in the early days instead of library focused approaches, user focused approaches should be the need of the hour. Therefore users should be provided with quality services tailored to the interest and needs of each of them. Thus the ultimate goal of KM is oriented towards the user. Information about each user can be obtained by analysing the records of user registration, surveys, circulation data, interlibrary loans, reference question statistics, use of e-journal and digital resources etc. User satisfaction and user needs should be assessed by the librarian through user surveys periodically. Therefore the main aim of KM is to provide users with a variety of quality services in order to improve the communication, use and creation of knowledge.

2.5. Human Resource Management

It is a real fact that the library staff having vast experience possesses expert knowledge. Such expertise possessed by them should be inventoried, indexed and updated and this should be made accessible through electronic databases created and maintained by libraries. The knowledge and experiences of the library staff should be appreciated, valued and shared. The library staff member who share their tacit knowledge and experience through writing, publishing, lecturing, tutoring or mentoring should be recognised by the higher authorities and should be rewarded which, in turn, is an encouragement for them. An organisational culture for sharing of knowledge and expertise should be established in the library and for this the Chief Librarian or the Library Director should take strong leadership and commitment. As learning organisation, libraries should allocate annual funds for providing continuing education and staff training to all its staff members periodically and this knowledge should be shared among all other staff members of the library. Prevent knowledge from becoming stagnant. Knowledge must be renewed and expanded.

3. KM & LIBRARIAN

The conventional function of libraries is to collect, store, process, retrieve and disseminate information to provide better and effective services to the clientele. The success of library depends upon their ability to utilise information and knowledge of its staff to better serve the needs of the society. There is a considerable opportunity for librarians to use their traditional skills to assume a new function of managing knowledge within the library which would complement the traditional library service function. Librarians as autonomous information professionals have a definite role in evaluating, filtering and managing information including skills of cataloging, classification, indexing, abstracting, documentation, etc. These are applied in the new information context such as the management of metadata, the design and application of search engines and the like. Other skills may also be useful in making the knowledge of the organisation, customer service orientation and their training skills.

Actually librarians are the ultimate knowledge managers. They are the custodians (have been the custodians) of documented knowledge for centuries. Therefore librarians can do KM better than anybody else. A wrong notion that crept into the minds of librarians and they still believe is that KM is simply managing information and explicit or documented knowledge which is what librarians did and are doing for many years. However they should understand that information and knowledge is not the same thing. Information is simply contextualised data and to transform into knowledge needs an added human element in it. Information tends to be tangible, whereas knowledge is informational – that is interpreted and synthesised. In addition many librarians may not know the important point that KM encompasses the whole organisation and not just bits in the library, and it includes tacit knowledge as well as explicit knowledge. Tools of KM consist of 70% services and 30% of technologies. Librarians or information managers provide 70% of these services. This indicates the potentiality of the role of librarians as knowledge managers.

There are a number of significant skills that librarians currently do not have. Perhaps this may be the reason why people are not routinely appointing library & information professionals as knowledge managers. A mind shift on the part of the librarians is essential if they are to have a place in the knowledge management circle. Librarians need to become more proactive, think more strategically and align our work more closely with the goals of the organisation as a whole. It is high time to understand that KM is more than information and technology and that tacit knowledge is of critical relevance today. If librarians have to play a significant role in the knowledge era, they have to start thinking outside the professional box and align every work they do with the broader objectives of the organisation in which their library is fitted. To do this they will need to work along with areas such as Human Resources, Information Technology and Senior Management. Such a team approach is essential in recognising librarians in the KM circle.

4. CONCLUSION

Organisations of all types are faced with tremendous competitive pressure nowadays. A variety of techniques were developed in the past, to enhance a firm's ability to react and cope with such pressures, including business process re-engineering, total quality management, outsourcing etc. Now information and knowledge have become increasingly recognised as competitive differentiators.

Knowledge is an asset. Knowledge sharing among employees and with customers and with business partners has a tremendous effect. KM is regarded as very important in business firms to gain competitive advantage over other business firms in the race, to add value to their products and to win greater satisfaction from their customers. The library & information professionals should learn a lesson from the business world. KM is very much important for the libraries as that of the business firms except the proprietary and money making concerns. It is to be remembered that librarians are the only sect of people having long and rich experience in managing information. Many such knowledge skills in the library & information sector can be applied to KM effectively.

As we entered the 21st century which is a knowledge age and since libraries are undergoing transformation and therefore should not lag behind in KM. On the other hand, librarians with vast professional knowledge and experience should lead the KM movement. In this endeavour IT and related systems are a great support and we should take benefit out of it. Further librarians & information managers should work in close association with IT professionals and others to develop a good KM system.

REFERENCES

1. Townley, Charles T. Knowledge Management and Academic Libraries. Available at http://www.ala.org
2. Wilson, T.D. The Nonsense of Knowledge Management. Information Research. Paper, No. 144. Available at http/ information R.net/ir/8-1/paper 44.html.
3. White, Tatiana. Knowledge Management in an Academic Library based on the Case study KM within OULS. *In:* World Library & Information Congress. Available at http:// www.ifla.org/iv/fla 69
4. Wen, Shixing. Implementing Knowledge Management in Academic Libraries: A Pragmatic Approach. Available at http://www.white-clouds.com/icle/clieg/c119
5. Lee, Hwa-Wei. Knowledge Management and the Role of Libraries. 3rd China -US Library Conference. Available at http://www.nic.gov.cn/culc/en/insex.htm
6. Cohen, Suzanne et al. Personalized Electronic Services in the Cornell University library. *D.Lib Magazine.* 6 (1-2). Available at http://www.dlib.org/dlib/april00/mistlebauer/ O4mistleba uer.html
7. Looney, Michael and Lyman, Peter (2000). Portals in Higher Education: What are they, and what is their potential? *EDUCAUSE Review,* pp 354. Available at http:// www.educause.edu/pub/er/erm00/article004/loon ey.pdf

8. Blair, David C (2002). Knowledge Management: Hype, Hope or Help? *Journal of the American Society for Information Science and Technology.* 53 (12), pp. 2; 1019-1028.

9. Koina, Cathie. Librarians are the Ultimate Knowledge Managers? *The Australian Library Journal.* Available at http://www.alia.org.ou

10. Church, Doug. From Librarian to Knowledge Manager and Beyond: the Shift to end-user domain. Available at http://www.sla.org/chatper/ctor/courier/v36n2alb.htm

11. Butler, Yuonnne. Knowledge Management if only you know what you know. STRAIT to the Future. ALIA 8th Asia Pacific Specials, Health and Law Librarians' Conference. Available at http://conference.alia.org.au/shllc/999/papers/butler.htm 1

12. Sravan Kumar, S. (2002). Librarians as Knowledge Managers. *In:* Workshop on Information Resource Management, 13 - 15, March. Bangalore: DRTC.

13
Entering Knowledge Society: Some Modest Indian e-Initiatives

C.R. Karisiddappa
Iqbalahmad U Rajgoli

ABSTRACT

The Knowledge Society demands people to be lifelong learners. Lifelong learning is a must in the real-life context of the knowledge society and covers "all purposeful learning from the cradle to the grave" of very diverse groups of learners in professional, community or individual context. Alongside the rise of e-commerce, e-health and even e-democracy, the Internet has been positioned as a potential saviour of lifelong learning and learning society. The information technology revolution is creating a new form of electronic, interactive education that should blossom into a lifelong learning system that allows almost anyone to learn anything from anywhere at anytime. This paper discusses the e-governance initiatives undertaken by the Government of India, non-profit and non-government organisations. Also highlights the importance of information literacy and lifelong learning in the Knowledge Society and proposes possible programmes and initiatives for implementation of information literacy and lifelong learning.

1. INTRODUCTION

Information Revolution has made a significant impact on the contemporary thinking and learning processes. Information is on the move and it calls for everyone to acquire intellectual skills such as the ability to scan, to make connections and to manipulate many forms of information to move towards a knowledge society. The important task is not to "know" but to "do" information – to be able to use it. Knowledge Society has become a buzzword of the 21st century. The Knowledge Society differs in scope and nature from 'literate society', 'learning society' and 'educated society'. Knowledge Society needs knowledge workers who form a dominant group of work force and they are always striving to keep their knowledge up to date.

A Knowledge Society is characterised by three important attributes, namely, creative capacity, innovative talent and ability to determine relevance. All this can be created and nourished by good vibrant education and training systems. The creative capacity is demonstrated by the generation of new knowledge and extensions to existing knowledge. The innovative talent is reflected in the improvements in quality to existing products and their functions. And a Knowledge Society successfully determines the relevance of the various creative abilities and innovative talents suitable to its specific needs by evolving appropriate knowledge systems. Much of the available knowledge, particularly that which is highly technical, cannot be absorbed without specific and extensive training in searching, evaluating and ethically using it for the problem at hand. Hence the importance of effective training systems.

The advances in Information and Communication Technologies (ICTs) are regarded as the most striking developments of the Knowledge Society. ICTs have helped enormously in generation, dissemination and communication of new knowledge required for economic growth along with the research and development activities around the world. The access to the nascent thought characterises the Knowledge Society. The important feature of the Knowledge Society is to keep up-to-date with the developments in the field of study and at work place.

2. IMPACT OF INTERNET ON INFORMATION AND COMMUNICATION TECHNOLOGY (ICT)

The impact of the Internet has enhanced widespread use of ICTs in generating and disseminating information through the networks. Today's citizens are flooded with more information than they can handle, and tomorrow's workers will need to know far more than any individual can retain. The number of Internet hosts worldwide grew by 35.8 per cent between Jan. 2003 and Jan. 2004, reaching a total of over 233 million, which represents a doubling of the growth rate in 2003. In terms of number of websites, as of June 2004 there were over 51,635,284 websites worldwide, 26.13 per cent more than a year before. With such a huge number of websites, it is unimaginable to comprehend the amount of information available in these websites. The reputed search engines are indexing these websites.

The Internet is the world's largest library. Massive information is available virtually on any topic. Infact, Internet is not only the largest but also appears to be most disorganised library. It lacks order and finding information is often time consuming, hit-or-miss and even frustrating. Invariably increasingly amount of unfiltered information is flashed on the Internet and thereby raising the questions about authenticity, validity and reliability. Apart from this, information is available through multiple media including graphical, aural and textual. These in turn will project special challenges in evaluating, understanding and using information in an ethical and legal manner. The uncertain quality and expanding quantity of information also pose large challenges for society. Mere abundance of information and technology will not in itself create more informed citizens without a complementary understanding and capacity to use information effectively. Due to a clearly visible information explosion, the ability to access, retrieve and evaluate information should constitute a significant part of the Knowledge Society. Learning how to identity; find, evaluate and use information effectively and efficiently to generate the meaningful information is very important for today's knowledge workers [Sawhney & Parikh, 2003]. Mere learning and getting certificates and degrees will not serve the purpose of Knowledge Society. In a Knowledge Society, the citizens should be lifelong learners. The message of the concept of lifelong learning is that each need to be learning all our lives long.

3. ICT INFRASTRUCTURE AND GROWTH OF KNOWLEDGE SOCIETY

Technology in general and Information and Communication Technology in particular have a very large potential in upliftment of society for a developing country like India. ICT is the driving force behind new global economy and is playing key role in education, public health, transportation, medicine, agriculture and communication. People, businesses and communities with ready access to information technologies are better equipped to participate actively in the decision making process at all levels of public life. ICT networks are now making it possible for rural India to participate in the development process in ways that simply were not possible in the past – by enabling her to take advantage of her natural, human, material and cultural resources.

India has made major contributions to ICT. The reduced tariff charges of telephones encouraged the use of mobile phones on a large scale. After identifying the need to develop the rural area, India had taken major steps towards rural communication and rural reconstruction. In this regard the outstanding contribution of Dr. Sam Pitroda is always remembered. Community Internet Centers were established all over, connecting the isolated villagers to the knowledge base. Government of India had established 487 community information centers in the Northern India, which is geographically isolated. The greatest advantage of ICT is the reach and the low cost of technology and data transmission. Technically, every individual can have a private or public access to a data terminal which connects him to each and every individual in the world. As Hitu points out the costs of building national level ICT infrastructure may be high but there are no equally effective alternatives and the cost of not investing in such infrastructure may be even higher. Further, once the infrastructure has been laid, the low-cost of propagation technology will help India move ahead through distance education, e-learning, distance health facilities (Telemedicine), better access to market information (e-commerce) and better governance (e-governance).

4. DAWN OF INTERNET IN INDIA

Further the Internet is regarded as the fifth network of the modern age. The first four networks were the telegraph, the railroad, the telephone and the electric network. Each of these networks had an enormous impact on how people live, work and communicates and the Internet is no exception. Ofcourse India is a late starter to the Internet phenomena still it is getting online at a remarkably fast pace. Internet services in India were started in 1991 through the ERNET to connect the various academic institutes and research bodies. Internet was introduced for commercial use in 1995 through the government owned VSNL as the sole Internet Service Provider (ISP). The last decade has seen the birth and growth of Internet as a phenomenon that has transformed the life of the people in several respects. In 1996 there were 0.05 million Internet connections with 0.25 million Internet users as compared to 10 million Internet hosts and 30 million Internet users in 2003. In order to address the challenges of cost of personal computers, cost of connectivity and IT literacy, Information Technology Task Force was formed in 1998. Accordingly, the IT Action Plan for India is also prepared containing 108 recommendations covering both bottleneck areas and broad promotional measures that are crucial for boosting IT in India.

The year 2000 saw another remarkable development in the application of ICTs in India. In order to boost e-commerce in India, the government passed the Information Technology Bill in May 2000. It is considered as the nations' bold initiative to set up regulatory and legal framework for e-commerce. It provides a legislation to facilitate e-commerce and to tackle the growing number of cyber crimes. The e-Governance initiatives undertaken in rural India saw another application of ICTs. High cost, software life cycle, ICT offer doesn't meet demand, lack of staff skills, difficult staff recruitment, staff reluctance and lack of client/supplier readiness are some of the barriers to the use of ICT in many countries. Although, India has a visibly good ICT infrastructure, but still it is not adequate to move up in the Networked Readiness Index of World Economic Forum where India has been ranked 39th for the year 2004-2005. This ranking has seen a jump of 6 places compared to the ranking for the year 2003-2004 where India was ranked 45th. The E-readiness rankings are published annually by Economist Intelligence Unit since 2000. E-readiness is the "state of play" of a country's information and communication technology infrastructure and the ability of its consumers, businesses and government to use ICT to their benefit. For the year 2006 E-readiness rankings, India is ranked 53rd compared 49 for the year 2005 [EIU, 2006]. Therefore the matter of the fall in the ranking is taken very seriously and efforts are made to provide good infrastructure facilities to match with the international standards.

5. E-GOVERNANCE INITIATIVES IN INDIA

Lack of information is one of the biggest obstacles to good governance and it dis-empowers poor people. Improving access to information is the most important reason to take the Internet to every village. Every villager does not have to own a computer. One Internet center for a group of villages is sufficient. Thus e-governance has to be taken to the grassroots. There are many advantages of e-governance. Once the Internet facility is provided to the rural area, it is easy to create e-identities for every people. This will help to check the identity of a applicant, for any service from passport to a ration card, with the help of applicant's identity number. The e-governance revolution will bring transparency in the affairs of the government, as all the information will be freely available on the net. For the proper and effective functioning of e-governance, the ICTs should be utilised for their widespread application.

New Delhi took the first step towards e-Governance, made the provision for Central Board of Secondary Education (CBSE) results via the Internet and showed the power of new technology in day-to-day life [Joshi, 2005]. Government agencies at state and national level took some of the bold initiatives to move towards complete e-Governance and these initiatives have been appreciated around the world. Many of the initiatives were implemented in the rural parts of the country to provide them an opportunity and facility to cope up the urban counter parts of the country with the help of ICTs. Some of the government and private e-Governance initiatives are worth mentioning.

5.1. Gyandoot

Gyandoot is a sincere effort of the rural-oriented ICT applications in India. Dhar district of Madhya Pradesh saw with the new millennium a massive revolution in ICT and governance. The Gyandoot Intranet project has won the CSI TCS Award for Best IT Usage and has also been awarded Stockholm Challenge IT Award. It was also adjudged winner in "Public Service and Democracy" category out of 109 IT project from all over the world. Computers have been installed at 30 places and are connected through an Intranet – The Gyandoot. Local rural youth act as entrepreneurs for running cyber cafes called Soochanalayas. From these Soochanalayas user-charge based services are given to the masses. Farmers have access to the Internet in the vegetable market for product prices and access to land records.

5.2. Pravana

Normally IT projects have been launched and sustained on the basis of government funding; Pravana is one such unusual and unique programme where government funds have not been utilised. Located in Ahmednagar district of Maharashtra. A cluster of 200 villages forms the Pravana cooperative movement. National Informatics Center (NIC) has ably assisted the 200 villages in commissioning appropriate software on the system. This initiative was taken by the villagers who were financially self sufficient and having aware of the benefits accrued from implementation of an IT network. This indeed is a healthy sign. Because elsewhere in the country many rural e-Governance projects fail in the early stages when villagers refuse to accept the advantages associated with computer networks. But in the case of Pravana telemedicine, distance education in Marathi, an agriculture information system and a medical information system have been successful and used by the progressive villagers.

5.3. Drishtee

It started initially with 12 member Indian ICT organisation. Drishtee Private Limited is one of the very few companies in the world that has become profitable by offering Information and Communication related services in rural India. With a manager and the staff of about a dozen and virtually no funding, Drishtee has successfully launched about a hundred kiosks throughout rural India. Using a tiered franchise and partnership model, it has enabled a wide range of rural services including access to government programmes and benefits, market-related information and private information exchanges and business transactions.

5.4. Warana Wired Village

This Project is supported by National Informatics Center and the state government. Under this Project village has a "facilitation booth" with wireless LAN for high-speed transmission of data for farmers on such essential issues as the best time for harvesting, product prices, new farming techniques, accounting procedures, method for processing ration cards and permits, market rivals, crop varieties and machinery, and pest management. Further this Project has extended the Internet connectivity to almost 70 villages in Kolhapur and Sangli districts of Maharashtra State. This initiative has enhanced farm productivity, increased the profits of farmers and helped the area's co-operative societies achieve an annual turnover of US $120 million.

5.5. SRISTI

The Project SRISTI is aiming at easing the task of accessing the innovation database of Honey Bee Network breaking the barrier of language and medium of data transmission. Understanding the tremendous potentiality of information and communication technology in furthering the cause of traditional knowledge and grassroots innovations, SRISTI has initiated a number of activities to network innovators, investors and entrepreneurs and facilitate the dissemination of knowledge and information pertaining to grassroots creativity. The initiatives have also taken particular care to facilitate peer learning among the innovators and traditional knowledge holders on one hand and with the institutions of formal excellence and world of entrepreneurship on the other hand.

5.6. NaiDisha

This is a Web portal dedicated to citizen services and is an ICT based interface between Haryana Government and its subjects. It stands for **N**ew **A**gent of **I**nformation – **D**istrict level **I**ntegrated **S**ervices of **H**aryana for **A**ll (NaiDisha). It is a step towards making government services available to citizens any time, anywhere via the Internet. Neither the time of the day, nor location hinders from obtaining information from this Web portal. NaiDisha brings State/Local Government and district administration closer to citizens as if they are only a mouse click-away from their Government and its services. The Web portal provides 22 services to people of Haryana. NaiDisha provides four distinctive services and they are (i) Government-to-Citizen (G2C), (ii) Citizen-to-Government (C2G), (iii) Government-to-Government (G2G) and (iv) Citizen-to-Citizen (C2C).

6. VILLAGE KNOWLEDGE CENTRES

M. S. Swaminathan Research Foundation has established Village Knowledge Centres in five villages at a radius of 13-21 kilometers from Chennai in the state of Tamil Nadu. Basically the knowledge centres are designed to provide agriculture-related information, education and training via ICT. These centres are equipped with PCs with Internet access, printers, CD-ROM and TVs/VCRs. They also provide the villagers with essential information on such matters like grain prices, women's health and rural welfare schemes. Provision is made to announce grâde 10 and 12 examination results, publicise events – even to provide updates on cricket matches. Ofcourse the emphasis is on socio-economic contexts, gender and local culture in this work. The centres are provided rent-free by the villagers. Each village has provided two to four volunteers with grade 10 education to help in the centres and, to date, nine volunteers (mostly female) have been trained in the basics of PCs, MS-Exchange, Word 97, I-LEAP in Tamil and system maintenance.

7. INVITE

An IBM and the Govt. of Karnataka jointly taken initiation to fuel the growth of Information Technology at the grassroots level. IBM India and BITES (Board of IT Education Standards) have launched this unique programme - Project INVITE (Initiative to Nurture a Vibrant IT Ecosystem), to promote academic excellence in Karnataka. The Department of Information Technology, Biotechnology and Science and Technology and BITES will participate in the Project, an ambitious initiative to enhance the local talent pool and leverage the ecosystem to fuel the growth of IT at the grassroots level. The Project compliments the IBM Academic Initiative, which helps universities to train the students on Open Source, Open Standards-based technologies and IBM Technologies for a more competitive workforce. The Project seeks to reach out to "IT-progressive" cities in the State that are rapidly adopting Information Technology to enhance e-governance and citizen services.

These are some of the few examples among many ICT enabled projects initiated in India to move towards complete e-Governance and Knowledge Society. The awareness is growing and it is evident from the initiatives undertaken successfully by some state governments and private companies in India. It is clear that only few state governments have embarked on implementing new and innovating use of IT for e-Governance, education and commerce. While presenting his report to the Prime Minister Dr. Manmohan Singh, the Knowledge Commission Chairman Mr. Sam Pitroda contended that instead of adopting e-governance technologies to help government employees process the data, it should be citizen-friendly to serve their purpose of getting things done quickly in a transparent way. In its report, the Knowledge Commission has urged the government to take up various e-governance projects to ministries on a mission mode and prioritise them according to their respective needs. Report also says that it has identified eight sectors of Central ministries. These Central ministries have been identified on the basis of the frequency of the citizens having direct interface with the government. And, if the services in these areas could be made available online, this will help the nation to save valuable time, energy and money in serving the citizens. The report also presented a list of areas falling under state governments in which the Union government could take initiatives on mission mode. But for these, the Central government has to work in close consultation with the state governments. The areas include land records, road transport, property registration, agriculture, treasuries, municipalities, gram panchayats, state commercial taxes, police and employment exchange.

8. EFFECTIVENESS OF E-GOVERNANCE INITIATIVES

By and large most of the e-Governance and

computerisation initiatives across the country use information and communication technologies as a means to achieve a more effective delivery of government services and better governance in general. e-Governance is a prime area of concern for state governments in India, not only as a means of achieving efficiency in the running of state departments, but, more importantly, as a means of providing an easy and effective way for citizens to access basic government services. The DataQuest and International Data Corporation carried out a survey (DQ-IDC e-Gov Survey 2006) to assess the availability of ICT infrastructure, the rollout of e-Governance projects of selected 18 Indian states and evaluate the impact of these projects on the delivery of government services to common citizens and corporates. The major findings are as follows:

* Kerala, Delhi and Gujarat emerge as the top three states in terms of overall perception in improvement of services through e-governance
* E-payment has emerged as one of the most successful e-initiatives for states like Goa, Gujarat and Chhattisgarh
* Police and security, judiciary and land-related functions remain pain points for most states
* The IT department emerges a clear winner in terms of initiatives
* Andhra Pradesh and Karnataka, synonymous with IT in India, have not quite made it to the top
* More states are rolling out e-initiatives in the areas of networking, land records, education,

and better information management

* Some of the areas where states have achieved moderate success have been those of e-payments, online provision of information and online ordering of documents, passport services and income-tax functions

There is a visible imbalance between the facilities provided through these initiatives and the utility by the public. Therefore for the proper utilisation, training and education becomes imperative where the people can be made self-learners and lifelong learners. The rural poor and the urban disadvantaged must be helped to become more empowered and self-reliant through education in order to enjoy better health and lifestyle, to be better informed about what is happening in the wider world. This is possible by teaching the lifelong learning skills through Information Literacy. To know the services provided by the government through these initiatives, one should be a informed citizen and have the ability to learn and relearn and become lifelong learner.

9. INITIATIVES FOR PROMOTING THE INFORMATION LITERACY ACTIVITIES

In the contemporary age learning to learn, learning to transform information into new knowledge, and learning to translate new knowledge into applications become more important than memorizing specific information. In this new paradigm, priority is given to analytical skills; that is, to the ability to seek and find information, crystallise issues, formulate testable hypotheses, marshal and evaluate evidence, and solve problems at hand. The new competencies that employers value in the Knowledge Society have to do with oral and written communication, teamwork, peer teaching, creativity, envisioning skills, resourcefulness and the ability to adjust to change. Many of these competencies involve social, human and inter-cultural skills that are not normally taught in science or technology-based disciplines. Information literacy training in collaboration between the teachers, media persons, computer technologies and librarians. A number of innovative programmes and seminal sets of standards and guidelines have to be developed in this area.

The e-Governance initiative undertaken throughout India, its services and positive benefits that the rural citizens can get from these programmes requires good publicity. In order to teach them skills required for realizing a information/service need, and developing the skills necessary to find, evaluate and use that information/service through these initiatives should be taught for the proper and effective utilis ation. To realise the dream of e-Governance and move towards a Knowledge Society, number of programmes needs to be undertaken which address the issues related to Information Literacy and lifelong learning. Information literacy forms part of the basic entitlement of every citizen in every country of the world, to freedom of expression and the right to information. It is thereby instrumental in building and sustaining democracy and good governance and represents a basic condition for any successful e-Governance programmes. To make India a Knowledge Society, people from all walks of life need to contribute towards the upliftment and proper implementation of the concept of Information Literacy and lifelong learning.

Government of India along with the State Governments and other competent organisations need to undertake some of the programmes/initiatives that are and needs to be implemented and practiced. Implementing Information Literacy programmes to users of the all types of libraries. Integrating Information Literacy across the curriculum at all levels of education.

University Grants Commission (UGC) may take the proper steps to induct the component of Information Literacy in higher education, so also the related bodies in engineering and other profession courses. In addition, the professional societies, academics and associations like ILA, SIS, IASLIC and IATLIS can make efforts to bring together the professional expertise along with academic and media experts to design and develop the viable Curriculum for various levels of education

10. CONCLUSION

In the emerging knowledge societies, an educated person will be someone who is willing to consider learning as a lifelong process. More and more knowledge, especially advanced knowledge, is acquired well past the age of formal schooling, and in many situations through educational processes that do not center on the traditional school. Information overload, the advent of high-functionality systems, and a climate of rapid technological change have created new problems and challenges for education and training. Information literacy is considered as a meta competency of the knowledge society. If one has to be successful in the knowledge society, he/she needs to acquire high level of information literacy skills. India essentially needs to transform in to complete knowledge society and hence the efforts be concentrated to develop the absorbing, analysing and integrating abilities of the people and to make them understand how to use information to bring real value to everything they undertake. Information literacy has become a global issue calling for grater attention. As a result several countries have taken initiation in starting the national as well as international programmes. These programmes are addressing many issues relating to technology and information skills. In the Information Age of the 21st century, information literate citizens will be the building stone for a society that is equitable and possesses economic growth potential. People will need information skills for the personal, professional and even for the entertainment activities. In the context of India, it is essential for librarians, teachers, technologists, media experts and policy makers to make all possible efforts to start the Information Literacy movement with a big bang.

REFERENCES

1. Splender, Dale (1998). The Knowledge Society: The Status of Science Education. *Australian Science Teachers Journal*, 44 (4), p. 2
2. Tilak, Jandnyala B G (2002). Knowledge Society. *Education and aid. Compare*, .32 (3), pp. 297-310.
3. United Nations (2004). E-commerce and Development Report 2004. New York: United Nations, p. 6.
4. Sawhney, Mohanbir and Parikh, Deval (2003). Powered by India. *In:* The Knowledge Economy in India / edited by Richter, Frank-Jurgen and Parthasarathi Banerjee. New York: Palgrave MacMillan, p.79.
5. Singh, Vikram and Suri, P.K. (2005). ICT for National Development. Proceedings of the 40th Annual National Convention of Computer Society of India, Hyderabad, 9-12 Nov., pp. 49-50.
6. Pandey, Sunil K, Kundu, Kumud and Bagchi, D (2005). ICT for National Development. Proceedings of the 40th Annual National Convention of Computer Society of India, Hyderabad, 9-12 Nov., pp.12-13.

7. Kajal, Hitu (2005). ICT for National Development: Proceedings of the 40th Annual National Convention of Computer Society of India, Hyderabad, 9-12 Nov., p.20.

8. Bakshi, Prashant (2005). Wired India. New Delhi: Knowledge World, pp. 45-71.

9. Joshi, Akshay (2005). Information Age and India. New Delhi: Knowledge World, pp. 143-181.

10. Economist Intelligence Unit (2006): The 2006 e-readiness Rankings: A White Paper from Economist Intelligence Unit. Available at: http://a330.g.akamai.net/7/330/2540/20060424215053/graph ics.eiu.com/files/ad_pdfs/2006Ereadiness_Ranking_WP.pdf

11. Panda, S and Chaudhury, S (2001): Telelearning and Telelearning Centres in India. *In:* Telecentres: Case studies and key issues /edited by C. Latchen and D.Walker. The Commonwealth of Learning, pp. 155-56.

12. ICT Initiatives. Available at http://www.sristi.org/cms/en/ict_initiative (Accessed on 17.01.2006).

13. The Hindu (2006): Inviting Academic Excellence. *The Hindu,* 30.01.2006. Available at http://www.hindu.com/edu/2006/01/30/stories/20060130004 80300.htm

14. The Statesman (2006): India's National Knowledge Commission Suggests Change on E-Governance. 06 Mar., New Delhi (Accessed on 10.03.2006).

15. DataQuest (2006): DQ-IDC Survey of 18 States: best e-Governed States 2006. *Dataquest,* XXIV (5), pp.20-47.

14

Blogging: A Teaching Tool in Library Education

Krishan Kumar
Jaideep Sharma

ABSTRACT

This paper examines the concept of blog ,its kinds, salient features, other related technologies, advantages and effects of using blogs and its usage as an effective teaching tool of education, particularly in Library and Information Science Education.

1. INTRODUCTION

The exact definition of "blogs" is still very much in flux. Basically, a blog or "Web log" is literally an online diary containing articles, comments, photos, Web links or other entries made by the creator of a blog called a blogger. A **blog** (short for **web log**) is a website where entries are input in chronological order but displayed in reverse chronological order. Thus, the latest entry would occur first.

A blog is and has always been more than the "online equivalent of a personal journal. Though consisting of regular (and often dated) updates, the blog adds to the form of the diary by incorporating the best features of hypertext: the capacity to link to new and useful resources. But a blog is also characterized by its reflection of a personal style, and this style may be reflected in either the writing or the selection of links passed along to readers. Blogs are, in their purest form, the core of what has come to be called *personal publishing* .In the hands of teachers and students, blogs become something more again. The Web is by now a familiar piece of the educational landscape, and for those sites where personal publishing or chronologically ordered content would be useful, blogs have stepped to the fore." (Downes, 2004)

A blog, is an easily created and updateable website. It is an easy to use website that allows people to publish to the Internet instantly. It is a website where you can quickly post your thoughts, views, bio-data and also interact with others, and also do lot more.

Blogs provide commentary or news on a particular subject such as food, library science, politics, or local news; some function like personal online diaries. A typical blog combines text, images. It may also provide links to other blogs, web pages, and other media related to its topic. The built-in provision for readers to leave their comments in an interactive format forms an important part of many blogs. "Most blogs are primarily textual, although some focus on art (artlog), photographs (photoblog), sketchblog, videos (vlog), music (MP3 blog), or audio (podcasting), and are part of a wider network of social media.The term "blog" is a portmanteau of the words web and log (Web log). "Blog" can also be used as a verb, meaning *to maintain or add content to a blog.* In May 2007, blog search engine Technorati was tracking more than 71 million." (blogs.http://en.wikipedia.org/wiki/Blogging)(accessed on July30, 2007)

2. BLOGS AND OTHER TECHNOLOGIES

The ability of Web applications to deliver a rich user experience has been increasing with new generations of light-weight protocols. For instance, Google has used a collection of technologies, called AJAX, consisting of standards-based presentation using XHTML and CSS; dynamic display and interaction using the Document Object Model; data interchange and manipulation using XML and XSLT; and asynchronous data retrieval using XMLHttpRequest; with JavaScript binding everything together.

The term "**Web 2.0**" has been coined to capture the flavor of new applications possible with these new technologies and their interactions. The features of these applications include a focus on services with cost-effective scalability, unique, hard-to-recreate data sources that get richer as more people use them, users as co-developers, harnessing collective intelligence, leveraging customer self-service, software that targets multiple devices, lightweight user interfaces and development models.

3. KINDS OF BLOGS

The simplest are the text-only blogs created by individual Web surfers to post their own eclectic and varied thoughts. Political parties, religious and professional bodies, businesses, trade and media organizations have started creating their own blogs, too. Very often, these contain various forms of multimedia content (digital videos, photos, audio). These postings are comparable to those available in traditional print or broadcast

The rapid developments in information technology are also changing the very nature of blogs, too. The popularity of digital audio players such as Apple's iPod has given impetus to the growth of blogs having audio content. Downloading these audio blogs, commonly known as "podcasts" like radio "on demand.", one formats.can choose and download a wide range of audio files , such as music, talk radio-like commentaries, discussions and lectures. One can then listen to them at one's convenience by means of a PC or a portable media player. The rapid adoption in the United States, Japan, and other countries, of cell phones with built-in digital cameras and wireless Internet connections is also changing the face and pace of blogging. Use of mobile, multifunctional handheld systems that serve as extensions of office environments is growing. BlackBerry, Palm One, and the Microsoft Compact Windows platform are cases in point. Enterprises are adopting location-based service applications and telecom providers have rolled out 2.5/3G broadband services. The adoption of 1XRTT/GPRS and EVDO/ EDGE services has soared and at the end of Q3 2004, Sprint reported 5.6 million 1XRTT subscribers. Marketers are beginning to experiment with mobile services. More than half of direct marketers in advanced mobile countries like the UK and Finland have adopted SMS for their campaigns to reach the mobile masses (Best And Worst Of European Mobile Site Design, 2005. Iris, Cremers, Forrester Report, December 2, 2005.) (Accessed on Aug 27, 2007). Many of them are ready to move to the richer, more interactive mobile Internet. As an example, airlines are using the new medium for services like mobile check-in.

4. SALIENT FEATURES OF A BLOG

Blogging or Web logging is basically an online diary or journal. Examine a typical blog, you would notice immediately a clear connection between it and a traditional diary. Often the entries are organized in reverse chronological order, the most recent entry posted first. Blogs contain views, wishes, comments, biodata etc. it may also contain anything else that the blogger may think to be relevant to his objective of the blog. Often, along with text, he may provide graphics, sometimes audio and video elements may be added.

Blogs are catching the fancy of both the educational community and the Internet community at large, is their ease of use. A blogger can edit or update a new entry without worrying about page formats or HTML syntax. Many easy to use, cost-efficient systems and tools have emerged in the area of personal Web publishing. These tools offer a new and powerful packages for the support of collaborative and individual learning that fits into the emerging patterns of contemporary information seeking behaviour and learning outside of formal educational settings.

5. BLOGGING AS A TEACHING TOOL

ICT has given us many teaching tools that can be employed by a teacher. Some of these are blogging, wikis, RSS feeds, lectures recorded on iPod, lectures available on the internet, etc. An instructor has many options available to him.

Open source blogging platform is being used in universities and colleges in the West as a teaching tool. Weblogs are becoming increasingly popular with teachers. The teachers are using them in the classroom in various ways. Teachers are noticing the effects weblogs have on their students' learning.

Access to and exchange of ideas produced by it, are beginning to bring a "transformative" effect on education. Academics are claiming that Blogs are changing education. There is a significant impact on teaching and learning. There is no doubt that in recent years, Blogging has exploded in its popularity. It has given educators and students an unprecedented opportunity to achieve self-expression and exchange of ideas in an easy way never thought of before. Anyone can access it. Anyone can respond to anyone else. It creates a kind of excitement that comes only from writing for a real and authentic audience instead of a circular file that only a teacher can see and comment upon. The thrill one gets can be a tremendous motivator for the students. A teacher can also use a class blog to challenge his students with frequent, short writing assignments designed to make them think hard and critically. Classroom Instruction Blog can enable a teacher to have a high-level, asynchronous conversation with his students that extends the boundaries of the traditional classroom into a whole new kind of world. It makes learning exciting and live.

Today, digital tools are available that make blogging extremely easy. Any body with a little training in IT can do it. Just compare it, with the effort it takes to upload files online via the File Transfer Protocol or build a web page using Hypertext Markup Language. The latter effort requires understanding of complex technology and its tools.

According to Nolan, "blogging looks at communication in different manner. Blogging is all about me. The location of the discussion is on the individual, not on the class. As a student, I would write about my personal experiences within the learning moment; how the lectures, discussions in class, readings intertwine with my own reflections and thoughts on the topic. The result is that a blog post can become a unique document of the learning process; one that is particular to each learner" (Dec21, 2006, p.R5). He can continue the blog from student days to his job. A blog can serve as a tool for communication. It enables the student to learn about of variety of ways to express himself, such as personal, public or private communication. He would learn what can be made public and what can remain personal or private. It can enable the teacher to get feedback from his students, so that he can improve his teaching. Nolan says, "I use blogs as to learn what my students think is important in the reading, and what I need to focus on in my lectures. In one scenario, I have students write a 350-word blog post on the readings before class. I can skim these posts and pick out any insights or omissions that I would like to take up. I can, at a glance, know that 120 students have done the readings, and, unlike other instructors, I don't have to hope that a significant percentage of students are prepared for class. I can use their blogs as raw material for developing quizzes and exam questions. I can use them as the starting point for research papers" (Dec21, 2006, p. R5). Blogs serve as indicator, whether or not the concerned student has done his assignment through his efforts or copied material wholesale, theirby raising the issue of plagiarism. These enable the instructor to get the feedback for revising the course, change of teaching strategies etc. It can be summed as follows:

* Instructor uses the blog as an online course management tool where s/he posts assignments, announcements, information and summaries of lessons.
* A weekly topic is posted and each student posts their thoughts on the topic.
* Post articles relevant to the course.
* Students post their thoughts regarding articles.

* Class discussions on course readings and lectures.
* Students post their writing assignments and homework exercises.
* Students exchange information related to the course's subject.
* Students post comments, questions and advice about the course to Instructor and fellow students.
* Students post their thoughts on what they are learning.
* Students use the blog as a writing portfolio.
* Students read each other's rough drafts of writing assignments and give feedback.
* Students and Instructor discuss news related to the course's subject.
* Students discuss class activities.
* Online students can get to know each other by reading and commenting on each others blog entries.
* Instructors post class times, rules governing classes, suggested readings, and exercises etc.
* Instructors provide links to Internet items related to their course.
* Instructors use blogs to organize class seminars

Educators have evidence that students write better when they have a real audience. It has been found that students' interest in writing and quantity of writing also improves when their work is published online and perhaps even more importantly, accessible to other readers for their comments.

6. THE EFFECTS OF USING A BLOG

The instant publishing on blogs makes students more able and willing to read, write, and discuss about topics related to their course work. knowing they have a real audience for whom they are writing. There is even a collaborative environment where involving giving and receiving of feedback. Therefore, students are forced by circumstances to dispay their best work.

Teachers using blogs in their classrooms find that students put more thought and effort into their blog writing, knowing that the teacher, parents and others may read their work on the Web, if made available to a wider audience. They make it sure that not only their teacher, but others who read it, will think of it as a good effort.

Students can strengthen their reading skills and strategies by exploring other's weblogs and hyperlinks. They will have to carefully read through these linked websites to decide which information is relevant and important to them. Not only that, but the students can build on their knowledge base by reading the content on the different linked websites.

Weblogs also enable the students to interact with their peers more much faster than a regular journal. Learners who happen to be shy in traditional class usually become more active online.

It has been found that blogs seemed to be used the most during the school day. Not that many entries are posted after school or during the summer.

There is a fear that the casual nature of writing on the web may encourage students to use incorrect style of writing violating conventions laid down in good writing. They may tend to use email style abbreviations, bad grammar, and poor spelling.

However, it depends on how the instructor uses the blog in the context of the classroom. Some teachers instruct their students that each entry be first written on paper, edited, and only after that posted onto the blog. Some teachers are of the view that weblogs is a different media that requires a different form of writing. Thus, they feel that a teacher should be more concerned with content, ignoring bad grammar.

There are also concerns about making the work of student's public when the same is published on the Internet. The teacher would be required to take written permission from the students before posting the same on the internet.

7. USE OF WEBLOG IN A CLASSROOM IN LIBRARY EDUCATION

There are three main uses of weblog in a classroom in library education. Use by the instructor as a personal journaling space, disussion space to be used by instructor and students, electronic portfolio of written work by students.

(i) Personal Journaling Space

It can be used as a personal journaling space by the instructor. He posts regular entries regarding, announcements, course information, course documents, new events, developments and trends in the field related to course, comments on the assignments and quizzes done by students etc

(ii) Discussion Space

The instructor may announce a topic for discussion, during a particular hour. The students can post their comments, views etc. the instructor can intervene, if the discussion goes off the track. At the end, he can sum up and add his comments.The students and the instructor can also post messages about assignments, quizzes, tests etc.

Weblogs can offer an extension of class discussions. If the discussion had to end due to time, then it can be continued online long after school is over. This allows students who did not get a chance to discuss, as well as the reticent students, to join in on the conversation. Students can post comments about certain topics, and other students can respond or start new ones.

An example of a blog on 'library education' course is illustrated in *http://lised.blogspot.com/search?q*

Tools and technology deal with matters related to access to the blog. It lists the tools he needs to use, how should learn their use, how should he go about, if there is problem. It is desirable that a worksop should be organized in the beginning of the session to instruct the students as to how to use the blog for learning purpose.

To get the best results, it is desirable that each learner must be provided with a lap top and the library school must have access to high speed wireless network (Wi-Fi). As an alternative, one personal computer may be provided to two students each, along with high speed internet.

The instructor plays a very important role in the effective use of blogging. At the very outset, he should lay down rules of the game. Each student must be respectful to each others ideas and comments. However, he must encourage them to express views openly without hurting others. They must be encouraged to read each others blogs and respond as early as possible giving their suggestions and comments. Each student must be expected to edit his entry properly before posting it. Each entry must be considered as a serious piece of writing, written with care and deep thinking. A class blog can be maintained, which provides access to the blog maintained by each student, where he is free express his ideas and feelings without interference from anybody including his instructor. This will give special feeling to him, feeling it as his own space. In the long run, this will serve as his journal that he can continue even after, he has passed the course. (Trimarco, 2004).

7. CONCLUSION

Blogging is a great tool that can be used by library educators in the field of library and information science to enhance quality of teaching and learning. It is becoming increasingly popular in higher education. The role of an instructor is very important in making it an effective tool.

It is easy to create a blog. However, it takes time to keep it updated. Once, one has formed a habit of updating, then it becomes an addiction. Many students and teachers do not want to learn this new technology. This can be a big handicap. The generation of students who are coming for higher education are often technology saavy. They find it easy and interesting to get into blogging. It may be pointed out that not all topics in library science are appropriate enough to be considered for discussion and dialogue purposes. Such topics may be less suitable for the purpose. This technology is highly useful for those students, who are shy and reserved in nature. Such students do not tend to participate in class discussion in a real class room. These kind of students have less hesitation in participating in discussion or giving their comments and opinions without inhibition. There is no doubt this media is excellent for developing communication skills and gaining knowledge.

REFERENCES

1. Downes, Stephen (2004). Educational Blogging. *EDUCAUSE Review,* 39 (5), pp. 14-26.
2. Farrell, Henry (2003). The Street Finds Its Own Use for Things," *Crooked Timber.* Available at (http://www.crookedtimber.org/archives/000516.html)
3. Nolan, Jason (2006), Blog is an Effective Teaching Tool. *Toronto Star,* p. R5.
4. Richardson, W. (2003). Web Logs in the English Classroom: More Than Just Chat. *English Journal,* 93 (1), pp. 39-43. (Accessed on February 21, 2005, from the Eric Firstsearch database).
5. Richardson, Will (2005). RSS: A Quick Start Guide for Educators (www.weblogg-ed.com) Ver. 1.5, Updated 3/29/05 Available at http://creativecommons.Org/licenses/by-nd-nc/1.0/ (Accessed on April 6, 2007)
6. Trimarco, R. (2004), Use of Blogs in Online College Classes. In: Encyclopedia of Educational Technology / edited by B Hoffman. Available at http://coe.sdsu.edu/eet/Articles/blogonlineclass/start.htm. (Accessed on June8, 2007)
7. http://www.oreillynet.com/pub/a/oreilly/tim/news/2005/0 9/30/what-is-web-20.html?page=5) (Accessed on Aug27, 2007)
8. US 2.5 and 3G Business Services. Lisa Pierce, Forrester Report. January 13, 2005. (Accessed on Aug 27, 2007)

15

Application of Information and Communication Technologies in Special Libraries

K. Mohamed Haneefa

ABSTRACT

This study was conducted to investigate the application of Information and Communication Technologies (ICT) in special libraries in Kerala. The following methods were used to collect data for the study: (a) questionnaire survey of librarians and library users, (b) semi-structured interviews with librarians and (c) observational visits in the libraries. This study was confined only to the automated special libraries in Kerala. The analyses revealed that though the libraries had hardware, software and communication facilities to some extent, ICT based resources and services were not reaching the users to the expected extent. This study recommends to enhance library automation and effective and efficient application of Information and Communication Technologies.

1. INTRODUCTION

The monopoly of libraries on information

provision is over. Today libraries are shifting their role from the custodian of traditional information resources to the provider of service-oriented digital information resources. Widespread use of computers, increased reliance on computer networks, rapid growth of Internet and explosion in the quality, and quantity of information compelled libraries to adopt new means and methods for the storage, retrieval and dissemination of information. Library automation, development of digital libraries and application of innovative information and communication technologies (ICT) have tremendously increased because it provides enhanced user satisfaction, cost effectiveness, rapid responses, and easier operational procedures. Libraries and Information Centres have been employing ICT and electronic information resources and services to satisfy the diverse information needs of their users. E-journals, CD-ROM databases, online databases, e-books, web based resources and a variety of other electronic media are fast replacing the traditional resources of libraries. While libraries automated their library management activities and procure expensive electronic resources, these may not be optimally used. This is the main concern of librarians around the world. There are lot of reasons to these state of affairs, like lack of sufficient funds, inadequate infrastructure, lack of qualified library professionals, etc.

2. BACKGROUND

Kerala is the most literate state in India. It has a number of special libraries attached to various research institutions, industries, departments and other corporate sectors. The late 1990s saw the introduction of ICT in special libraries in Kerala. Majority of the libraries have been partially automated their house keeping operations. Libraries attached to the central government autonomous institutions are better in library automation and application of ICT. These libraries offer diverse information resources and services. They subscribe e-journals, CD-ROM databases, online databases, web based resources and a variety of other electronic resources. They participate in library consortia and build digital libraries. However, these libraries have been hampered by many constraints to embark successful application of ICT for their operations, resources and services. Therefore a need was felt to conduct a study to assess the application of information and communication technologies in special libraries in Kerala. The study also tried to identify the major factors that promoted or hindered the application of ICT.

3. OBJECTIVES OF THE STUDY

The aim of the study was to investigate the current application of information and communication technologies in special libraries in Kerala. In order to fulfil this aim, the following specific objectives were identified:

* To assess the current state-of-the-art Information and Communication Technology Infrastructure in Special Libraries in Kerala.
* To evaluate the contemporary use of Information and Communication Technologies in Special Libraries in Kerala.
* To compare the Information and Communication Technology status among the Special Libraries in Kerala.
* To identify and analyse the specific factors that promoted or hindered the application of

Information and Communication Technologies in Special Libraries in Kerala.

* To assess to what extent users are satisfied with Information and Communication Technology resources and services in Special Libraries in Kerala.
* To suggest measures for improvement of existing resources and services and implementation of Information and Communication Technologies.

4. RESEARCH DESIGN

To meet the main aim and specific objectives of the study, a combination of quantitative and qualitative research methodologies along with a comprehensive literature review had been employed. Three main methods were used in data collection: questionnaire survey of librarians and library users, semi-structured interviews with librarians and observational visits in the libraries. Structured questionnaires were prepared and administered to chief librarians. The purpose of the questionnaires was to obtain data regarding the current application of ICT in special libraries in Kerala. These questionnaires were distributed to chief librarians with a cover letter indicating the significance of the study and the intended plans for the results. Telephone and face-to-face interviews were conducted with chief librarians using a semi-structured interview schedule. Observational visits were also conducted in the libraries to collect information about the current application of ICT and to assess the degree of the utilisation of electronic information resources. The purpose of the interviews and observational visits was to complement the quantitative information obtained by the questionnaires with more detailed qualitative information. Structured questionnaires were also prepared and administered to library users. The purpose of these questionnaires was to obtain data regarding the current use of ICT based resources and services in special libraries in Kerala.

This study was confined to the automated special libraries of Kerala. The Directory of Libraries in India, Directory of Scientific and Technical Libraries in India and Directory of Libraries in Kerala were used to identify the names, administrative status and addresses of libraries for the study. Since the directories were dated, information was verified telephonically and through personal visits. Thirty-One automated libraries with information and communication technologies were identified for the study. But despite several attempts one institute library did not permit data collection, so it was excluded from the list. Finally, the study was confined to 30 libraries. The thirty libraries belonged to four categories of institutions, viz., central government, state government, central government autonomous, and state government autonomous. Since the use of ICT requires certain minimum infrastructure and qualified fulltime library professional and also electronic information resources and related equipments require substantial financial commitment by libraries, government departmental libraries and technical libraries were excluded from the study.

5. DISCUSSION

The data collected by the above mentioned tools were analysed and inferences made based on standard statistical methods. The quantitative data from the questionnaires were converted into machine-readable form and imported into the statistical analysis package SPSS. The investigator used content analysis to code responses from the open-ended questions, interviews and observations. Analysis of the data obtained through the questionnaires, interview schedules and the observation using both quantitative and qualitative measures provided an in-depth interpretation for fulfilling the six research objectives.

5.1. ICT Infrastructure

ICT infrastructure is usually considered with respect to its main areas, which are: hardware, software, and telecommunication. The infrastructure remains the main bottleneck to the development of ICT in libraries. Sufficient infrastructure is very essential for the successful application of ICT in libraries. Library management software plays a key role for the success of library automation. Responses indicated that the organisations surveyed used a wealth of different software packages depending upon particular applications. The libraries were more interested in commercial software packages. There were 11 software packages preferred by 23 libraries (Figure 1). CDS/ISIS was used more in libraries (23.3 per cent) than any other software. Libsys software was a distant second with 16.7 per cent of the libraries. Seven libraries reported to had developed the library management software in-house. The other software packages used were Alice for Windows, SLIM++, LibSoft, Winisis, Winsoft, Winlis, Chronicles 2001, E-grandhalaya, and LibsuitASP+.

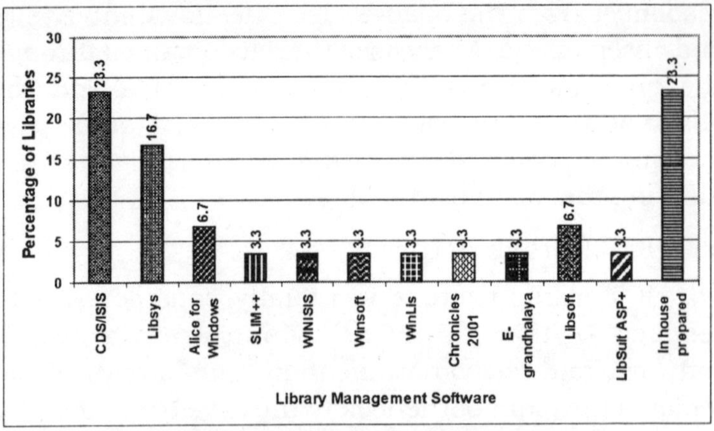

Fig. 1. Use of Library Management Software

5.2. Electronic Information Resources

Electronic information resources are becoming increasingly important to libraries of all types and sizes. The explosive growth of Internet and widespread reliance on computer networks accelerated the use of electronic information resources to a great extent. The use of electronic information resources in special libraries in Kerala are explained under the following sub headings.

5.2.1. Internet

The Internet has become an indispensable resource for libraries worldwide to enhance the collection, improve services and operations. The librarians were asked to indicate the extent of use of Internet in their libraries. All the institutions under study had access to the Internet in the library or information centre. Majority (63.3 per cent) of the libraries had leased line connection, and a few (36.7 per cent) libraries had access to Internet through dialup connection. Though there were five Internet Service Providers, namely VSNL, NICNET, ASIANET, Sathyam and BSNL, majority of the libraries were accessing Internet through the VSNL. All the libraries of State Government institutions and majority (53.8 per cent) of the Central Government autonomous institutions and State Government autonomous institutions (57.1 per cent) were using Internet for Selective Dissemination of Information (SDI) services. Majority (61.5 per cent) of the libraries of Central Government autonomous institutions were using Internet for acquisition work. All the libraries of State Government institutions and majority (57.1 per cent) of the State Government autonomous institutions were using Internet for current awareness service (CAS).

All the libraries were providing E-mail and World Wide Web facilities. Majority of the libraries of Central Government autonomous institutions were providing FTP, Telnet, ListServe and Usenet/Newsgroups services. Libraries of the Central Government autonomous institutions were considerably better in Internet based resources and services.

5.2.2. Electronic Databases & Online Journals

E-journals are becoming increasingly prevalent in the information landscape of libraries. The librarians were asked to indicate the extent of use of e-journals in their libraries. Majority (66.7 per cent) of the libraries under study were providing access to electronic journals. It is found that most (92.3 per cent) of the libraries of Central Government autonomous institutions and about half of the State Government institutions were providing electronic journals in their libraries.

The analysis revealed that a very few (20 per cent) libraries had commercial online databases, both bibliographic and full text. Most of these libraries were attached to the Central Government autonomous institutions. Nearly 57 per cent of the institutions had CD-ROM databases. It is found that 25 per cent of the Central Government institutions, 53.8 per cent of the Central Government autonomous institutions and 14.3 per cent of the State Government autonomous institutions were using it for retrieving bibliographical information. A few libraries (28.6 per cent) of the state Government autonomous institutions, and Central Government autonomous institutions (23 per cent) were using it for retrieving both full text and bibliographical information. A very few of the libraries were using databases of internal records.

It is revealed that only two libraries had a separate digital library. The main components of these digital libraries were electronic databases, full text e-journals through Science Direct, Emerald, etc., publications of the institute research community, e-books, discussion groups, online news, CD-ROM databases, in house databases, publication databases, etc. A few (36.7 per cent) libraries had digital library initiatives and they were started creation and digitisation of some of their collections. But majority (56.7 per cent) of the libraries had no digital library or digital library initiatives.

5.3. Library Consortia

Only three special libraries in Kerala were participating in library consortia and this was for accessing electronic journals. One library in the State government institutions was participating in the INDEST consortia for accessing E-journals. Two libraries of the Central Government autonomous institutions were participating in the CSIR Consortium on e-journals.

5.4. Use of ICT Based Resources and Services

Users were asked whether they use any of the ICT based resources and services and the responses are summarised. The electronic resource/tool used by the largest percentage of the users was the e-mail. Majority (65.6 per cent) of the users indicated that they had access to e-mail from the library. The next most widely used resource was WWW, which was being used by nearly 60 per cent of the users. Majority of the users had access to bibliographical databases (54.8 per cent) and used floppy disk (52.2 per cent). A good number of them used CD-ROM (47.6 per cent), printer (44.2 per cent), e-journals (45.4 per cent) and OPAC (41.6 per cent).

A good number (42.4 per cent) of the library users indicated 'inadequate ICT infrastructure' as their reason for dissatisfaction. Other reasons were 'users are not trained for ICT based information services' (35.1 per cent), 'Inadequately trained library professionals in ICT application' (20.2 per cent), 'Limited computer literacy among library users' (17.5 per cent), 'Inadequate publicity for the ICT based resources and services' (15.6 per cent), 'Rigid ICT use policies implemented by the library' (6.3 per cent) and 'Discouraging attitude of library professionals towards their users' (4.9 per cent).

5.6. Recommendations

The numerous views and comments offered by the librarians and the library users have enabled the investigator to offer some feasible suggestions for the successful application of information and communication technologies in libraries. The following suggestions can be offered in developing countries like India to enhance the automation of libraries and application of information and communication technologies.

Libraries need better funding/finance, if they are to give more productive and effective information resources and services. In order to access electronic resources such as e-journals and databases, substantial amount of money is needed. Therefore sufficient funds should be made available by the authorities for library automation, development of digital resources and application of information and communication technologies. It should be noted that a library, which has better resources performs better. Libraries should have state-of-the-art infrastructure including hardware, software and humanware. They should procure sufficient hardware like servers, computer terminals, printers, scanners, barcode scanners, data capture unit, CD-Tower, CD-writers, DVD drives, VCD players, UPS, etc. It should be maintained properly. Software is the life blood of hardware. Libraries should also install very good software packages to operate all the library management activities. The software should be an integrated version with online help and OPAC/ WebOPAC facilities. Librarians should have skills to evaluate software, which will enable them to identify appropriate software for their libraries. Local area networks (LAN) should be set up in all libraries. LAN is very essential to access electronic information resources and to provide OPAC.

In view of the increasing importance of electronic information resources and the widespread use of ICT, it is suggested that libraries should strive a right choice between printed and electronic resources. Most of the special libraries in Kerala have a good collection of information resource in hardcopy, however, they lack service oriented electronic information resources. These libraries must go a step ahead and provide electronic resources like e-journals, bibliographic databases, full-text databases, CD-ROM databases, multimedia databases, and access to web based resources, etc.

This study has seriously considered the lack of skill and expertise of library staff as the major factor that hindered the application of ICT in special libraries in Kerala. Hence, it urges the authorities to appoint qualified library professionals in the libraries. The library professionals should combine ICT and library and information science qualifications, skills, competencies and expertise. There are lot of skills related to library automation and application of ICT. Library professionals should have skills to handle ICT products, particularly library management software, operating system, telecommunication products, DBMS, data and file management, DTP, word processing, etc. They should have skills to apply ICT for service management in general and information processing, search and retrieval in particular. This involves collection and organisation of data in electronic form, indexing techniques, selection and evaluation of sources, searching techniques, etc. Information retrieval skills include online searching as well as searching CD-ROM databases. They should also have Internet skills, programming skills and skills required for networking, system administration, hardware maintenance and troubleshooting, system migration, etc.

A significant effort is required to increase the awareness of new technologies among the library professionals in special libraries in Kerala. Majority of the library professionals have inadequate knowledge about library automation and application of ICT.

Libraries should promote ICT awareness and knowledge by providing short-term courses, organising workshops, seminars, conferences, and public lectures. They should provide training in hardware, software, communication facilities, and digital library. In-house training programmes are more effective for libraries. A separate budget should be allocated for training whenever a new technology is acquired even if it is highly expensive. Librarians should initiate orientation programmes for staff and users for newly implemented systems and technologies.

Development of digital libraries is a main activity of all types of libraries. Realising the importance and potential of digital libraries and digital collection, it is suggested that the special libraries in Kerala should take initiative in planning and implementing digital libraries so as to keep pace with the modern trends. While problems and challenges still exist in Indian context, there is an urgent need to establish digital libraries.

Library consortium is a collective activity of any group of libraries towards a common goal. The collective strength of consortia facilitates the libraries to get the benefit of wider access to electronic resources at affordable cost and at the best terms and conditions. The consortia-based subscription can be successfully deployed to meet the pressures such as diminishing budget, increased user's demands and rising cost of electronic resources. Special libraries in Kerala can form consortia based on their affiliations like consortium of ICAR institutes, consortium of CSIR institutes, consortium of State Government autonomous institutes, consortium of Government departmental libraries, etc.

The contemporary electronic environment

predominated by innovative information and communication technologies indicate the pressing need to educate and train the library professionals. The present library and information science curriculum in the universities in India is not supporting the appropriate skills and expertise to be able to handle the digital libraries and application of ICT. In this context a new model curriculum integrating the traditional and, modern knowledge has to be devised and implemented. ICT should be a core component of formal Library and Information Science education in India. Library schools need to upgrade their syllabi regularly according to the job market and future requirements. LIS schools should promote research and development in ICT.

6. CONCLUSION

This investigation has provided a useful summary of the application of ICT in special libraries in Kerala. Though the libraries had hardware and software facilities to some extent, ICT based resources and services were not reaching the users to the expected extent. This state of affairs has been largely due to inadequate finance, inadequate infrastructure and inadequately trained library professionals. The skill and expertise of library staff in ICT based resources and services were not adequate. Majority of the libraries had commercially prepared library management software and CD-ROM databases, but very few of them were using commercial online databases. Majority of the libraries had no digital library or digital library initiatives. Only three libraries were participating in library consortia. The use of Internet for library and information services was found to be very less. ICT based resources and services of majority of the libraries were very poor and not adequate. The electronic resource used by the largest percentage of users was the e-mail. Central Government autonomous institutions were better in the use of various ICT based resources and services. To overcome this unfortunate situation, library management in developing countries need to review their policies and, instead of heavily depending on traditional information resources, should set aside adequate resources for collecting digital information. They also need to give priority to staff training, and user education in regard to ICT based resources and services. The study concludes that most of the special libraries in Kerala need proper ICT infrastructure including hardware, software and humanware and library staff have to be trained properly to make use of the resources optimally both conventional and digital resources.

REFERENCES

1. Adams, J.A. and Bonk, S.C. (1995). Electronic Information Technologies and Resources: Use by University Faculty and Faculty Preference for Related Library Services. *College and Research Libraries,* 56, pp. 119-31.
2. Ali, A. (2004). Application of Information Technology in the Educational Media Libraries in Delhi. Proceedings of the XX IATLIS National Conference on Globalization of Library and Information Science Education. Chennai: University of Madras, pp. 89-96.
3. Amekuedee, John-Oswald. (2005). An Evaluation of Library Automation in Some Ghanaian University Libraries. *The Electronic Library,* 23 (4), pp. 442-52.
4. Barlow, Lisa J. and Graham, Margaret E. (1999). The Use of Information and Communication Technologies in Commercial Libraries in the UK, *Program,* 33 (2), pp. 109-28.
5. Furness, Karen L. and Graham, Margaret E. (1996). The Use of Information Technology in Special Libraries in the UK, *Program,* 30 (1), pp. 23-37.
6. George, P. Joshi. (1994). Library Automation in Kerala: an Evaluation, MLISc Dissertation, University of Calicut.

7. Haider, Syed Jalaluddin. (1998). Library Automation in Pakistan. *International Information and Library Review,* 30, pp. 51-69.

8. Hewitson, A. (2000). The Use and Awareness of Electronic Information Services by Academic Staff at Leeds Metropolitan University. *Library & Information Research News,* 24 (78), pp. 17-22.

9. Hewitson, A. (2002). Use and Awareness of Electronic Information Services by Academic Staff at Leeds Metropolitan University - a Qualitative Study. *Journal of Librarianship and Information Science,* 34 (1), pp.43-52.

10. Kasirao, V. (2000). Application of Information Technology (IT) in Special Libraries, Information and Documentation Centres (LIBIDOCS) in Chennai: a Study of its Impact on LIS", *In:* Proceedings of the Seventh National Convention for Automation of Libraries in Education and Research on Information Services in a Networked Environment in India. Ahmedabad: INFLIBNET Centre, pp.245-52.

11. Kumar, Bharat. (2003). Automation in University Libraries of Haryana. *ILA Bulletin,* 39 (3), pp. 15-21.

12. Mohamed Haneefa, K. (2005). Electronic Information Resources in the Special Libraries of Kerala, *Kelpro Bulletin,* *9*(1-2), pp.53-58.

13. Mohamed Haneefa, K. (2006). Information and Communication Technology Infrastructure in Special Libraries in Kerala. *Annals of Library and Information Studies,* 53 (2), pp. 31-42.

14. Moorthy, A.L. and Karisiddappa, C.R. (2001). Information Infrastructure and Use of Electronic Media in Indian Libraries". *In:* Proceedings of the First South Indian Library Conference on Role of University and College Libraries in the Changing Information Scenario. Hyderabad: Potti Sreeramulu Telugu University, pp. 148-62.

15. Moscoso, Purification. and Molina, Teresa Malo De. (1999). And After Automation, what? Spanish Libraries and the Challenge of Modernization. *Journal of Librarianship and Information Science,* 31 (2), pp.111-17.

16. Rehman, S and Ramzy, V. (2004). Aareness and Use of Electronic Information Resources at the Health Sciences Centre of Kuwait University, *Library Review,* 53 (3), pp. 150-56.

17. Sinha, Manoj Kumar (2004). Scenario of Automation and Networking of Library and Information Centres (LICs) of Northeastern region of India: an Evaluative study. *In:* Proceedings of the Second International CALIBER on Road Map to New Generation of Libraries Using Emerging Technologies, February 11-13, New Delhi. Ahmedabad: INFLIBNET Centre, pp. 61-72.

18. Thapa, Neelam and Sahoo, K.C. (2004). Problems and Prospects of Automation with Special Reference to Special Libraries in Jabalpur. *IASLIC Bulletin,* 49 (3), pp. 171-81.

19. Vicente, A., Crawford, J. and Clink, S. (2004). Use and Awareness of Electronic Information Services by Academic Staff at Glasgow Caledonian University. *Library Review,* 53 (8), pp. 401-7.

16

Archival of Digital Resources

Challenges and Issues

T.K. Mohammed Sageer
T.A.Abdul Azeez

ABSTRACT

Information explosion and exponential growth of literature has created a number of challenges and opportunities for information professionals. With the advent of Word Wide Web and Internet, the present day libraries have witnessed a flood of information resources in digital media in addition to traditional print media. The archival of digital resources poses challenges to library professionals. Archival concerns include deciding what to digitise, formats for texts and images, quality of images and costs. Digital Preservation refers to the various methods of keeping digital materials alive into future. This paper discusses the need for digital archiving, objectives of archiving and issues related to archiving of digital resources. It also discusses the various steps involved in the process of digital archiving.

1. INTRODUCTION

The information explosion and exponential growth

of literature has created a number of challenges and opportunities for information professionals. It is interesting to note that from the age old traditional libraries to the present day digital libraries, the major functions of the libraries remain the same: selection, procurement, organisation, preservation and dissemination of knowledge. In all these areas tremendous changes have been taken place due to technological revolutions like the advent of World Wide Web (WWW), unprecedented advances in Information and Communication Technology (ICT), etc.

With the advent of Word Wide Web and Internet, the present day libraries have witnessed a flood of information resources in digital media in addition to traditional print media. Digital resources include e-books, e-journals, conference proceedings, CD-ROM databases, online databases, multimedia databases and so on. In addition, a wide spectrum of relevant digital resources is freely available on the web for libraries to incorporate into their digital collection and to make them available to users. The digital media offers great potential to libraries and information centers such as wide access to resources, less storage space, remote access and long term preservation.

Digital preservation (1) means preserving the digital medium that holds the digital information by storing it in the correct environment and following agreed storage and handling procedures; copying the digital information into newer, fresher media before the old media deteriorates. Preservation concerns include deciding what to digitise, formats for texts and images, quality of images and costs. Digital Preservation refers to the various methods of keeping digital materials alive into future. It includes everything from electronic publications on CD-ROM to online databases and collection of experimental data in digital format and maintains the ability to display, retrieve and use digital collections in the face of rapidly changing technological and organisational infrastructures and elements.

2. NEED FOR DIGITAL ARCHIVING OF RESOURCES

Digital archiving is defined as long-term storage, preservation and access to information that is born digital (created and disseminated primarily in electronic form) or for which the digital version is considered to be the primary archive. In a broader perspective, it should also include the digitisation of materials from other media.

Long term preservation and archiving generally mean keeping an object safe from harmful effects such as loss, damage, destruction, etc. It is to be assured that information of enduring value is to be protected for present and future generations. Most of the information generated today originates in digital form, including scientific research data, scholarly publications, records of administration, creative expressions in arts and music. However, few organisations have the means to preserve digital information for future reference. The vast ocean of knowledge in digital media should be made available and usable for future generations.

3. OBJECTIVES OF ARCHIVING

The major objectives of archiving (2) are:

1. To make information survive for future use
2. To provide world wide accessibility
3. To make the information easy to use and handle

4. To maintain the historical value of information
5. To prevent the information from deteriorating factors

4. ISSUES OF ARCHIVING OF DIGITAL INFORMATION

Archiving of digital information has many issues and challenges and important among them are discussed below.

4.1. Permanent Accessibility

Usually publishers of electronic journals provide access privilege to their journals for the prescribed subscription period only. In this context it is significant to note that in the case of print subscription, the libraries will have the print copies of the journals subscribed in their collection, even after the libraries stop the subscription. But, in the case of electronic journals the things are entirely different. As long as we continue subscription we are permitted to access the archives. Once we discontinue subscription we won't have access to archives including the period for which we had subscription. However, some publishers like Springer arrange complimentary "limited perpetual" access to the subscribed content for one or two years and after expiry of complimentary access further access can be assured by paying a maintenance fee. Publishers of e-journals also have software-controlled mechanism for checking sequential downloading of the articles of a particular issue. Hence there is no scope for downloading an entire issue and storage of the same on a secondary storage media. In the case of discontinuing an electronic subscription, the library will have absolutely no issues of journals for the future use of their patrons.

4.2. Uncertainty of Publishing Industry

It is well known that publishing industry is prone to mergers, cessation and stoppages. In such circumstances the libraries have no guarantee for accessing archives of the e-journals. In addition, many publishers upload their gigantic digital contents with third party server firms and there is no clarity or assurance how long the arrangement will last.

4.3. Durability of the Media

Shorter life span of electronic media is another important issue of electronic archiving. The scientific journals are in existence for a long time in print medium and they are well preserved in libraries. Now the format is changed from print to digital. At present most of the e-journals are published in PDF format. As the technology advances, the present medium and format may change within a short span of time.

4.4. Technological Advances

Archival initiatives may also consider unprecedented pace of technological developments in hardware and software. Today's software and hardware may be outdated tomorrow. Issues like interoperability and standards must be considered in this context. We must also take security measures against unauthorised access either through password authentication or by IP authentication.

4.5. Intellectual Property Right

Copyright issue is another issue for Archives. Generally copyright of a journal article or document rests with the publisher of the document. When we subscribe to a digital content, we are only "licensed to access" that content during a particular period. We may or may not have rights to access that digital content in future. So, at the time of setting up of the Archives, issues of copyright have to be settled with the creators of digital contents.

5. DIGITAL ARCHIVING PROCESS

Digital archiving process involves copying the digital information into newer media before the old media become so obsolete that the data cannot be accessed. This is referred to as copying or refreshing. In this process integrity of digital information is preserved. Digitisation refers to all of the steps involved in the process of making collections of materials available in digital medium. The various equipments needed for digitisation includes Computers, Scanners, Digital Cameras, Software and Storage medium. The process includes all of the following steps and more depending on what you're digitizing:

* Get financial resources, staff, equipment, build technical knowledge
* Project management
* Selection of collections/materials
* Scan or digitize materials
* Transcribe, markup, index
* Create metadata
* Quality control
* Process images
* Mount it all on the web
* Preserve and maintain archival media and online collections

Before moving to the technical details of a project, the following questions are to be considered:

* Why do you want to digitise materials?
* Who is your audience?

* Who owns the materials?
* Who is the copyright holder for the intellectual property of the materials?
* What is your timeframe for the project?
* How is the project being funded?
* Who will be responsible for different stages of the project?
* How will you digitize the materials?
* How will you describe the materials & what metadata scheme will be used?
* How will you provide access to the collection?
* How will you preserve and maintain the collection and digitized materials?

The steps involved in the digital archiving process is schematically represented below:

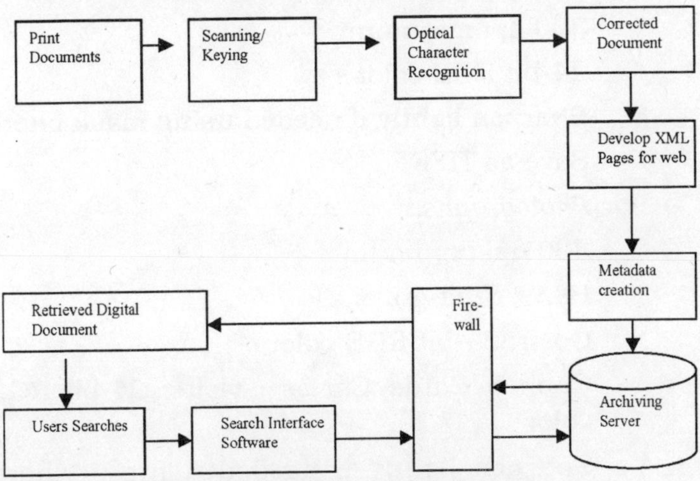

Fig. 1. Digital Archiving Process

5.1. Scanning of Documents

In this process, the scanning of documents is an initial process. The documents should not be scanned below 300 dpi resolution. Basically the resolution depends on the physical condition of the document. The scanned images are typically stored in file formats like JPG, TIFF etc. The final out put is converted to a convenient format like PDF that allows various security measures to be incorporated to prevent modifications and other manipulations. The process of scanning documents involves:

- Create a master image, saved as a TIFF (Tagged Image File Format) File
- Generate derivative or access images from this master image
- Save the master images onto CD-R disks or other long term storage and mount the access images on a web server for public access

For *manuscripts and printed materials* use the following guidelines:

* 300 dpi minimum
* 24-bit RGB color
* Sharpen lightly if needed using mask filter
* Save as TIFF

For *Photographs*:

* 300 dpi minimum
* B&W: 8-bit grayscale
* Color: 24-bit RGB colour
* Cabinet Cards/Cartes d'visite: 24-bit RGB color
* Sharpen lightly if needed using unsharp mask filter
* Save as TIFF

Image Derivatives : Several common types of derivative images may be created from master images.

* **GIF (Graphics Interchange Format)** This

format is only currently used for creating thumbnails and 1 bit bitonal (black & white) images.

* **JPEG (Joint Photographic Experts Group)** This format is widely used for creating medium and high resolution images for Web delivery.
* **PDF (Portable Document Format)** From Adobe, this compressed format requires users to have the Adobe Acrobat Reader software installed on their machine (a common default on newer machines and browsers). It offers the benefit of re-sizing on screen and easy printing of documents. This format is most commonly used for printed documents.

5.2. Preparation of Text Files

The scanned files may be processed to separate the text and images before saving into PDF formats. The next process is to rectify the errors and make text files error free with the help of Optical Character Recognition (OCR) process. This process involves proof reading and checking quality of text files. After all the above processes, the text is converted to mark up languages like XML, HTML etc. along with complete tagging that enables the database to be integrated with any web applications.

5.3. Server Installation

A high power archiving server can be installed for this purpose with Internet access for remotely accessing the archival. The server shall have access to a high end hard disk drive of around 2TB capacity. The server will have strategic configuration such as dual processing and mirroring capabilities. Suitable archive software can be identified and installed to host the data in the server.

5.4. Search Interface

For information retrieval from the server, a user-friendly search interface can be developed in HTML/ASP/PHP and placed in the home page of the archive. The databases can be connected via CGI scripts and other scripting languages with the help of an HTML/ASP/PHP front end. XML based metadata description support can be provided to enhance the retrieval capacity. State-of-the-art Fire-wall software also can be provided for effective data security.

6. CONCLUSION

The archiving and long term preservation of vast wealth of digital information is considered as a social service to the generations to come. While attempting archiving of digital resources, enough care should be taken to overcome the issues discussed above. It is true that significant advances have been taken place in the areas of repository architecture and design, standards and metadata, but not many fruitful efforts are made in the direction of preserving the digital information heritage of the country.

REFERENCES

1. Rakesh, Prasad (2006). Preservation of Library Resources in Digital Environment. *University News*, 44 (11).
2. Ram, Mange et al (2005). Digital Preservation: a Challenge to Libraries. *Library Progress* (International), 25 (1).

17

Knowledge Management in Digital Environment: An Overview

M. Nagarajan
P. Sivaraman
M. Surulinathi

ABSTRACT

This paper is aimed to discuss the concept of knowledge Management, types of knowledge, critical success factors of knowledge management, and the advantages of knowledge management in detail.

1. INTRODUCTION

New technologies have changed the way organisations view and use knowledge. Information can now be collected, analysed and distributed in ways not previously possible. Databases help to collect, store, filter and make sense of this information. Groupware allows communities of practice to grow beyond the limits of time and place. Network makes it possible to disseminate information to millions simultaneously. Electronic Performance Support Systems (EPSS) can be used to support cognitive skills and provide technical expertise.

But it's not just technology that is driving the excitement around Knowledge Management. Knowledge Management is exciting because it makes sense to executives. They know that there are rich resources nestled in the minds and hearts of their organisations. They want access to those resources and to hold onto them as the organisation.

Geography and management are also fueling the interest in Knowledge Management. Employees are everywhere and often on their own because they are mobile or the only person in a remote location. Organisations are leaner and there are fewer middle managers to coordinate the flow of information. KM helps people and ideas reach each other.

At the same time, the bulk of the work that needs to get done falls under the umbrella of "knowledge work." Leading businesses, like Microsoft, Intel, or Yahoo! are less about selling products or services and more about providing services, knowledge and innovation. What's different is that while people have always needed knowledge to do their work, now knowledge (using, sharing and creating) has become the work.

2. WHAT IS KNOWLEDGE MANAGEMENT?

Knowledge Management is planning, designing, building, operating and maintaining the knowledge Management System. Knowledge Management is managing knowledge of

* Information in Document
  — Sounds
  — Images and

  — Text
* Knowledge in People Heads
  — Collaboration
  — Storytelling
  — Community of Practice
  — Mind mapping
* Organisational Memory
  — Knowledge Re-use
  — Community of Practice
  — Lesson Learning
* Conversion of Information to Knowledge
  — Logical intelligence
  — Collaborative Intelligence
  — Sensory Experience
  — Intuition
  — Technology Experience
* Learning Methods
  — Discovery Learning
  — Constructivist Learning
  — Task-based Learning
  — Goal-based Learning

Knowledge Management (KM) is about getting the right knowledge to the right people at the right time through a collection of technological tools, non-technological tools and philosophies. There are essentially two perspectives on Knowledge Management. The first views knowledge as an object that can be captured and transferred. The second views knowledge as a process that is unique to each individual. Each perspective contributes to the possibilities. The first led to the development of systems that encourage the efficient collection and dissemination of knowledge. The second led to the creation of "communities of practice," or groups of individuals who communicate because they share work practices, a profession or other interests. What is important to remember about Knowledge Management is that it's not just one initiative, it's the integration of many initiatives working together to ensure that knowledge is created and shared throughout organisations. How exactly this is done is unique to each organisation.

3. DEFINITIONS

According to Ouitas et al. , "Knowledge Management is to discover, develop, utilize, deliver and absorb knowledge inside and outside the organization through an appropriate management process to meet current and future needs".

According to Batt, "Knowledge Management is a process of knowledge creation, validation, presentation, distribution and application."

According to Horwitch and Armacost, "Knowledge Management is the creation, extraction, transformation and storage of the correct knowledge and Information in order to design better policy, modify action and deliver result"

According to Wikipedia, Knowledge Management refers 'to a range of practices used by organisations to identify, create, represent, and distribute knowledge for reuse, awareness, and learning across the organisations'.

According to Barth, "Unless you feel a burning need to inject into conversations concepts like heuristics, reintermediation, probabilistic concept correlation or syntactic morphological disambiguation, no one should feel compelled to call it "knowledge management" at all".

4. APPLICATION

To serve customers well and remain in organisation must reduce their cycle times, operate with minimum fixed assets and overhead (people, inventory and facilities), shorten product development time, improve customer service, empower employees, innovate and deliver high quality products, enhance flexibility and adoption, capture information, create knowledge, share and learn.

None of this is possible without a continual focus on the creation, updating, availability, quality and use of knowledge by all employees and teams, at work and in the marketplace.

5. TYPES OF KNOWLEDGE

Explicit and Tacit Knowledge

* The term tacit knowledge first introduced in 1966 by Michael Polanyi : The Tacit dimension.
* Nonaka & Takeuchi in 1995 used it as : Knowledge-Creating Company
* Explains the power of knowledge creation in an organisation and the roles between individual and organisation and between explicit and tacit knowledge

Explicit knowledge:

* Codified
* Transmittable through formal, systematic language
* Theoretical
* Objective

* Rational
* "There and then"
* Context-free (to some extent)
* "Knowledge of mind"
* Easily transmitted and stored
* Documents
* Databases etc.
* Approximately 5% of all knowledge

Tacit knowledge

* Embodied
* Personal
* Context-specific
* Includes cognitive elements
* Subjective
* Experience
* Here and now
* "Knowledge of body"
* Mental models (beliefs, perspectives, paradigms etc.)
* Difficult to share and transmit
* Estimate: 95% of all knowledge

6. STAGES IN KNOWLEDGE MANAGEMENT SYSTEM

Identify Knowledge

* Knowledge Gap
* Core Competencies
* Knowledge Domain
* People and skills

Collect Knowledge

* Buying Knowledge – Recruiting
* Merging the Organisations
* Outsourcing
* Rending Knowledge – Consultant
* Joint Venturing
* Data entry
* OCR and scanning
* Voice input
* Pulling information from various sources
* Searching for information to include

Select Knowledge

* Assess the value of Information
* Find the insight

Store Knowledge

* Expert System – Storing of expert knowledge
* Repository
* Keep and Index the knowledge dynamically

Share Knowledge

* Selective Dissemination of Information
* SECI Model

Create Knowledge

* SECI Model

Apply Knowledge

* Perform Support System
* Problem Solving and Task analysis

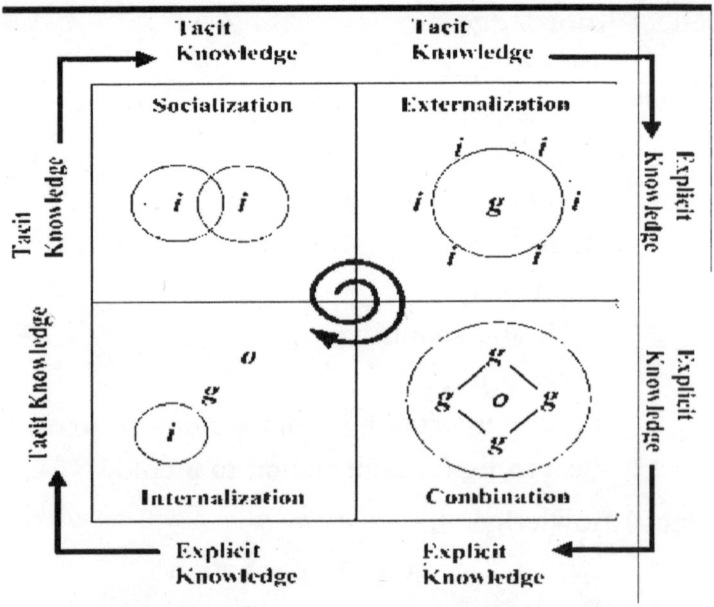

Fig. 1. The Key Elements of the SECI Model

7. SUCCESS FACTORS

Using the lessons learning from early adopters, many organisations have effectively providing their employees with the tools they need for managing and sharing knowledge. Yet, it is easy to forget to account for certain critical elements that enable knowledge sharing.

An elementary success factor of knowledge management is to have a common understanding of the terms "knowledge management" and "knowledge sharing" and how they apply to your situation and needs. Some organisations choose not to use these terms at all because they are not accepted within the culture. By recognising this fact, an organisation is actually adhering to a critical success factor of KM: listen to your employees and customers.

APQC defines KM as an emerging set of strategies

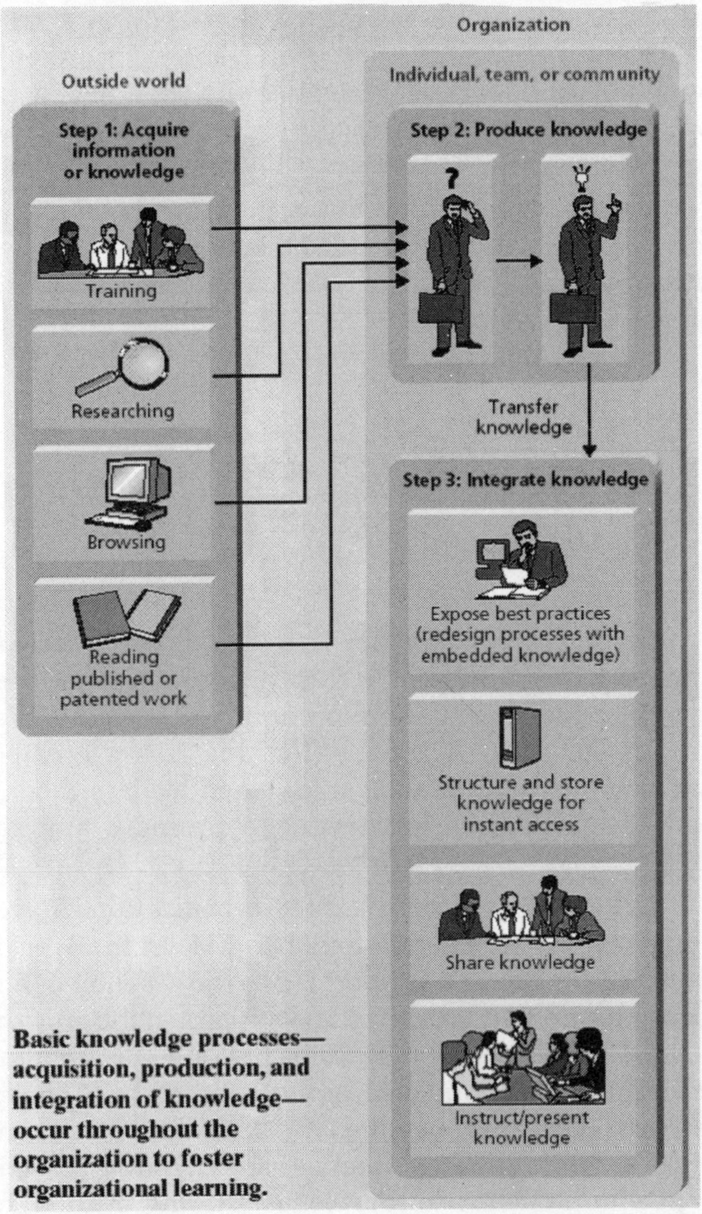

Fig. 2. Knowledge Life cycle Model

and approaches to create, safeguard, and use knowledge assets (including people and information), which allows knowledge to flow to the right people at the right time so they can apply these assets to create more value for the enterprise.

The success of a KM initiative depends on many factors, some within our control, some not. Typically, critical success factors can be categorised into five primary categories:

* Leadership;
* Culture;
* Structure, roles and responsibilities
* Information Technology Infrastructure; and
* Measurement;

Leadership

Leadership plays a key role in ensuring success in almost any initiative within an organisation. Its impact on KM is even more pronounced because this is a relatively new discipline. Nothing makes greater impact on an organisation than when leaders model the behaviour they are trying to promote among employees.

Several other best-practice organizations have demonstrating this commitment to KM. At the World Bank, the president's support led to the creation of an infrastructure that promoted and supported the growth of communities of practice (CoPs) not only throughout the organisation, but also around the globe. Today, the World Bank has sustained its KM initiative through its CoPs. Its knowledge managers constantly search for new approaches to knowledge sharing. Although leadership plays a critical role in the success of the KM initiative, the "culture" factor can be even more important to the success of KM.

Culture

Culture is the combination of shared history, expectations, unwritten rules, and social customs that compel behaviors. It is the set of underlying beliefs that, while rarely exactly articulated, are always there to influence the perception of actions and communications of all employees. Cultural issues concerning KM initiatives usually arise due to the following factors:

Lack of time : The goal is not to encourage the employees to work more, but to work more effectively. The processes, technologies, and roles designed during a KM initiative must save employees' time, not burden them with more work. This can only be accomplished if the employees' work patterns are accounted for during the initial design and planning phase of the initiative.

Unconnected reward systems : Organisations have to maintain a balance between intrinsic and explicit rewards in order to encourage employee behavior. The most effective use of explicit rewards has been to encourage sharing at the onset of a KM initiative. If the attendees don't find value in either the meetings or the information on the system, providing incentives will not sustain their participation. People share because they want to, they like to see their expertise being used, and they like being respected by their peers.

Lack of common perspectives : Sharing must be inspired by a common vision. The people affected by the new process or technology must all buy in to this vision and believe it will work.

No formal communication : When designing and implementing KM initiatives, ensure that employees and customers know about the changes occurring in your organisation. It has been hypothesised that a person needs to hear the same message at least three times before it registers in the brain. Hence, communication should be pervasive and ingeminating. While implementing KM within your organisation, market yourself. Make sure everyone knows what you are attempting to do, and build anticipation for the launch.

If your organisation naturally has a tendency to share knowledge, enabling knowledge sharing becomes a little easier. If your organisation harbors a knowledge-hoarding culture, don't give in to it. Remove negative consequences to sharing. People want to share their knowledge. They want others to know they are knowledgeable. Break down some of the existing barriers to knowledge sharing, and give people the tools and environment they need. By designing KM initiatives around your culture, you will be initiating a cultural change.

Structure, Roles and Responsibilities

Although there are many ways that organisations structure the governance of their KM initiatives, APQC has found common elements among best-practice partner organisations: a steering committee, a central KM support group, and stewards/owners throughout the organization who are responsible for KM. It is a combination of a centralised and decentralised approach.

The Steering Committee usually consists of executives at the top level. They promote the concept and provide guidance, direction, and support. The central group usually consists of people with advanced project management, facilitation, and communication skills. The stewards, or owners, are responsible for knowledge sharing and acquisition within the business units. Like the core KM group, the stewards are change agents for the organisation. They model and teach employees the principles of knowledge sharing using a common vocabulary.

Although the structure is put in place to establish ownership and accountability, if there is no overall ownership of knowledge and learning within the organisation and the leadership does not "walk the talk," it will be difficult to sustain any sharing behaviour.

Information Technology Infrastructure

Without Information Technology infrastructure, an organisation cannot enable its employees to share information on a large scale. Yet the trap that most organisations fall into is not a lack of IT, but rather too much focus on IT. A KM initiative is not a software application; having a platform to share information and to communicate is only part of a KM initiative. Following are some KM success factors related to IT.

Approach : The people who are charged with implementing KM must take the time to understand their users' needs. Matching the KM system with the KM objectives is essential.

Content : With a similar focus on users' needs, establishing great content involves having processes in place to acquire, manage, validate, and deliver relevant information, when and where it is needed.

Common platforms : A standard organisation wide architecture ensures the sustainability and scalability of KM efforts. By understanding the organisation's infrastructure at a high level, the Steering Committee can guide the KM team in picking the appropriate technology. Sometimes organisations realise that they need a complete overhaul of their IT infrastructure before they can expect their employees to share knowledge. This enables organisations to build on the existing architecture by using off-the-shelf software that was written to support these platforms, thus avoiding costly customised packages.

Simple technology : If it takes more than three clicks to find knowledge on your system, users will get frustrated. Of course, you have to temper that with the amount of information being delivered and the complexity of information demanded by the user. Another common mistake made in information delivery is the emphasis on explicit knowledge. Although technology is primarily used to deliver explicit knowledge, placing too much emphasis on it causes the user to lose the context in which the information was shared and leads to misunderstanding on how to interpret the knowledge.

Adequate training : KM is enabled by adequate technology and people who know how to use it. Best-practice examples reveal that the central KM group should spend most of its time (after deployment) teaching, guiding, and coaching users how to use the system to interact, communicate, and share information and knowledge with one another.

Measurement

Most people fear measurement because they see it as synonymous with ROI (Return on Investment), and they are not sure how to link KM efforts to ROI. Although the ultimate goal of measuring the effectiveness of a KM initiative is to determine some type of ROI, there are many intervening variables that also affect the outcomes.

Because many variables may affect an outcome, it is important to correlate KM activities with business outcomes, while not claiming a pure cause-and-effect relationship. Increased sales may be a result not only of the sales representatives having more information, but also of the market turning, a competitor closing down, or prices dropping 10 percent. Due to the inability to completely isolate knowledge-sharing results, tracking the correlations over time is important.

There is a final imperative concerning critical success factors, which transcends KM and applies to all interactions: Listen! Listen to your users, customers, and managers-whichever audience for which you are designing. They will tell you how you can meet their needs and have a successful KM initiative.

8. ADVANTAGES OF KM

* Knowledge has been and continues to be the key to success and competitive advantage for every organisation.
* Effectively managing the processes of actively disseminating and of actively applying knowledge to making an organisation successful is Knowledge Management
* Competitive advantage is achieved through developing and implementing both creative and timely business solutions that reuse applicable knowledge and that use newly created knowledge, which is commonly called innovation.

9. SUMMARY

In summary, Knowledge Management involves connecting people with people, as well as people with information. Creating competitive advantage today requires developing and leveraging organisational knowledge. Leading edge firms consider their knowledge to be a strategic asset and actively and explicitly manage it as such. It's up to you to lead your teams to craft, communicate, and instill KM practices throughout your organisation. Knowledge for its own sake does not help the organisation unless it turns into action. To add value, give a competitive edge, create new opportunities and improve profit, organisations, teams and individuals have to make a real change in the way they see and do things. This means going beyond analyzing, reporting, benchmarking and sharing. They have to transform information and knowledge into action in the digital environment.

REFERENCES

1. http://www.providersedge.com/kma/km_overview.htm
2. http://defcon.sdsu.edu/1/objects/km/defining/index.htm#qgAn
3. http://www.providersedge.com/docs/km_articles/Critical_Success_Factors_of_KM.pdf
4. http://www.providersedge.com/docs/km_articles/KM_-_The_Road_Ahead_for_Success.pdf
5. http://www.unsw.adfa.edu.au/units/research/BAM2005%202.pdf

18

Competitive Intelligence in the Context of Knowledge Management

Santosh A. Navalur
Savita N. Nayak

ABSTRACT

Knowledge Management is the process through which corporate knowledge is used to improve organisational performance. As a part of Knowledge Management, Competitive Intelligence (CI) is a process for gathering usable knowledge about the external business environment. That knowledge leads to improve the performance, flexibility and competitiveness of the organisation. In this paper, we have made an attempt to give brief information about relationship between knowledge management and competitive intelligence, meaning and definitions, goals and objectives, activities, tools and techniques, information sources, process and phases, benefits and some common problems of Competitive Intelligence.

1. INTRODUCTION

In order for organisation to remain globally competitive, new tools for decision-making are required. Of these tools, it is internationally recognised that Competitive Intelligence, as a part of Knowledge Management, is fast becoming a norm rather than the exception to assist management with decision-making in the modern knowledge-based organisation.

2. KNOWLEDGE MANAGEMENT & COMPETITIVE INTELLIGENCE

There is a strong link between these two disciplines. *Knowledge Management* is the process through which corporate knowledge is used to improve organisational performance. Essentially it looks at managing internal knowledge processes, developing the efficient usage of all information required for corporate decisions. *Competitive Intelligence* is a process for gathering usable knowledge about the external business environment. Competitive Intelligence focuses on turning external information into the intelligence required for tactical or strategic decisions relating to the business environment. Without an effective knowledge management process, gathered Competitive Intelligence is likely to collect dust, there is no proper process to turn the information into something usable. Even if immediate actions are taken based on collected Competitive Intelligence, it must be integrated into the internal knowledge systems to develop any long-term learning. This learning is a crucial element to enable companies to become skilled at spotting trends and adapting to business change. So Competitive Intelligence is a part of Knowledge Management System.

3. COMPETITIVE INTELLIGENCE

Competitive Intelligence (CI) as the ethical programme for selection, collection, interpretation and distribution of publicly held information about the competitors, market trends, business environment and organization itself that has strategic importance to make the strategic decisions which will aims to further the goals and objectives of an organisation in order to remain globally competitive. The term is often viewed as synonymous with Competitor analysis but Competitive Intelligence is more than analysing competitors, it is about making the organisation more competitive relative to its existing set of competitors and potential competitors. Customers and key external stakeholders define the set of competitors for the organisation and, in so doing, describe what could be a substitute for the business, votes, donations or other activities of the organisation.

According to the Society of Competitive Intelligence Professionals: A systematic and ethical program for gathering, analyzing, and managing external information that can affect your company's plans, decisions, and operations."

Leonard Fuld has defined Competitor Intelligence as "highly specific and timely information about a corporation."

Benjamin and Tamar Gilad have defined that "Business intelligence [an alternate term for competitive intelligence] is the activity of monitoring the environment external to the firm for information that is relevant for the decision-making process of the company."

3.1. Goals & Objectives

Common goals of CI

* Detecting competitive threats
* Eliminating or lessening surprises
* To increase managerial flexibility
* Enhancing competitive advantage by lessening reaction time
* Finding new opportunities
* Making optimal use of information sources
* Enable to put competitive actions in context
* Broadens awareness of competitive situation

Objective of CI

The objective of Competitive Intelligence is not to steal a competitor's trade secrets or other proprietary property, but rather to gather in a systematic and legal manner a wide range of information that when collated and analysed provides a fuller understanding of a competitor firm's structure, culture, behavior, capabilities and weaknesses.

3.2. Activities of the CI

The activities of the CI are focused on Information gathering and information analysis to support the organisation to be competent, some core activities of CI are:

* Identify competitors, markets, customers, suppliers, or other variables in the environment to be monitored. Identify what information is to be collected.
* Specifically identify possible sources of information and collect the information from these sources.

* Evaluate the validity, reliability, and usefulness of the information collected.
* Gather information collected from different sources and integrate them.
* Interpret and analyse the information for strategic or tactical significance. Draw conclusions and recommend actions.
* Disseminate and present analysed findings to management.
* Respond to ad hoc inquiries for decision support.

3.3. CI Tools and Techniques

Different types of CI tools and techniques are available for different requirements of the CI activities, they are:

* *Contacting Government Agencies* can yield valuable data for the CIP, but may often require excessive lead-time.
* *Searching Online Databases* is a faster method of finding competitive information, although it is more expensive. With increasing sophistication and affordability of information technology, this technique is expected to become less expensive. Database search does not provide information that has not been released to the public or that has not yet been collected.
* *From Companies and Investment Community Resources* — Some types of data that are not widely available from databases can be procured by contacting the corporation itself or from investment community sources.
* *Surveys and Interviews* —Surveys can yield

plenty of data about competitors and products, while Interviews can provide more in-depth perspectives from a limited sample.

* *Drive-by and On-site Observations* of the competitor's [full or empty] parking spaces, new construction-in-progress, customer service at retail outlets, volume and pattern of [suppliers' or customers'] trucks, etc. can yield useful CI information about the state of the competitor's business.
* *Competitive Benchmarking* is used for comparing the organisation's operations against those of the competitor's.
* *Defensive Competitive Intelligence* involves monitoring and analysing one's own business activities as the competitors and outsiders see them.
* *Reverse Engineering* of competitor's products and services may yield important CI information about their quality and costs.

3.5 Information Sources for CI Activities

The aim of the Competitive Intelligence is analysis and dissemination of information to support the organisation to compete in the global market. The main sources of information for CI activities are categorised as following :

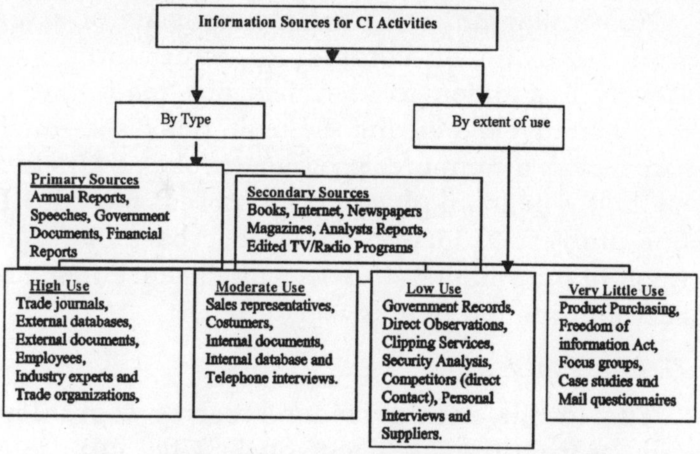

Fig. 1. Information Sources for CI Activities

3.6. CI Process

The process of CI analysis might be divided into an arbitrary number of steps. Friedman (1997), Barndt (1994), Kahaner (1996), Meyer (1987), and Heuer (1999) identified the following general phases in CI process, which are grouped as main phases and mini phases.

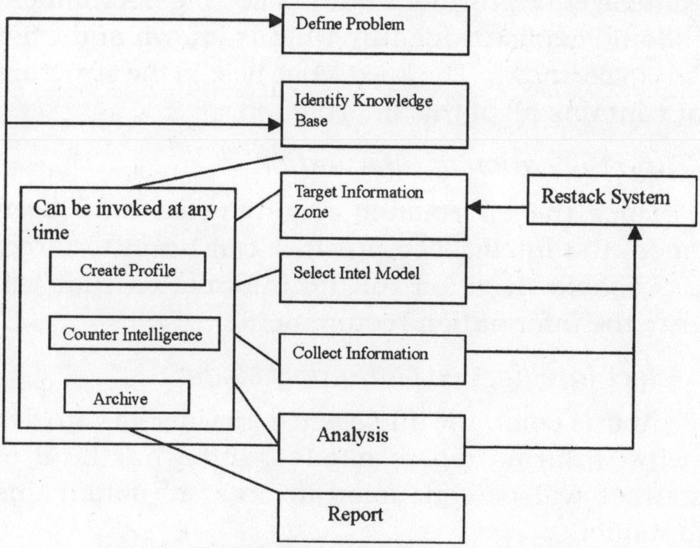

Fig. 2. Competitive Intelligence Process

Above diagram of CI process consists of seven phases that can be completed sequentially and iteratively. In addition, we identified four "mini-phases" that can be invoked during the main phases in much the same way a computer program invokes a function or method. The main phases of CI process includes 1) Define problem 2) Identify knowledge base 3) Target location of information 4) Select Intelligence mode 5) Collect information 6) Analysis 7) Report

1. Define Problem

The intelligence provider receives a problem statement from the intelligence user. The purpose of defining the problem is to ensure that the intelligence provider understands the needs and desires of the intelligence user. The defined problem describes all of the criteria for a successful operation.

2. Identify Knowledge

After the problem has been defined and before the intelligence provider begins collecting information, he should explicitly identify what is known and what needs to be known. The knowledge base is the structure that contains all of this information.

3. Target Location of Information

Once the information requirements have been defined, the intelligence provider can begin to target the probable "location" of the information that will satisfy the information requirements.

4. Select Intelligence-Gathering Mode

At this point, the intelligence provider has an idea of what information is needed and what kind of resources will be consumed in order to obtain this information.

5. Collect Information

After weighing the modes for gathering the information, the intelligence provider begins to pursue the information that was targeted in the previous phase. In general, the intelligence provider should begin by mining information that is internal to the organisation and then move to external sources.

6. Analysis

In this phase, the intelligence provider generates possible solutions (hypotheses) to each of the mission requirements that are contained in the mission statement.

7. Report

Once all of the collection and analysis are complete, the intelligence provider's findings must be put in a form that provides value to the intelligence user. The intelligence product consists of the evidence, hypothesis evaluations, and recommendations.

The other phases of CI process include: Create profile, Retask the system, Counterintelligence, Archive, The main phase report can also include the sub-phases 1) Create Profile (mini-analysis phase that is used to acquire certain kinds of information) 2) Counterintelligence (intelligence provider identifies what are pieces of information that represent a competitive advantage to the intelligence user) 3) Archive (consists of storing all of the information that makes up a certain intelligence operation according to the terms or features that characterise the operation). 4) Retasking the system is the mechanism for performing a loop in the larger "intelligence analysis" process. It can be invoked at any point in the process. But it will most often occur after the completion of an iteration of the collection phase (in one mode or another). In this phase, the intelligence provider deliberately moves information, which has been collected and intermediately stored, into the knowledge base.

3.7. Benefits of CI

Important Benefits of CI are:

* Reliable network of field sources for fast data collection
* Optimal use of information sources
* Early warning of threats and opportunities
* Increased managerial flexibility
* Shorter cycle times from ideas to implementation
* Disseminates intelligence to decision-makers on a need-to-know basis
* Transforms data into timely, pertinent and meaningful information/intelligence

These all benefits will help to improve the performance, flexibility and competitiveness of the organisation.

3.8. Common Problems for CI

* Managers don't value intelligence
* Managers consider intelligence a luxury
* Inability to incorporate it into strategy
* Managers believe "I know my industry!"
* Unskilled people try to perform intelligence
* Managers hoard information
* The function doesn't meet the real needs and concerns of decision makers

4. CONCLUSION

Competitive Intelligence is a Knowledge Management technique which bringing together many activities to aggregate data and synthesize information concerning the competitive environment, or to assess competitor's strengths and weaknesses. Its structure ensures accuracy and validity of information while ensuring the propriety of competitors' information within legal and ethical boundaries.

REFERENCES

1. Haravu, L J. Lectures on Knowledge Management: Paradigms, Challenges and Opportunities. Bangalore.
2. Sammon, William L. et al (1985). Business Competitor Intelligence. New York: John Wiley & Sons
3. http://en.wikipedia.org/wiki/Competitive_intelligence
4. http://www.infotoday.com/it2001/presentations/jmiller.ppt
5. http://www.scip.org/

19
Mobile and Wireless Communication Technologies in Knowledge Management in Marginalised and Rural Communities

A. Neelameghan

ABSTRACT

This paper defines the terms information society, knowledge society, cyberspace and highlight their features. It emphasises that Knowledge Management will facilitate empowering rural and indigenous communities on the one hand and enable the sharing and use of the wealth of tacit community knowledge for the good of the nation, the global community of nations and nation states. The concern is not only the need to empower the marginalised communities through information out-reach programmes but also to collect and record the community knowledge, make efforts to understand their cultures, and leverage on the wisdom they possess for the good of the society. Recent developments and extension of ICT applications points to the possibilities of bridging the digital divide and better management of rural community knowledge. Attempts to use ICTs to reach out to indigenous and marginalised rural communities with a view to empowering them through implementation of e-governance, providing access to a variety of government documents relevant to the life of rural communities, village kiosks, land-sat imaging and remote sensing, geographical information systems etc.

1. INFORMATION SOCIETY, KNOWLEDGE SOCIETY, CYBERSPACE

Information society : A society in which "the creation, distribution and manipulation of information has become the most significant economic and cultural activity with application of computers and telecommunications in many sectors of the economy" in contrast with societies in which the basis of economic development is primarily industrial and/or agrarian.(http://whatis.techtarget.com/definition/0,,sid9_gci213588,00.html). The term was popularised in Europe in the mid 1990s (cf. the Bangemann Report on *Europe and the global information society,* 1994)

Knowledge society : A society that creates, shares and uses knowledge for the prosperity and well-being of its people. Features of the emerging knowledge society include the convergence of information and communication technologies (ICTs) enabling almost seamless access, in the expanding digital space, to vast and varied information and knowledge sources from anywhere at any time.

Cyberspace : A virtual space covering many hundreds of web pages networked by hypertext links. These web pages and the information resources they hold can be surfed / navigated and accessed from any computer (PC, tabletop, laptop, handheld devices, etc) connected to the Internet. Cyberspace being a multi-media domain of words / text, images, and sound, is becoming a key element in the development of the information society.

2. GLOBALISATION AND EXPANDING CYBERSPACE

The Internet is not only the largest library in the world but also a large commercial market with numerous companies maintaining websites to provide information about themselves and their products and services, facilitating online trading and other business transactions. Government departments, non-governmental organisations, research centres and almost every other type of institution, big and small, vie with each other to be noticed on the Internet. Practically any kind of information can be placed on the Internet / WWW – technical report, research papers, learning materials, games, legal, medical, religious / spiritual offerings, kitchen recipe, market information, disaster warning messages etc.

It has enabled national, regional and global video-conferencing and democratic debate and has spurred a whole variety of virtual person-to-person and group contacts and exchange of messages, news and views in many different languages and interactions among different cultures. The reach is almost immediate and world-wide. These developments give people the perception of elimination of distance and time in the communications context and the creation of a global village

A consequence of the expanding cyberspace and globalisation is the growing interdependence among peoples of the world. Implicit in this is the need to share both knowledge and wisdom among people.

However, wisdom calls for an understanding of the limit(s) that humans must respect or place on the use of the knowledge they gain.

During the past two decades, in many countries, the movement of at least parts of their society from a mainly paper-based communication to electronic (digital) communication has been accelerating thanks to the sharp decline in the cost of powerful PCs and communication devices and their wider accessibility. However, in many developing countries and among marginalised communities of the developed countries the benefits of application of information and communication technologies (ICT) have largely been minimal. There is always the challenge of the ICT savvy sections of society exploiting such under-privileged and marginalised communities (locally, nationally, and/or internationally) while the latter's hope of crossing the digital divide to be part of the mainstream has not been fulfilled to any significant extent. Some would even say that the digital divide has been widening in many dimensions.

3. KNOWLEDGE MANAGEMENT

Knowledge management (KM) is usually defined in relation to an enterprise environment. In that context KM is concerned with organisational processes that integrate data and information processing capacity of information technologies with peoples' creative and innovative capacity, including their tacit knowledge. It examines issues of organisational adaptation, survival, and competence in the context of discontinuous change. Common to these definitions is the emphasis on knowledge as the intellectual capital or asset of an enterprise and leveraging an organisation's knowledge resources to enable it to adapt, survive and compete in the face of increasingly discontinuous change. (Allee (1997), Davenport (1998), Haravu, 2002, chapter 3; Malhotra, (1998), Nonaka and Takeuchi (1995), Svelby (1997)). These authors generally consider two dimensions of KM, namely, Collaborative dimension and Semantic dimension as important. Neelameghan and Chester (2007) have proposed that it is useful and possible to widen the scope of KM, beyond the enterprise environment, applying it to community knowledge management. In so doing we need to take into consideration not only the collaborative and semantic dimensions but also other dimensions, such as, Structural/Organizational dimension, Technological dimension, Policy and Legislative dimension, Cultural dimension (which influences the semantic dimension, and people's perceptions and priorities), Spiritual dimension, Space dimension, and Time dimension. In fact, equity and justice in governance call for such widening of the scope of KM. This will facilitate empowering rural and indigenous communities on the one hand and enable the sharing and use of the wealth of tacit community knowledge for the good of the nation, the global community of nations and nation states. It will accommodate trans-generational and multi-generational transfer of knowledge and education, both formal and informal. In relation to a particular community some of these factors may influence KM more than the others; and they may play an enabling role or create barriers to communications and knowledge transfer.

Human behavioural characteristics differ from place to place within a country and across national boundaries; they vary over periods of time too. In other words, they are influenced by space and time, culture and other factors. The organisational dimension of a community as a whole and of its programmes influence the communication and information flow patterns - e.g. dominantly oral, written, or ITC-enabled; top-down, bottom-upward, spiral, horizontal, trans-generational, or a combination of these.

4. RURAL AND INDIGENOUS COMMUNITIES: COMMUNITY KNOWLEDGE

In most developing countries over 70 per cent of the population live in rural areas. They are mostly illiterate or semi-literate. They live in vast numbers of rural villages, often spread out, into small communities. But they form a vital cog in the national economy as they produce the raw materials of food, clothing, and shelter that are converted into consumable products, used and enjoyed by a much larger population in the urban and semi-urban population nationally and even internationally. They constitute a vital base of a democratic socio-political system, and usually have strong family and community bonds and democratic processes for making decisions. Living close to nature they acquire knowledge of and have a stake in, nurturing and preservation of nature's offerings – their environment - for survival and well being. They have skills in crafts, use of colours, and an integrated view of wellbeing – the totality of physical, mental and spiritual. Much of this applies to the marginalised indigenous communities in the technologically and economically advanced countries as well.

Thus, these communities possess a fund of valuable native knowledge relating to the environment, the earth, climate, food, medicinal plants and animals, social and cultural value systems, ethnic music and the arts. Such knowledge is essentially locale specific, and may not even be found in modern textbook sources.

For example, certain South Pacific Islanders have a detailed categorisation and description of some thirty-five varieties of a single species of fish. This is important information for their daily life: it informs them when particular variety(ies) will appear and where in the sea, which of them have food and/or medicinal value and so on.

Regarding the wisdom of local communities and management of forest wealth, Justice P.N. Bhagwati writes: "There is so much traditional wisdom amongst these tribals and forest dwellers accumulated over the years, that they are able to live in harmony with nature. Nature and environment are as much a part of their daily existence as food, shelter and clothing and they are continuously in communion with nature. Our plan for forest management must, therefore, take into account the human beings who live in the forests and nothing should be done which would affect their daily existence or their means of subsistence." (Seshia *et al.* eds. [2005], quoted inside book jacket)

In regard to management and use of forest wealth, it is important to take into account the internal dynamics and knowledge of the local indigenous communities. "The local knowledge and management of forest / tree resources for cultural / religious purposes is set within the complex social framework of the area. Conservation of tree resources through propagation of cultural and religious beliefs can best be understood in the context of control by the rural elite" (Kumar, 2001, p. 2897). "In comparison to western scientific conservation models, which advocate the creation of national parks and sanctuaries, the conservation of bio-diversity in these people-declared-managed sacred groves is more effective. This may be due to the fact that these sacred groves are intimately connected to the social life of the communities and, such as in the case of Hariyali sacred grove, form an integral part of the cultural identity of the community. Rituals associated with the grove and annual festivals associated with the presiding deity serve to bind the community while strengthening the social bonds and relationships. Therefore, it is evident that sacred groves serve an important social function. This is clearly not the case with national parks, which may completely alienate local communities from the area, cutting off all ties and relationships that the community had previously." The well-researched documentation *Traditional wisdom in natural resource management: the only way to conserve* (Seshia et al. eds. [2005]) describes the wealth of environmental knowledge acquired by indigenous local communities of Uttaranchal, North India. The recent UNESCO publication (Haggan and Baird, eds., 2007) records a wide range of knowledge gained by fisheries folks in many parts of the world, which could be incorporated with great advantage into fisheries science and management. Such is the wealth of tacit social knowledge of the communities – that is, community knowledge.

The knowledge gained by rural and indigenous people through observation and experience is largely embodied in folklore and shared by word of mouth for centuries and passed down the generations. This knowledge needs to be recorded, (may have to be recreated), processed, disseminated and utilised. For instance: "Myths can tell us a great deal about what happened in the past and were important in establishing what happened here (Seattle) 300 years ago," remarks Brian Atwater, U.S.Geological Survey. "Along the Oregon and Washington coast, there are Native American stories about boulders, called a'yahos, which can shake to death anyone who stares at them. In addition, Ruth Ludwin, a seismologist in Seattle, discovered tales of villages being washed away and of whales and thunderbirds locked in flights." The new science of geomythology is being harnessed by researchers who believe folklore can save lives. (McKie, 2005). By utilising the knowledge / folklore of the natives they will feel their participation in and contribution to the nation's progress. *See also* Neelameghan and Chester, 2007

5. INTERNATIONAL CONCERN

Koichiro Matsuura, Director General, UNESCO, in his Message on the occasion of the International Day of the World's Indigenous People, 9 August 2006 emphasised: "As custodians of cultural diversity and biodiversity, embodied in natural and cultural heritage – tangible as well as intangible -, indigenous peoples, and particularly women, must be proud of their role as mediators in the safeguarding and transmission of traditional knowledge, while taking their rightful place in a globalised world .... Indigenous cultures are an asset for future generations and a potential source of regeneration. By highlighting the strong ties between culture and nature, tradition and modernity, they provide an inclusive and truly global vision of the world."

"The fact that the culture(s) of indigenous people are in danger of dying out cannot fail to be a matter of concern .... These populations number some 350 million individuals in more than 70 countries in the world and represent more than 5000 languages and cultures. Today many of them live on the fringes of society and are deprived of basic human rights, particularly culture rights."

Even two decades ago in 1987, J.M. Cobo, United Nations Special Rapporteur, in the *Study of the Problem of Discrimination Against Indigenous Populations* , expressed concern thus: "It is essential to know and understand the deeply spiritual special relationship between indigenous peoples and their land as basic to their existence as such and to all their beliefs, customs, traditions and culture ... Their land is not a commodity which can be acquired, but a material element to be enjoyed freely."

An implication of these concerns is not only the need to empower the marginalised communities through information out-reach programmes but also to collect and record the community knowledge, make efforts to understand their cultures, and leverage on the wisdom they possess for the good of the society.

6. ICT APPLICATIONS

Recent developments and extension of ICT applications points to the possibilities of bridging the digital divide and better management of rural community knowledge. Attempts to use ICTs to reach out to indigenous and marginalised rural communities with a view to empowering them through implementation of e-governance, providing access to a variety of government documents relevant to the life of rural communities, village kiosks, land-sat imaging and remote sensing, geographical information systems etc. The following selected documents report on the subject:

Garai, Atanu and Shadrach (2006). *Taking ICT to every Indian village: opportunities and challenges – a collection of four papers*. New Delhi, IN: OneWorld South Asia; 134 p

Willard, Terri and Andjelkovic, Maja, *eds*.(2005). *A developing connection: bridging the* policy gap between the information society and sustainable development Winnipeg, Manitoba, CA: International Institute for Sustainable Development; 210 p.

Slater, Don and Tacchi, Jo (2004). Research, ICT innovations for poverty reduction /Edited by Ian Pringle and Savithri Subramanian. New Delhi, IN: UNESCO; 91 p.

6.1 Spread of Wireless Technology and Cell Phone use

Front-runners among the ICT applications for rural connectivity are: wireless and mobile communication technologies. Features of these devices of particular interest to multi-cultural, multilingual, semiliterate and illiterate communities include:

* Overcoming language-barriers;
* Dissemination of images, learning materials, etc. in local languages;
* Enhancement of collaboration and cooperation and facilitation of joining voices / forces, that is connectivity for collaboration even at global distances;
* Recording, collection and use of the knowledge and experience of the marginalized communities; and
* Relatively low-cost of the equipment

The spread of telecom facilities – wireless technology and cell phones – into the rural areas is enabling rural traders and others to obtain market information for their products, to contact village and/ or taluck and district officials not only to get information but also obtain certificates and other documents. Information kiosks and tele-centres are also playing useful roles by providing information and connecting people in rural areas among themselves and with NGOs, government offices, etc. Mobile phones are seen to bridge the digital divide in developed as well as developing countries. In a recent report on GSMA, a recommendation was the extension of mobile phones to different segments of the peoples of Africa. This is considered the fastest way to bridge digital divide in the countries of that continent (Biniyat, (2006)).

6.2. Mobile Communication in Rural India

According to a study commissioned by Nokia and conducted by the Center for Knowledge Societies (CKS), "mobile communication is revolutionising economic and social life in rural parts of the country, generating a wave of local entrepreneurs, and creating greater access to social services".

"In the rapidly growing mobile phone market, six million new mobile subscriptions are added each month. The research predicts that by the end of 2007, one in five Indians will own a phone, while three quarters of the population will be covered by a mobile network by the end of 2008."

Dr Aditya Dev Sood, the author of the Report, pointed out that new adopters of mobile phones have found their incomes rise, as a result of increased productivity made possible through mobile communications. Sood says, "While mobile phones are widely seen merely as a communications medium, they should really be seen as a new and essential form of infrastructure that will transform a host of other service sectors in rural economies around the world."

The new mobility could be used to bridge the socio-economic digital divide between rural and urban areas. Of the new subscriptions a significant number are from rural areas "with scarce infrastructure and facilities, high level of illiteracy, low PC and Internet penetration." Sood points out that "new adopters of mobile phones have found their incomes rise, as a result of increased productivity made possible through mobile communications."

3.3. WiMAX for Wireless Broadband Access

Amit Sharma, President, Motorola India, says: In rural India where 70 percent of the population is spread out, telecom penetration is a meagre 2 per cent and data connectivity is practically non-existent. Internet connectivity, though growing, is still low. India has just about seven million Internet subscribers of whom only 1.3 million have access to broadband connections, way below the target of 20 million set for 2010.

"Last mile access has been a major constraint in the growth of connectivity. ... Fortunately, an alternative is available. India can avoid the unwieldy and challenging process of hardwiring its 3.2 million square kilometers — the seventh largest area in the world — by using next-generation broadband wireless technologies such as WiMAX. WiMax will allow India to make the leap from voice (2.5G) to voice/data/video/ TV (4G), both cost-effectively and quickly.

"WiMAX is a global, standards-based technology that can provide wireless broadband access to both urban and rural areas. Technology experts around the world say that going wireless is the best and only way forward for developing countries wanting to provide data services to the masses, given their limitations of infrastructure and time.

"WiMax can also complement another trend in emerging markets — mobile devices, and not personal computers, will drive the next wave of growth in connectivity. India has over 130 million mobile phones against less than 20 million PCs. .... PC usage is restricted to the educated elite and businesses. However, every electrician, carpenter and delivery boy is today comfortable with, indeed dependant on, a mobile phone to conduct his/her business. In the future, more consumers will access the net on their phones than on PCs; even more so, when WiMax makes high-speed data, video and TV possible on handheld devices.

"The early gains of partial wireless connectivity in rural India can be seen in the stunning success of ITC's e-choupal project, which has empowered thousands of farmers in remote hamlets by enabling them to optimise price-discovery through access to updated information. WiMax could accelerate the pace of such connectivity thousand-fold, unleashing the potential and the power of the rural economy."

It is reported that "with a constructive public-private partnership, WiMax could become a truly powerful engine of socio-economic transformation."

REFERENCES

1. Allee, Verna (1997). The Knowledge Evolution: Expanding Organizational Intelligence. Boston, MA: Butterworth-Heinemann
2. Bhatnagar, S., and Schware, R. (Eds). (2000). Information and Communication Technology in Development: cases from India. New Delhi: Sage Publications
3. Biniyat, Luka (2006). Mobile Fastest way to Bridge Digital Divides in Africa, says GSMA. (Vanguard).
4. Blagsvedt, Sean and Veeraraghavan, Rajesh. Available at http://research.microsoft.com/~rajeshv/warana.htm:
5. Chester, Greg and Neelameghan, A. (2006). Information Professional: Knowledge and Skill Development for Serving Marginalized and Rural Communities. *Webology,* 3(3); article 29. Accessible at http://www.webology.ir/2006/v3n3/a29.html

6. Cobo, J.M. (1987). Study of the Problem of Discrimination against Indigenous Populations". United Nations Special Rapporteur.

7. Davenport, Thomas, H. and Prusak, Laurence (1998). Working Knowledge. Boston, MA: Harvard Business School Press

8. Haravu, L.J. (2002). Lectures on Knowledge Management: Paradigms, Challenges and Opportunities. *In:* Sarada Ranganathan Endowment Lectures Series, 22, 2000 / edited A. Neelameghan. Banglore: Sarada Ranganathan Endowment for Library Science

9. Harkin, James (2006). Social Networking. *The Guardian,* April 15. Available at http://www.guardian.co.uk/commentisfree/storylO... 17 54398.00.html

10. Hirwade, Mangala and Rajyalakshmi, D. (2006). E-content Awards: and Initiative for Bridging the Digital Divide in India and Worldwide. *D-Lib Magazine,* 12(11), p. 10. Available at http://www.dlib.org/dlib/November/hirwade/ll/hirwade.html

11. Kumar, B.R (2006). AIR's Broadcasts did make a Difference: a Phenomenal Success was achieved in Production through Sustained Broadcasts during the 'Green Revolution Period'. *The Hindu Magazine,* 2006-12-31, p. 14.

12. Kumar, S. (2001). Indigenous Communities' Knowledge of Local Ecological Services. *Economic and Political Weekly,* 28 July.

13. Mckie, Rob (2005). Ancient Legends give early Warning of Modern Disasters: the New Science of Geomythology is being Harnessed by Researchers who believe Folklore can Save Lives. *The Observer* (Guardian Newspapers Limited), 4 December.

14. Malhotra, Yogesh (1998). Knowledge Management, Knowledge Organization and Knowledge Workers: aview from the front lines. Available at http://www.brint.com/interview/mail.htm

15. Matsuura, Koichiro (Director General, UNESCO). Message on the Occasion of the International Day of the World's Indigenous People', *9 August 2006.*

16. Neelameghan, A. (2006). E-Communities, Community Knowledge, and Knowledge Management. *Know Genesis*

International Journal for Technical Communication, 1(2), pp. 21-27

17. Neelameghan, A. and Chester, Greg (2006). Environmental Knowledge and Marginalized Communities: the last mile connectivity. *Webology,* 3(1), March.
18. Nonaka, Ikujiro and Takeuchi, Hirotaka (1995). The Knowledge Creating Company. Oxford, UK: Oxford University Press.
19. Rose, J. (2000). Multipurpose Community Telecentres in Support of People-Centered Development. *Information Studies,* 6(1), pp. 5-28.
20. Seshia, Shaila et al (Eds) (2005). Traditional Wisdom in Natural Resource Management: the only way to Conserve. Dehra Dun, Uttaranchal: Rural Litigation & Entitlement Kendra.
21. Soni, Vikram (2005). Tribal People and Preserving Prime Forests. *The Hindu,* 29 November.
22. Svelby, Karl Erik (1997). The New Organizational Wealth: Managing and Measuring Knowledge-based Assets. San Francisco, USA: Berrett-Koehler Publisher.
23. Swaminathan, M.S. (2005). Mission 2007: Every Village a Knowledge Centre. *The Hindu,* 25 November.
24. Wolf, Richard K. (2006). The Black Cow's Footprint -Time Space and Music in the Lives of the Kotas of South India Delhi.

20

Globalisation, Information Society and the Future of Libraries

K. S. Raghavan

ABSTRACT

Libraries have always played an important role in identifying, selecting and acquiring resources of value to its user community and organizing these for easy access and retrieval. What is expected of them in the changed information environment with a huge volume of digital electronic information available on networks including the World Wide Web is to extend their activity to include relevant networked resources also. There is also a new important role that libraries will have to perform in future in addition to their traditional role in functioning as a portal for external information resources. A major factor that has affected and that will continue to affect all knowledge transaction activities and all the players in these activities including the libraries in the coming years will be the increasing globalisation of economic activities.

1. PREAMBLE

My association with Dr. Bavakutty dates back to 1969 when both of us were students of the Master's Degree Programme in Library Science at the University of Delhi. The fact that we two were the only South Indians in that batch of twelve brought us closer. I soon discovered that we had common areas of interest – especially Colon Classification and S.R. Ranganathan's ideas. A couple of months after we graduated from the University of Delhi, I joined the American Center Library in Delhi and Bavakutty joined the Farook College near Calicut in Kerala as librarian. But in a couple of years both of us entered the teaching profession; I joined the University of Mysore and Bavakutty joined the University of Kerala. An interesting component of the library science teaching programmes in Indian in the 1970s was the educational tour. Although a visit to Kerala University was not normally a part of the tour itinerary of the University of Mysore, Mysore and the Mysore University Library were very much a part of the tour itinerary of the Kerala University library science students. Bavakutty and another common friend of ours – Sri Augustine, also on the faculty of library science of the University of Kerala – would bring a batch of students from the Kerala University almost every year to Mysore. We would get to meet each other and we would regularly share experiences, opinions during these meetings and through correspondence. The contacts intensified after Bavakutty moved to the University of Calicut and I moved to the University of Madras. For the last 30 years we have been continuously interacting with each other on professional matters; we have met at conferences, workshops and many other professional meetings. I have been closely associated with the academic activities of the University of Calicut during the last 30 years. The broad area of Bavakutty's work has been: '*libraries in institutions of higher education*' while mine has been '*Knowledge organisation*'. An area that touches all aspects of our profession is that of globalisation and its impact on information work and service. I chose, therefore, to write on this subject for the festschrift volume being planned in honour of my friend, Dr. M. Bavakutty.

2. INTRODUCTION

It is a truism that Information has always been important to the society. It is also true that the basic goal of the information profession has more or less remained unaltered for centuries: To provide efficient, effective, convenient and cost-effective access to relevant information and information resources to those who are in need of it.

Library is one of the several social institutions that the society has created to handle certain knowledge transaction activities. We need to realise that there are many other players in this activity such as authors, the publishing industry, the database industry, the telecommunication networks that facilitate data transfer and communication, to name a few. In recent years a few parallel systems that play a complementary role to that of the library have also come into being; e.g. MIS, Knowledge Management Systems, especially within the corporate sector, document delivery mechanisms, information analysis and consolidation centres – to mention a few. These institutions, and more particularly, the libraries are in the process of fundamental changes as a consequence of the major shifts and transformations taking place in the environment in which they operate. The present generation of information systems including libraries has been the result of the steady progress in computerisation of most aspects of library functions that began in the late 1960s and early 70's:

* The computerized library catalogues, the development of circulation systems, the development of the integrated library systems which appeared in many libraries in the early 80's.
* Development of the OPAC revolutionised catalogue searching and brought about the notion that libraries could be distributed and that catalogues did not necessarily represent the stock held within that particular building.
* The development of the online database industry
* The availability of full-text e-journals and other scholarly material.
* The Internet and the web that have transformed the knowledge transaction processes fundamentally.
* Many of the earlier developments, e.g. OPACs, Online databases, full text resources, etc have re-emerged as web compliant databases providing even an average library with the opportunity to search huge collections of data.
* The digital library; the virtual library.

As a consequence of these developments, the library has become somewhat less central in the knowledge transaction process / scholarly communication process, particularly when the library has not been able to embrace the newer developments. A survey by the OCLC on users' perception of libraries has a number of interesting findings about what the future holds for libraries. Responses were collected from a representative sample of 3,300 information consumers from Australia, Canada, India, Singapore, the United Kingdom and the United States (OCLC, 2005). The report provides the findings and responses from the online survey in an effort to learn more about:

* Library use
* Awareness and use of library electronic resources
* The Internet search engine, the library and the librarian
* Free vs. for-fee information
* The "Library" brand

The findings indicate that information consumers still view libraries largely as places to borrow print books. The findings are both important and relevant in the context of the fact that of the respondents:

* 96% had visited a library
* 72% were library members
* 57% were library users several times in a year
* In response to the query: "*Where do you start an info search?*", the survey indicated that just about 1% of the respondents thought of the library website as the place to begin their search where as 82% named search engines as the first preference.

The following table summarises the responses that provide a comparative overview of users' perception of libraries vis-à-vis search engines measured in terms of some important attributes (Table 1).

Even in terms of users' perception of the sources that provided worthwhile information search engines scored over the library. Obviously libraries need to re-position themselves and define their role in the knowledge transaction processes. At least three

Table 1

Attribute	*Libraries*	*Search Engines*
Trustworthy/credible sources	60%	40%
Accurate, quality information	56%	44%
Reliable/always available	28%	72%
Cost Effective	25%	75%
Easy to use	15%	85%
Convenient	11%	89%
Fast	8%	92%

different perceptions of what the future holds for the library exist:

View 1 : ICT enthusiasts see the physical library being replaced by digital media networks rather than buildings dispensing books and other resources

View 2 : Dismiss the revolution in ICTs as largely irrelevant to print culture; they believe that acquiring more resources and setting up more libraries will restore the vitality of this institution

View 3 : ICTs are seen as an enhancement rather than a substitute for print media

Among these the last appears to be the most realistic assessment of the emerging scenario. The ICTs are enabling and necessitating restructuring and enhancement of the library both as an institution and in terms of practices employed. Even the present scenario is characterised by the degree to which the libraries are being wired for effective deployment of the new ICTs; geographically distributed, more organisationally specialised and networked libraries; and more technologically dependent on electronic media in all aspects of their administration and service delivery, and more uncertain about their future role.

Undoubtedly technology has been a major player in bringing about transformations in the library scene. However, there are more fundamental changes and transformations taking place that will have far reaching impact on library & information services and may even alter the fundamental notions of what should be the role of the library in an organisation. A major factor that has affected and that will continue to affect all knowledge transaction activities and all the players in these activities including the libraries in the coming years will be the increasing globalisation of economic activities. In recent years the impact has been of such an order that there have even been questions raised on the continued need for and relevance of libraries in the emerging scheme of things. While it is difficult to agree with the suggestion that libraries as a component in the knowledge transaction system may become irrelevant in the near future, there is no question that fundamental changes are necessary if libraries and the library / information profession have to remain at the center stage of knowledge transaction activities.

3. GLOBALIZATION

The terms 'Information Society' and 'Globalisation' have been in use for sometime now. The term '*Knowledge* Economy' is of more recent origin; the term '*Globalisation*' appeared in the late 1980s in the *Harvard Business Review*. These have primarily been employed to emphasise the transformations that have been taking place in recent decades in the society. The term '*globalisation*' as a subject matter probably had its origins in the context of economics of growth and development. In an economic sense "globalisation might mean capital market integration, goods and service market integration, migration agreements, cultural interchange, or some combination of all these" (T. N. Srinivasan, 2001). Globalisation is believed to help in long-term economic growth and poverty reduction. The establishment of the World Trade Organisation (WTO) in 1995 definitely hastened, and to a certain extent, even streamlined the process of globalisation. The phenomenon has been characterised by:

* Globalisation of markets
* Globalisation of work force for spatially distributed operations
* Outsourcing of Business Processes
* The importance of and need for Sustained Technological Innovation in the face of growing competition
* Growing Consumer Awareness
* Involvement in increasingly complex range of products, processes and services

One factor that has greatly accelerated the process of globalisation is the rapid and breathtaking developments in ICTs. Globalisation and ICTs have combined to transform the way in which individuals and organisations function and have practically touched every aspect of life. The terms 'Information society' and 'Knowledge society' have come into vogue in this context and emphasise a society in which the creation, distribution, diffusion, uses and applications of Information are a significant economic, political, and cultural activity. They refer to the changes taking place as a consequence of the increasing importance of 'knowledge' and 'information' as economic factors in the growth and development of organisations and nations, and the impact of ICTs on activities and processes related to information and knowledge generation, accessing, transfer and communication, use and application. 'Knowledge society' which is both a cause of and integral component of the process of globalisation is a 'a society that makes extensive use of information networks and information technology; generates large quantities of information and communication products and services, and has a reasonably large and diversified content industry' (Jeskanen-Sundström, 2001). The crux of the issue lies in the accelerating (and unprecedented) speed at which knowledge is created, accumulated, communicated. Equally important is the rate of depreciation of the value of a piece of knowledge / information in terms of economic relevance and value. A new kind of organisation is spearheading the phenomenon: knowledge-based communities, i.e. networks of individuals striving, first and foremost, to produce and circulate new knowledge and working for different, even rival, organisations. Libraries and other information institutions have been significantly affected by these developments.

4. THE FUTURE

What are the implications of these changes for libraries? The most likely possibility is that libraries will become a fusion of physical and virtual realms. This is something that has already happened to a significant extent. Libraries are trying to address a multiplicity of issues:

* Increasing amounts of diverse resources in a variety of formats - print and electronic
* Rapid changes in publishing, scholarly communication, and related technology
* The concept of a library collection will be

redefined. Aggregators and publishers will continue to bundle multiple titles into single price packages available through license agreements.

* There will be a growing volume of information, including scholarly information, available via open access initiatives such as open access journals, open digital archives, institutional repositories, etc.
* Publishers and aggregators will market directly to users, bypassing libraries. Information discovery tools built on the technologies of Google, Yahoo and others will seamlessly index information available through open access as well as licensed materials.
* The growing and diverse information needs of the ordinary citisens in the emerging knowledge society (community information)

Throughout history the role of the library has been to serve as a storehouse, an archive of important documents. The library contained the foundational building blocks of information for all humanity. In medieval times, books were far too expensive for most people to own. The process of democratisation of access to knowledge began in the middle of the 15th Century with Gutenberg unveiling his printing press to the world. This printing revolution was responsible for getting over 500,000 books into circulation before the end of that Century. Libraries have, since, tried to build large and comprehensive collections of books and other materials, and have largely been funded and maintained by the state or other institutions. We have moved far away from that situation where information was scarce and precious. Today information is vast and readily available, and in many cases, free. A considerable amount of the information for which people had to visit libraries earlier is now available online. As a result a vast majority of people with specific information needs no longer visit libraries. Of course there are those who read for pleasure who continue to patronise the public library and the scholar who continues to depend to a significant extent on the resources of a library. Thomas Frey, Executive Director of the DaVinci Institute has identified certain key trends that are affecting the future of the library. These include:

* Communication systems that are continually changing the way people access information
* New technologies, especially that will emerge
* Information storage technologies
* Search Technologies
* Speech Recognition technologies
* The new era of Global Systems
* Transition from a product-based economy to knowledge- based economy
* Libraries will face a transition from a center of information to a center of culture

5. SUMMARY

There is no question that the demand for access to information will grow and the library will continue to be among the most effective and efficient means of providing access to information especially in the less developed countries. In the academic world, real scholarship will continue to depend on libraries. Perhaps the single most important role of the library will be to serve as a portal / knowledge gateway to evaluated quality information resources – both in-house and distributed network resources. This will be a major requirement given the problem of information overload and the limitations of available search engines in directing end users to quality information resources. To a certain extent many libraries have been doing this via their websites. This represents merely an extension of the traditional role of the library to serve as a portal to quality print information resources based on an assessment of the needs and requirements of its customers. Libraries have always played an important role in identifying, selecting and acquiring resources of value to its user community and organising these for easy access and retrieval. What is expected of them in the changed information environment with a huge volume of digital electronic information available on networks including the World Wide Web is to extend their activity to include relevant networked resources also. There is also a new important role that libraries will have to perform in future in addition to their traditional role in functioning as a portal for external information resources. The library, especially the research and special library, should also emerge as a portal / gateway to the outside world for the scholarly information generated within the organisation. This requires that the library should play an active role in creating and maintaining institutional repositories and in developing effective search mechanisms for these to both showcase and provide access to scholarly research output of the organisation. In the corporate sector, it is likely that more and more organisations will create parallel systems for knowledge sharing (Knowledge Management Systems). In other words another clear implication of the transformations taking place is the need to understand that the *'information service'* sector even within an organisation is by no means limited to the library. These suggest that the greatest challenge that the information profession in India (and probably elsewhere too) will face in the coming years is the possibility of questions being raised about its continued relevance triggered by the emergence of a parallel and a more sophisticated information management profession. It does indeed appear that organisations have begun to see investments in IM /KM as important for their growth. The important question is whether this sector will look to the LIS schools and their educational programmes for their information manpower needs? The profession needs to seriously examine what needs to be done, especially to our manpower development programmes to ensure that information professionals will continue to make a difference as they indeed did for the scholarly community of the 20th Century? There is a need to re-define the boundaries of our profession in order to continue to be relevant in terms of developing and providing human resources for the typical 21st Century workplaces, which require knowledge and skills of a different kind and of a different order.

REFERENCES

1. Frey, Thomas. Available at http://www.davinciinstitute.com/page.php7I D=120 (Accessed on 9th October 2007)

2. Jeskanen-Sundstrom, H. (2001). ICT Statistics at the New Millennium -Developing Official Statistics - Measuring the Diffusion of ICT and its Impact. IAOS Satellite Meeting on Statistics for the Information Society 2001: Tokyo. P. 4. Available at http://portal.unesco.org/ci/en/files/12851/10711588385uis.pdf/uis.pdf (Accessed on 10th October 2007)

3. OCLC (2005). Available at http://www.oclc.org/reports/2005perceptions .htm. (Accessed on 8th October 2007)

4. Srinivasan, T. N. (2001). *(quoted in* N.S.S. Narayana, *Ed.* Political Economy of Trade, Finance and Development: Selected Papers of T. N. Srinivasan. New Delhi: Oxford University Press, p. 4)

21
Information Literacy and Digital Libraries in the Higher Education Scenario

R. Samyuktha

ABSTRACT

The outcome of the challenges is the 'Digital Divide' which warrants a need for the society to become Information Literate to be economically progressive. There has been several Information Literacy initiatives across the globe. Global resources of Information Literacy and initiatives in India are examined with special focus on role of Information Literacy and Digital Libraries in the context of higher education.

1. INTRODUCTION

The emergence of the Information Age has posed several challenges to society at large and more so to education and libraries. There is an unprecedented plethora of information and the rapid trends in technology to manage it with functions of storing, organising and accessing information. The outcome of the challenges is the 'Digital Divide' which warrants a need for the society to become information literate to be economically progressive. There has been several Information Literacy initiatives across the globe – Europe, Australia, America, and Asia for the last one decade which aim at educating the community at large.

2. SCOPE

This paper attempts to analyse Information Literacy (IL) in different dimensions that are as follows:

* What is Information Literacy?
* Why is Information Literacy essential?
* For whom is Information Literacy targeted?
* How Information Literacy is / can be implemented?

Global resources of Information Literacy and initiatives in India are examined with special focus on role of Information Literacy and Digital Libraries in the context of higher education.

3. WHAT IS INFORMATION LITERACY?

To have a lucid understanding of the term *'Information Literacy' (IL)* the following definitions would probably be more comprehensive. 'Information Competency' or 'Information fluency' are synonymously used by a few. The terms bibliographic instruction, library instruction, computer literacy are also often used in conjunction with the term 'Information Literacy'. Information Literacy' is defined as -*"the ability to locate, and use information to become independent life-long learners"*– Commission on Colleges, Southern Association of Colleges and Schools (SACS). Criteria for Accreditation, Section 5.1.2 [Library and other Information Resources] services. 10th Ed. Dec. 1996.

"the ability to know when there is a need for information, to be able to identify, locate, evaluate and

effectively use that information for the issue or problem at hand" —*National forum in Information Literacy*

"includes practical skills involved in effective use of information technology and information resources, either print or electronic"—*J.Shapiro and S K. Hughes*

Information Literacy is a new liberal art which extends beyond technical skills and is conceived as the critical reflection on the nature of information itself, its technical infrastructure and its social, cultural and even philosophical context and impact.

Many of the definitions have been derived from that originally produced by the American Library Association (ALA).

..............................."To be information literate, a person must be able to recognize when information is needed and have the ability to locate, evaluate, and use effectively the needed information. Producing such a citizenry will require that schools and colleges appreciate and integrate the concept of information literacy into their learning programmes and that they play a leadership role in equipping individuals and institutions to take advantage of the opportunities inherent within the information society. Ultimately, information literate people are those who have learned how to learn. They know how to learn because they know how knowledge is organised, how to find information and how to use information in such a way that others can learn from them. They are people prepared for lifelong learning, because they can always find the information needed for any task or decision at hand" — *American Library Association, 1989, p. 1.*

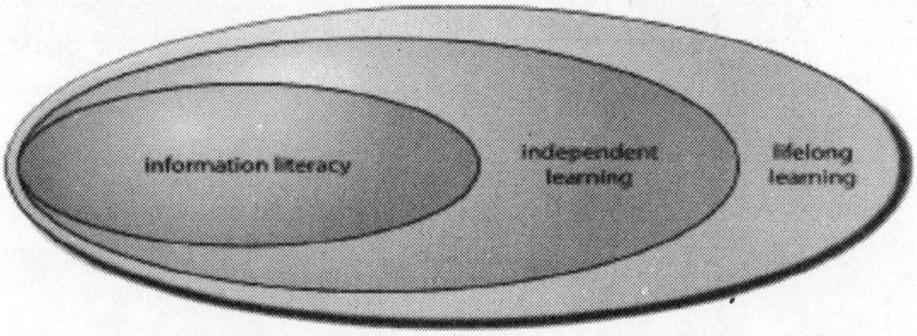

Source: Bundi (2004. p.5)

Fig. 1. Relationship between Information Literacy and Lifelong Learning

Information literacy is the larger umbrella which encompasses the different types of literacy such as Tool literacy, Resource Literacy, Social Structural Literacy, Research literacy, Publishing Literacy, Digital Literacy...

Tool Literacy : the ability to use print and electronic resources including software.

Resource Literacy : the ability to understand the form, format, location and access methods of information resources.

Social Structural Literacy : knowledge of how information is socially situated and produced. It includes understanding the scholarly publishing process.

Research Literacy : the ability to understand and use information technology tools to carry out research including discipline – related software.

Publishing Literacy : the ability to produce a text or multimedia report of the results of research.

Digital Literacy : refers to a way of reading and understanding information that differs from what we do when we sit down to read a book or a newspaper.

The competencies of Digital literacy invariant to

technology changes include :

* knowledge assembly skills – ability to collect information from diverse sources;
* internet searching - based on search engines;
* hypertext navigation; and
* content evaluation;

4. WHY INFORMATION LITERACY?

Information Literacy is of prime importance to empower and transform students........as independent learners with necessary skills; both generic skills as well as skills which are specific to certain disciplines or subject areas. Olsen and Coons describe why IL education is required in an academic environment.

* to understand the variety of content and format of information;
* to understand standard systems for the organisation of information ;
* to develop the capability to retrieve information from a variety of systems in various formats successfully navigate within the libraries.
* to develop the capability to organise and manipulate information for various access and retrieval purposes;
* to write correct bibliographic citations for book, journal articles and conference papers
* to use a bibliographic file management package to organise downloaded citations and personal files of references

Changes in library services such as the following warrant IL programmes:

Catalogue : online catalog with web-interface and

remote accessibility

Collection : online access to subscribed databases, including bibliographic records, full- text articles, e-books and so on; library web sites leading to selective online documents and resources

Circulation : online access to e-books; online renewal of checked-out materials

Instruction : online instruction; in-person instruction with online components

Interlibrary loan & document delivery : online ILL request, and articles delivery via e-mail in addition to traditional delivery

Reference : online reference including simple e-mail reference and real-time virtual reference

Reserve : online accessible electronic reserve

Hence, the changed roles of librarians pose challenges such as

* reduction in traditional face to face teaching in the library, replaced by virtual learning environment
* lack of control over access to information
* print has lost its monopoly as a format for information storage
* increased access in technology has altered the way the students study
* spectrum of eresources increasing the resource base

Librarians need to change the way they plan and reach out through IL education. Librarians specially subject specialists should work as resource liaisons, develop strategies for planning and implementation of IL programmes accommodating different learning styles reducing time and teaching repetitiveness eg.

Orientation, Training Programmes, Workshops, Discussion Forums, Product Presentations, etc. They should update their skills and be competent to educate and guide the stakeholders.

5. INFORMATION LITERACY – TARGET GROUP

In the context of Digital Libraries and higher education, Information Literacy is targeted at the postgraduates, research scholars, faculty, scientists, administrators. Beside this any individual who is interested in accessing and using scholarly information would be benefited.

6. IMPLEMENTATION OF INFORMATION LITERACY

Information Literacy depends largely on the symbiotic efforts of faculty, academic administrators, librarians and other information technology professionals. Involvement of every one of them is extremely essential for the successful implementation of Information Literacy. Though librarians have been teaching the effective use of information resources for several decades popularly understood as bibliographic instruction or library orientation to develop library skills, there has been a paradigm change in the formats of availability of information. Hence the need to enhance the searching or retrieving skills needs to be paid attention to. In institutions of higher education research being the major objective, calls for Information Literacy to supplement their information needs. Information Literacy programmes could be organised at different levels, for freshmen, research scholars and faculty. Information Literacy could be incorporated into curriculum to be effectively and progressively used through their study, research or teaching.

As consumers and producers of information within the higher education environment, it is important for students to be able to build on a foundation of IL skills for e-learning. Faculty – Librarian partnerships which support both formal and informal learning communities will be the best way to help students reach this goal.

Librarians can develop instructional websites with sources specifically recommended for a course, sites with sources pertaining to a particular discipline or subject, online tutorials for basic information research skills, online IL modules, such as multi session tutorials which can lead students directly to web based databases, search engines and information sources. Examples:

* User Guides
* Information Literacy Tools
* Curriculum guides
* Subject guides
* Open Sources

7. INFORMATION LITERACY INITIATIVES IN INDIA

Initiatives at various universities or institutions of higher learning are in process but at different levels and there is a need for awareness and networking of these initiatives. Creating digital libraries, building institutional repositories of the institution's research / scientific output, compiling subject gateways linking to global resources, organising information literacy programmes to utilize all of them are some of the major initiatives in India being a developing country.

An International Information Literacy Workshop was organised in India by Punjabi University with the support of UNESCO in Oct 2005 to promote Information Literacy in South and South East Asia. They resolved that Information Literacy should be introduced within national curricula at all levels including life long learning programmes to make the stakeholders independent learners and critical thinkers. There is a need for social responsibility to leverage the benefits of higher education for the under privileged.

Recently the Department of Library and Information Science, University of Kerala proposed to implement an Information Literacy Programme in colleges affiliated to its University.

8. GLOBAL INITIATIVES OF INFORMATION LITERACY

A few of the global initiatives could be accessed in detail at the following URLs:

UK- IL model (SCONUL 1999)

www.sconul.ac.uk/publications/99104Rev1.doc

UK- Pedagogy for IL

http://dis.shef.ac.uk/literacy/project/index.html

US IL competency Standards for Higher Education approved by the Academic College and Research Libraries (ACRL 2000)

www.ala.org/acrl/ilcomstan.html

Australia - IL Standard developed by Council of Australian University Libraries (CAUL 2001) based on a revision of US standard. www.caul.edu.au/caul-doc/InfoLitStandards2001.doc

Australia - Standards for the curriculum developed by Queensland University of Technology www.library.qut.edu/au/infolit/

Australia & New Zealand - IL framework: principles, standards and practice developed by Australian and New Zealand Institute for IL . www.caul.edu.au/info-literacy/InfoLiteracy Framework.pdf

9. CONCLUSION

Developing research competencies by guidelines for IL in the curriculum have led the digital libraries to create a strategic edge in integrating exploration and research in the online world. Faculty – Librarian partnerships should exercise collaborative efforts in planning systematic and comprehensive IL programmes. Thus, IL contributes to the vision of grooming educated students and facilitate skills for becoming life long learners.

REFERENCES

1. ACRL (2000). Information Competency Standards for Higher Education. Available at www.ala.org/ala/acrl/acrlstandards/standards.pdf (Accessed on 14, October 2006)
2. Andretta, Susie (2005). From Prescribed Reading to the Excitement or the Burden of Choice. *In:* Information Literacy: foundation of e-learning Aslib Proceedings: *New information perspectives,* 57 (2), pp. 181-190
3. Bawden, David (2001). Information and Digital Literacies: a Review of Analysts. *Journal of documentation,* 57 (2), pp. 218-259
4. Bundi A (Ed.) (2004). Australian and New Zealand IL Framework. Principles, Standards and Practice. Edn 2, Australian and New Zealand Institute for IL (ANZIIL), Adelaide. Available at www.caul.edu.au/info-literacy/InfoLiteracyFramework.pdf (Accessed on 20, October 2006)
5. Joshua, Ami (2006). Information Initiatives in India. *Hindu Times,* May 11. Available at http://www.digitaldivide.net/community/Informatio nlndia (Accessed on 14 October 2006)

6. Maria, Ana, Correia, Ramalho and Teixeira, Jose Carlos (2003). Information Literacy: a Integrated Concept for a Safer Internet, *Online Information* Review, 27(5), pp. 311-320

7. Rockman, Ilene F. (2003). Information Literacy, a Worldwide Priority for the Twenty-first Century. *Reference Services Review,* 31 (3), pp. 209-210

8. Yi, Hua (2005). Library Instruction goes Online: an Inevitable Trend. *Library Review,* .54 (1), pp. 47-58.

22

Concept of Bibliometrics, Scientometrics and Informetrics

S.L.Sangam
Keshava

ABSTRACT

This paper defines the terms Librametrics, Bibliometrics, Scientometrics, Informetrics, Cybetmetrics and Webometrics. It further describes the bibliometrics laws and their application in libraries and library & information science research.

1. INTRODUCTION

Universe of knowledge is a complex output of man's intellect in the form of documented literature. Now a day the division of subjects, in the universe of knowledge into sciences, humanities or arts is almost unwarranted. In other way this is called 'Information Explosion' often termed as 'white plague' posed, many problems, and challenges among library and information professionals. Identification and selection of documents is an example for such challenges. So there is a need of special technique or effort to face these challenges.

Bibliometric / Scientometric study is one such useful technique (of series of techniques) which helps to solve the problems, challenges posed by so-called information explosion. Over the years, several new terms have appeared on the horizon representing quantitative studies in library and Information Science. They were known as: 'Librametrics' in 1940's, 'Bibliometric' in 1960's, 'Scientometrics' in 1970's and 'Informetrics' in the midth of 1980's. And now with the advent of information technology two new concepts namely 'cybermetrics' and 'webometrics' are emerged in 1990's.

2. LIBRAMETRICS

The term Librametrics has two roots: Libra and Metrics. The word 'Libra' connotes 'library' and 'metrics' means measurement. The term librametry was formally introduced by Ranganathan in the year 1948 at the Aslib's Annual Conference held in Leamington Spa. But as the librarian of the Madras University Library he practiced various librametric techniques way back in 1925, in order to solve day-to-day library problems and to streamline the day-to-day library activities, services for their clientele and also for the betterment of library professional as a whole.

Sengupta defined Librametrics as, "Quantitative analysis of various facets of library activities and library documents by the application of mathematical and statistical calculus to seek solution to library problems.". According to Ravichandra Rao, bibliometrics and librametrics is nothing but "Information process and information handling in libraries and information centres by quantitatively analysing the characteristics and behaviour of documents library staff and library users."

Within the sphere of libraries, Dr. S.R. Ranganathan and other Indian Scientists had suggested several areas for the application of quantitative analysis in library and information systems and services. The following uses below account only for some of them.

* Librametry in the day-to-day work of a library
* Librametry in organising national or state library systems.
* Operations research in library work.
* Librametry and book selection.
* Librametry and classification.
* Library administration.
* Library services.

3. BIBLIOMETRICS

The study made by Cole and Eale on 'The History of Comparative Anatomy Part – I: A Statistical Analysis' is considered to be the first bibliometric study, where for first time in 1917, the expression of statistical analysis has been used in the literature. Hulme was the first to use the expression 'statistical bibliography' in 1923 and later many others used it. Gross and Gross's study is considered to be the third study in the field based on citations. After Hulme this term used by Henkle in 1938 in his article – 'The Periodical Literature of Bio-Chemistry', by Gosnell in his dissertation in 1943 and later in his article of 1984. Fusscler in 1948 and 1949, Raising in 1962, Berker in 1996 and Pritchard in 1968 and 1969 have used the term statistical bibliography in their works. Pritchard suggested the word 'Bibliometrics' in 1969 in preference to statistical bibliography.

3.1. Bibliometric Laws

The quantitative analysis of Bibliometrics, developed three basic Bibliometric Laws that is Lotka's Law (1926) predicting the productivity distribution of various authors, Zipf's Law (1933) describing the word-frequency ranking and the Bradford's Law of Scattering (1934) explaining 'distribution of documents (usually journals) in specific discipline or problem areas.'

3.1.1. Lotka's Inverse Square Law

In 1926, Alfred J. Lotka proposed his inverse square law correlating contributors of scientific papers to their number of contributions. His law provided fundamental theoretical base for bibliometric studies involving authorships. He was interested in determining "the part which men of different calibre contribute to the progress of science." For this he checked the decennial index of 'Chemical Abstracts' 1907 – 1916 and counted the number of names against which appeared 1,2,3 etc., He tabulated the data for 6,891 names, beginning with letter 'A' and 'B'. Similarly the data from the Auerbach's Geschieftafeth der Physik was also collected for the 1325 physicists. Lotka then plotted the graph on a logarithmic scale, the number of authors against the numbers of contributions made by each author and he found that in each case the points were clearly scattered about a straight line, having a slope of approximately two to one. On the basis of these data, Lotka deduced a general equation, for the relation between the frequency 'y' or persons making 'x' contributions as follows:

$$x^n y = \text{constant}$$

and for the special case n = 2, constant is 0.6079. Further he summarised the results as follows:

"In the case examined it is found that the number

of persons making two contributions is about one-fourth of those making one contribution, the number making 'n' contributions is about $1/n^2$ of those making one and the proportion of all contribution is about 60 percent.

In other words, for every 100 authors contributing one article, 25 will contribute two articles, about 11 will contribute 3 articles and 6 will contribute 4 articles and so on. Though, the law was based on the study of chemistry and physics literature later it has generated much interest and attracted the attention of researchers and it has been applied and tested in many other fields.

3.1.2. Bradford's Law

Samuel C. Bradford first formulated his law in 1934 but it did not receive wide attention until the publication of his book 'Documentation' in 1948. He, while searching for papers in two journals 'Applied Geophysics' and 'Lubrication', noticed that the scatter of such papers among the scientific journals had a common pattern. He described it as... "If a large collection of scientific journals are arranged in order of decreasing productivity of papers relevant to a given subject, then they may be divided into three zones so that each zone produces 1/3 of the total relevant papers. The first, the nucleus zone, contains a small number of highly productive journals, say n_1 ; the three zones contains a larger number of moderately productive journal, say n_2; and the outer zone containing a still larger number of journals of low productivity say n_3. He enunciated his law of scatter as:

$$n_1 : n_2 : n_3 = 1 : \alpha : \alpha^2 \text{ where } \alpha \text{ is constant.}$$

Bradford also plotted graphs of the cumulative

number of sources by plotting cumulative total of relevant papers R (n) on a linear scale along the y-axis and the number of journals (n) on a long scale.

3.1.3. Zipf's Law of Word Occurrence

Zipf developed and extended an empirical law, of least effort. He said that there is a relationship between the rank of a word and its frequency of occurrence in a long text. In a long textual matter if the words are arranged in their decreasing order of frequency then the rank of any given word of the text will be inversely proportional to the frequency of occurrence of the word i.e. If 'r' is the rank of a word and 'f' is its frequency, then mathematically zipf's law can be stated as follows: rank (r) a1 / frequency (f) or rf = C, where 'c' is a constant.

Thus, these three laws are respectively based on number of authors contributing in a discipline or other field; distribution of articles in a set of journals; and ranking word frequency in a particular set of documents.

4. INFORMETRICS

According to Brookes, the term 'Informetrics' was first proposed by Otto Nacke of West Germany in 1979 (18). An FID Committee with broadly defined objectives in the provision of research and technical data subsequently given this name. However, the term was not widely adopted until 1987 when B.C. Brookes at the First Conference on Bibliometrics and Theoretical Aspects of Information Retrieval held at Diepenbeek, Belgium suggested that the term "Informetrics" is the most appropriate term to cover bibliometrics, scientometrics, and other quantitative studies related to Information Science and it should be included in the name of Second International Conference on the subject. Egghe and Rossueau also stated in the proceedings of the conference that the term 'Informetrics' was favoured besides the terms 'Bibliometrics' and 'Scientometrics'. The Third International conference on Informetrics, held in Bangalore in 1991. 'Informetrics' was used as a generic term to mean "The use and development of a variety of measures to study and analyse several properties of information in general and documents in particular". Obviously, Informetrics comprises of Bibliometrics and Scientometrics.

Tague-Sutcliffe defined the term as "The study of the quantitative aspects of information in any form, not just records or bibliographies, and in any social group, not just scientists".... (20). It can incorporate utilise, and extend the many studies of the measurement of information that lie outside the boundaries of both 'Bibliometrics' and 'Scientometrics', and she continues to say that,

Although in practice the scope of "Informetrics" is very broad, ... two phenomena that have not, in the past, been seen as part of 'Bibliometrics' and 'Scientometrics' but fit within the scope of 'Informetrics' are: Definition and measurement of information; and Types and characteristics of retrieval performance measures

Informetrics involves studies in: The growth of literature in subjects; How much literature is contributed by various individuals, groups, organisations, countries; How much exists in various languages; How the literature on a subject is scattered viz., over documentation types, language, periodicals. And how quickly the literature on some subject becomes out of date viz., studies of obsolescence. One very important group of informetrics studies with such phenomena as: which authors are most cited, which journals are most cited.

5. SCIENTOMETRICS

The term Scientometrics originated as a Russian term for the application of quantitative methods to the history of science. This term was introduced and came into prominence with founding of the journal named 'Scientometrics' by T. Braunin 1977, originally published in Hungary and currently from Amsterdam. Scientometrics used to mean communication process in science including socio-cultural aspects and appears to be almost synonymous to science of science with more stress on quantitative aspects. It also used as a generic term for a system of knowledge, which endeavours to study the scientific (and technological) system using a variety of approaches within the area of science and technology studies. Thus Scientometrics is a part of the sociology of science and has application to science policy making.

5.1. Definitions

The term 'Scientometrics' is a field which applies quantitative methods to the study of science as an information process. It is a scientific discipline, which performs reproducible measurements of scientific activity and reveals its objective quantitative regularities. Further, Scientometric methods include statistical and thesaurus methods, and indicators as to the number of citations, terms etc.

According to Pouris, 'scientometrics is for science what econometrics is for economics" (21). Therefore it is 'Application of quantitative techniques (systems analysis, mathematical and statistical techniques etc.) to scientific communication (science output, science policy, science administration etc.)' with the objectives of

* Developing science indicators;
* Measuring the impact of science on society; and
* Comparing the output as well as the impact of science at national and international levels.

According to Tague-Sutcliffe, 'the study of the quantitative aspects of science as a discipline or economic activity'. Thus Scientometrics involves studies in:

* Sociology of Science
* History of science
* Growth of science and scientific institutions
* Behaviour of science and scientists.
* Science policy and decision-making.

6. CYBERMETRICS

Cybermetrics is one of the recently emerged field in the line of metric studies. It has gained much popularity since the mid-1990's with the advent of Information Technology. As it is mainly concerned with the computer-science-based approaches, it has superseded all other metric studies in this Internet Era.

6.1. Definitions

Cybermetrics is proposed as a generic term for 'The study of the quantitative aspects of the construction and use of information resources, structures and technologies on the whole Internet drawing on bibliometric and informetric approaches'. It is defined as 'quantitative study of Internet-related phenomena'. Cybermetrics thus encompasses statistical studies of discussion groups, mailing lists, and other computer – mediated communication on the

Internet including the WWW. Besides covering all computer-mediated communication using Internet applications, this definition of cybermetrics also covers quantitative measures of the Internet backbone technology, topology and traffic. The breadth of coverage of cybermetrics implies large overlaps with proliferating computer-science-based approaches in analyses of web contents, link structures, web usage and web technologies.

A range of such approaches has emerged since the mid-1990s with names like Web Ecology (e.g. Chi etal. 1998: Huberman, 2001). Web Intelligence (e.g. Yao et.al. 2001) : Web Mining (e.g.Etzioni 1996: Kosala & Blockeel. 2000: Chen and Chau 2004) and Web Graph Analysis (e.g. Chrakbarti et.al. 1999: Kleinberg et.al. 1999)

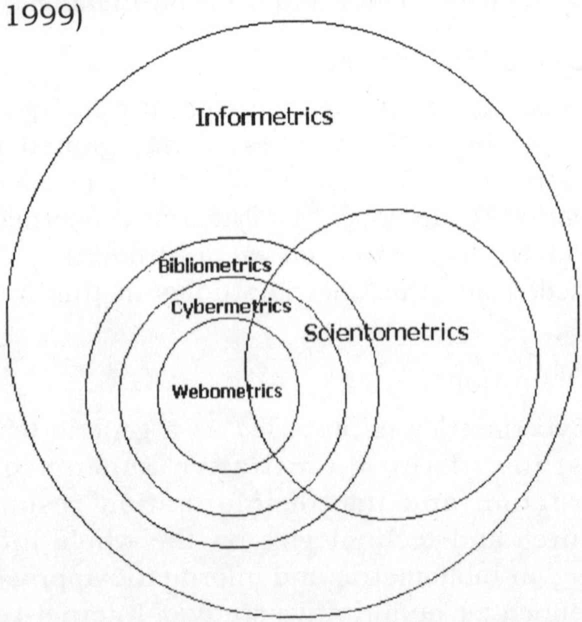

As shown in the above figure, the field of cybermetrics exceeds the boundaries of bibliometrics, because some activities in cyberspace normally are not recorded, but communicated synchronously like in chat rooms. Cybermetric studies of such activities still fit in the generic field of Informetrics as the study of the quantitative aspects of information "in any form" and 'in any social group" as stated by Tague-Sutcliffe (1992). The inclusion of webometrics expands the field of bibliometrics, as webometrics inevitably will contribute with further methodological developments of web-specific approaches. As ideas rooted in bibiometrics, scientometrics and informetrics contributed to the emergence of webometrics, ideas in webometrics might contribute to the development of these embracing fields.

7. WEBOMETRICS

A range of new terms for the emerging research field has been proposed since the mid-1990s, for instance, netometrics (Bossy, 1995); webometry (Abraham, 1996); interentometrics (Almind and Ingwerser, 1996); webometrics (Almond & Ingwerser 1997); cybermetrics (journal started 1997 by Isidro Anguillo); web bibliometry (Chakrabarti et al.,2002). Webometrics and cybermetrics are currently the two most widely adopted terms, of ten used as synonyms.

7.1. Definitions

Bjorneborn and Ingwerser used an information science – related definition of webometrics as "the study of the quantitative aspects of the construction and use of information resources, structures and technologies on the WWW during on bibliometric and informetric approaches" (23). This definition thus covers quantitative aspects of both the construction side and the usage side of the web embracing the four main areas of present webometric research : a) web page content analysis; b) web link structure analysis; c) web usage analysis (e.g. exploiting log files of users searching and browsing behaviour); d) web technology analysis (including search engine performance).

According to Almind Thomas and Ingwersen Peter, webometrics is defined as "Research of all network-based communications using informetric or other quantitative measures is called webometrics" (24).

8. CONCLUSION

Most of the librametry /bibliometrics/ informetrics studies applied in the library and information field are concerned with the different types of uses and degrees to which user needs are satisfied. The studies are becoming more analytical than descriptive. Such studies may be grouped as: a) to make a careful and intensive study of the library situation, b). to measure the adequacy of library collection for present and possible future library programmes and c) to discover mathematical and statistical models for various phenomenon which we experience in library and information work and studies.

REFERENCES

1. Senugupta (1985). Bibliometrics: A Bird's Eye View. *IASLIC Bulletin,* 30 (4), pp. 167-174.
2. Ravichandra Rao (1988). Librametry to Informetrics: Developments in India. *In:* Information Systems, Networks and Services in India: Developments and Trends / edited by V. Rajaraman. Bangalore: Ranganathan Centre for Information Studies, pp. **187**— 209.
3. Pritchard, Alan (1989). Statistical Bibliography or Bibliometrics. *Journal of Documentation,* 25 (4), p. 348
4. Fairthome, R A. (1969). Empirical Hyperbolic Distributions (Bradford. Zipf-Mandelbort) for Bibliometric Description and Prediction. *Journal of Documentation,* 25, p 319.

5. British Standards Institution (1976): British Standard of Documentation Terms. London: BSI, p. 7.

6. Hawkins, D T (1977). Unconventional Uses of On-line Information Retrieval Systems: Online Bibliometric Studies. *Journal of American Society for Information Science,* 28 (1), pp. 13-18.

7. Rising, L Miks (1962). Statistical Bibliography in the Health Sciences. *Bulletin of the Medical Library Association,* (50), p. 450-461.

8. Nicholas, D and Ritchie, M. (1978). Literature on Bibliometrics. London: Bingley, pp. 9-10.

9. Potter, W G (1981). Introduction to Bibliometrics. *Library Trends,* 30, p. 5

10. Sengupta (1990). Bibliometrics and its Applications. *In:* (Ed). Information Science and Libraries / edited by Pushpa Dhyani, New Delhi: Atlantic, p.256.

11. Egghe, L. (1988). Methodological Aspects of Bibliometrics. *Library Science with a slant to Documentation and Information Studies,* 25, p. 179-191.

12. Sangam, S. L. (1989). Obsolescence of Literature in Economics. *ILA Bulletin,* 25(2):p59.

13. The Oxford New English Dictionary on historical principles. Oxford: Clarendon, 1933(vol.7):p33.

14. Funk and Wagnalls New Standard Dictionary of the English Language. New York: Funk and Wagnalls, 1942:p 1704.

15. McGraw Hill Dictionary of Scientific and Technical Term. New York: McGraw Hill, 1974.

16. Line, M B and Sandison, A. Obsolescence and Changes in the Use of Literature with Time. *Journal of Documentation,* 30 (3), 283.

17. Brookes, B C (1971). Use of Scientific Periodicals. *Nature,* (232) Aug., p. 439.

18. Brookes, B C (1989). Biblio-, sciennto-, informetrics???: What are we Talking About?. *In:* Informetrics 89/90: Selection of Papers Submitted for the Second International Conference on Bibliometrics,Scientometrics and Informetrics, London , 5-7 July 1989.

19. Ibid

20. Tague-Sutcliffe, J. An Introduction to Informetrics.

Information Processing and Management, 28(1), pp.1-3.

21. Pouris (1989). Scientometric Assessment of Agricultural Research in South Africa. *Scientometrics,* 17(5-6), pp. 401-413.
22. Bjorneborn, L and Ingwersen, P. Perspectives of Webometrics. *Scientometrics,* 50 (1), pp. 65-82.
23. Bjorneborn, L and Ingwersen, P. Towards a Basic Framework of Webometrics. *JASIST Special Issue.*
24. Almind,T C and Ingwersen, P. Informetric Analysis on the World Wide Web: A Methodological Approach to "Intemetometrics". Centre for Informetric Studies, Royal School of Library and Information Science. (CIS Report 2).
25. Subramanyam, K. (1983). Bibliometric Studies of Research Collaboration. *Journal of Information Science,* 6(1), pp.333-338.

23
Perspectives of Digital Preservation

N.R. Satyanarayana

ABSTRACT

Deals with the problems posed by storing digital information in the Electronic Libraries as digital information, due to its nature and format, presents problems of its preservation such as for viewing, scrambling, translating, copyright and custodianships. As a vast number of resources are now being committed to reformatting into digital form, librarians are faced with the problems of digital longevity, choice, quality, integrity, and access, i.e., whether digital information will continue to be accessible over a long period of time. This paper throws light on the general problems of information in digital form and looks closely at the main key factors, as preservation remains an ill-defined concept when applied to the development of library collection.

1. INTRODUCTION

The amount of information and the multitude of formats it is recorded on have been growing exponentially over the last few years. Without consistent and reliable access to information sources from both past and the present, the sum of a society's knowledge can not keep on advancing. The information of the ages has traditionally been placed in the custody of librarians. The very idea of losing information sends a shiver up the spines of most librarians. Digital information is no less important than its analog counterparts. Both require that efforts be expanded to preserve the wealth that they contain.

2. THE SHORT SPAN OF DIGITAL INFORMATION

Though the advent of electronics storage is fairly new, a substantial amount of information stored in electronic form has deteriorated and disappeared. This is because electronic formats are more fragile and must rely on technology that is constantly changing. Marcum states that the rapid change in the means of recording information, in the formats for storage and in the software for use (all) threaten shorten the life of information in the digital age in a few years. The threat is that much digital information will be, if not already lost'.[1] As innovations in computer hardware storage and software industries continue to grow at a rapid pace, records originally created in digital form and those that have been converted retrospectively from traditional to digital formats become vulnerable to what has been termed 'technological obsolescence'. New devices and software that can yield greater storage and processing capabilities are regularly being replaced on a three to five year cycle.[2] Under the very best of storage conditions, digital media is still fragile and has a limited shelf life. Given the incredible rate of change in technology, even the most fragile media may outlive the technology that can read it. Therefore, the greater threat to information in digital form is technical obsolescence not the inherent fragility of any given medium.[3]

To prevent further loss, we need to come to grips with the problems of longevity in the digital world. In the following paragraphs, five key factors have been discussed that pose digital longevity problems:

* The Viewing problem
* The Scrambling problem
* The Inter-relation problem
* The Custodial problem
* The Translation problem

2.1. The Viewing Problem

Digital information created in the past requires the maintenance of an infrastructure and knowledge base in order to view it. For example, to view an older word processing file one needs software that understands the encoding schemes of the original software and can display that properly on the screen without this, all one will be able to see is gibberish. But to keep these file alive over time, we will need to also keep software needed to run it, or keep knowledge of the encoding scheme and be able to produce software that uses the encoding scheme to properly display our digital files on the screen. Digital information requires an elaborate set of knowledge and/or computing environment in order to decipher it. It is usually encoded and to view it requires applications software, which runs on a particular operating system and which needs a particular hardware platform. It is usually stored on a physical device (like a hard disk drive, floppy disk, or CD-ROM) which requires a particular type of driver connected to particular type of computer. Most of today's word processors can not read files created with older word processors. In fact, today's word processors (such as Microsoft Word) can not even read files created with earlier versions of the same word processors. How can we ever hope that the files we create today will be readable in our environments 100 years from now? [4]

2.2. The Scrambling Problem

In order to solve short-term problems resulting from the use of digital technology, we have engaged in practices that may result in long term problem. In the past, because large scale storage was costly and bandwidth was fairly narrow, many repositories responded to these constraints by compressing their master images or multimedia. The reason was that compressed master files take up less storage, are easier to deliver to users with slow network connections, and are more convenient to handle internally. There are a number of problems created by compression. Common lossy image compression formats such as JPEG essentially try to throw away information that is not too distinguishable to the human eye (colours that are close to one another get combined; spectral ranges beyond human perception are eliminated). But we don't yet understand whether some of this eliminated data will prove useful to future applications that will employ machine (rather than human) vision-applications that may perform functions such as colour analysis comparing and overlaying images, etc. use of lossy compression today may preclude certain use of these images in the future. Both lossy and lossless compressions add still another level of complexity to the encoding of a file making it even more difficult for future archeologists trying to decipher its content. The level of complexity that scrambling adds makes to difficult to believe that anyone will be decode today's scrambled files even 50 years from now. [5]

2.3. The Inter-relation Problem

In the digital world, information is increasingly inter-related to other information. The World Wide Web is primary example of how any given work may incorporate or point to a number of other works. On today's web, it is difficult to strive to make our own work persists when they point to and integrate with works owned by others. Because our current scheme for referencing web files (the URL) is based upon a files location, any time the location of file we refer changes, our links break and users experience the most common error message on the Web ("404 not found"). Usually this problem is caused by some simple reorganisation at the pointed-to Website (the renaming of a file, or of a folder/directory somewhere above it in the storage hierarchy, or the renaming of a server, etc.) but this common act of file/site management wreaks havoc on any works that point to or incorporate files from the sites.

Another critical subset of the Inter-relation problem is the issue of determining the boundary of a set of information (or even of digital object). Today, the boundaries of digital work are no longer confined to a single file. Frequently, a webpage will incorporate images, graphics, and buttons that are stored in separate files. Even traditional works like a journal article, report, or essay are frequently broken up into several separate files which are either assembled together at viewing time by a user browser, or remain separate linked files that a user must click between. If we want to take action to preserve one of these complex works, we need to develop guidelines on where the boundaries of the work lie. If a work incorporates pieces owned of managed by another organisation (icons, logos, images, text, etc.) does saving a copy of those pieces raise intellectual property question? [6]

2.4. The Custodial Problem

Though a number of traditions have developed concerning which organisations should take responsibility for preserving and maintaining various types of analog material (correspondence, manuscripts, printed matter), no such traditions exist yet for digital material. As a result of this, much current material originating in digital form falls thorough the cracks and is unlikely to be accessible to future generations. A major question we face in the coming years are: who should be responsible for saving material in electronic form? Should individuals carrying this responsibility themselves or should social entitles (such as business, libraries, archives and professional societies) aggressively intervene to save material? And how will they decide what to save?

Another critical question is: How should they go about saving it? Our field still needs to develop guidelines and best practices so that organisations and individuals who want to make the effort to try to make digital information persist will know how to do so.

2.5. The Translation Problem

When content is translated into new delivery devices (such as digital forms), the change of form often serves to change part of the meaning. Conversions from analog to analog face this problem, as do conversions from analog to digital (a photograph of a painting is not the same as that painting, and a digital representation of an object is not the same as that object.[7] Because we can make identical copies of digital files, this has led some people to make mistaken belief that digital-to-digital conversion will not face the same translation problems that analog-to-digital conversion face. This is not true because though the bits in the file's contents may be identical, the applications environment used to view the file most certainly will be different. In fact, the very reason for converting the file is because we are unable to successfully sustain that application's environment overtime. Many people have experienced this as their word processor successfully: imports a document created with an earlier version of the same word processor, while losing formatting (such as entering, underlining, and font changes) or punctuations.

3. WAYS TO IMPROVE DIGITAL LONGEVITY

Any long-term preservation strategy for digital information must incorporate cooperative relationships among physically dispersed locations and organisations. We need to develop international cooperative projects where organisations are willing to store and refresh redundant copies of works that are really under the custodianship of other organisations.

Current intellectual property laws inhibit an archive or library from preserving information in digital form, particularly since much of the digital information they acquire is licensed rather than owned. A recent study on copyright by the National Academy of Science (National Research Council 2006) strongly recommended that intellectual property laws be changed to permit these institutions to legally preserve information in digital form and that significant funding be allocated to digital preservation.

We have to gain more experience in applying the two strategies: i.e., emulation and migration for digital longevity.

4. THE ROLE OF METADATA

Metadata is the best way to minimising the risks of a digital object becoming inaccessible properly used, metadata can-

* Identify the name of the work, who created it, who reformatted it and other descriptive information.
* Provide unique identification and links to organisations, files or databases which have more extensive descriptive metadata about this work.
* Explain the technical environment needed to view the work, including applications and versions numbers needed, decompression schemes, other files that need to be linked to it, prove critical for properly viewing these files in the future.

5. CONCLUSION

Rapid technological obsolescence combined with relatively short-lived media means that digital information must be actively managed. In digital environment we need to better understand how information relates to other information. In particular, we need further clarify about what constitutes the "boundaries" of information objects. When we are trying to save something (particularly are hypertexts or hypermedia object) we need to know what pieces are really need to say. Finally, we need to develop a concrete set of guidelines that can be used by people and organisations wishing to make information persist.

REFERENCES

1. Marcum, Deanna B. (1996). The Preservation of Digital Information. *Journal of American Librarianship* , 22, November, pp 451-454
2. Headstrom, Margaret (Digital Preservation: a Time Bomb for Digital Libraries. Available at http://www.uky.edu
3. Taskforce on Archiving of Digital Information. Available at www.rlg.org/ArchTF/tfadi
4. http://www.gets.ucla.duc/-howard/copyright/
5. http://sunsiteberkeley.edu/longevity
6. Commission of Preservation and Access. Available at http://clir.org
7. Basser, Howard. The changing Museum *In:* Proceedings of the 50th Annual Meeting of the American Society for Information Science / edited by Ching-chin Chen. NJ. Learned Information, pp. 14-19

24

Current Trends in IT and its Application in Academic Libraries

D. Shivalingaiah
K. Manjunatha

ABSTRACT

There have been significant changes in academic library services in recent years. Technology particularly Information Technology (IT) supported devices, resources and services are constantly changing the information landscape. The potential of the internet offers the possibility of universal access to everything. These unparalleled changes are empowering the younger generation more knowledgeable, tech-savvy and making them less patient. These changes are challenging information service providers to realign their products and services to serve users more efficiently within short time.

In this paper, the authors provide an outline of chronological development of IT products and services in academic libraries followed the current IT trends and the forces that are driving such technological innovations.

1. INTRODUCTION

Technology remains one of the primary drivers of change in the ways that people work, seek information, communicate, and entertain themselves. The functions, techniques, and principles of information technology in the organisation have spilled over into other aspects of modern society. It created innovative forms of information and communication that has also altered the rules of communication in social life. The emergence of Internet, particularly, the World Wide Web (WWW) as a new media of information delivery triggered proliferation of web-based full-text online resources. Increasing numbers of publishers are using the Internet as a global way to offer their publications to the information seekers. DiMaggio et al. (2001) purport that the Internet is different from earlier communication technologies, as it offers different modes of communication (broadcasting, individual searching, group discussion) and different kinds of content (text, audio, visual images) in a single medium. Castells (2001) believes that the Internet is a type of technology that is even more deeply embedded in social history since it is, "a technology of communication".

In an academic environment, no unit has been transformed by technology than library. It is causing important changes in the ways and means of functions of libraries. It is fueling increased user demands and expectations for information resources and their timely delivery. The libraries and information centres, as heavy consumers of electronic journals and online databases, stand to benefit greatly from this technology-driven revolution. Libraries in digital era are not necessarily be linked to a physical space or a single organisation, although many have grown – and will continue to grow – out of a single entity, which may have a physical base, collections and services as well as digital ones (PRG, 2006). In most cases, the digital library will bring together content and services from a range of commercial and non-commercial suppliers. They should enable any citizen to access all human knowledge anytime and anywhere, in a friendly, multi-modal, efficient, and effective way, by overcoming barriers of distance, language, and culture and by using multiple Internet-connected devices.

Baker (2006) points that forecasting the future is going to be complex, partly because of the significantly greater number of "players" or providers in the digital library environment than was the case even five years ago and partly as a result of the increased diversification of requirement, expectation and usage amongst user communities. The future physical libraries – where they exist – will be areas encompassing a set of resources, facilities and services in which digital/web-based research and learning can take place. But they will be just one part of a much larger organisational whole that places greatest value on maximum access – whether in terms of timeframe or type. Digital support for users will be a critical success factor, with the opportunity to provide: signposts for personal learning, and the development of individual thinking; encouragement for innovation as well as wider take-up. Strong mechanisms will be needed to manage this support, not least in the light of the fact that fewer people will travel in person to a physical space. The libraries need to understand and address these new challenges and reorganise their physical space to make technology-enabled resources both more readily available and widely used.

2. BRIEF HISTORY AND DEVELOPMENT OF IT IN LIBRARIES

Technology is not a new concept to libraries. It is rooted in their functions as they have been the laboratory or floor for testing any innovation in technologies related to production, processing, preservation and presentation of knowledge. Reprographic machines, varieties of book binding, stack systems, card catalogue/cabinet, and card punching are some of the examples of technology in libraries. The changes in technology became more visible with the invention of computers. In 1960s the IBM invented computers for computing scientific calculations. A white paper developed by Sun Microsystems (2003) traces the evolution of library automation (*http://www.sun.com/edu/whitepapers/pdf/digital_library_trends.pdf*). According to this paper, the milestones in technology in libraries are as follows:

* The automation entered libraries in 1970s with the introduction computing machines in libraries for scientific calculations.
* The next phase was development of integrated library systems (ILS) to perform library functions online and ILS led the emergence of MARC.
* Networking became a focus during 1980s and network supported LIS softwares developed during this period. Libraries began utilising new application systems for automation of resource sharing, union catalogues and inter-library loan modules.
* As the 1980s ended, libraries and computing centres were tackling communications, relational databases, and information distribution challenges. Intranets provided campus

connectivity using TCP/IP communication standards.

* The 1990s saw greater use of campus communication infrastructures and commercial communication systems to create and store information and then to deliver it from libraries to end users. Large databases from periodical, magazine and journal publishers became increasingly available in digital format- at first on CD-ROM; later via online services. .
* During the period 1998-2002 the Internet, the web, computer languages and tools have matured to enable creation of rapidly increasing number of digital resources that need to be controlled, served and preserved by libraries. Open archives initiative (OAI), metadata, Unicode etc. are the trends during that period.

Since 2002, the IT innovations are more visible in development of hardware and software. The significant development in hardware is related to innovation of laptops, RFID (Radio Frequency identification Device), Wi-Fi-wireless connections, miniaturised digital storage device and mobile technologies. The developments in softwares related to innovations web designing, wikis, blogs, podcasts, RSS (Really Simple Syndication), web OPACs, librarian 2.0 etc.

3. CURRENT IT TRENDS IN ACADEMIC LIBRARIES

Invention of computer has transformed almost every aspect of how the library provides its services and performs its work behind the scenes. This resulted in automation of library in-house operations, online public access catalogue (OPAC), remote access, digitisation, and creation of digital libraries. The findings of research conducted by Primary Research Group of Academic Library Technology Directors (2005) reveals that:

* Most libraries have some kind of wish list for the digitization for their special collections, particularly their photographic collections. More thought needs to be given to the integration of special collections in to library catalogues over the web, or in partnership with other institutions.
* Some of the other findings related to: implementation of wireless access, policies towards laptops in the library, establishing digital depositories, preserving scholarly access to potentially temporal digital media, use of e-books, services for distance learning students, use of URL resolvers, web site development and management, use of virtual reference, investment in library software, IT staff size and staff skill composition, range of IT staff responsibilities, use of outsourcing, catalogue enhancement software, website search engine policies, use of CMS (content/ collection management system/software, technology education and training, information literacy, and library printing technology.

Frey (2005) traced ten key trends that are affecting the development of the next generation library. He also mentions that these are not the only trends, but ones that have been selected to give clear insight into the rapidly changing technologies and equally fast changing mindset of library patrons.

Trend #1 : Communication systems are continually changing the way people access information;

Trend #2 : All technology ends. All technologies commonly used today will be replaced by something new;

Trend #3 : We haven't yet reached the ultimate small particle for storage. But soon;

Trend #4 : Search Technology will become increasingly more complicated;

Trend #5 : Time compression is changing the lifestyle of library patrons;

Trend #6 : Over time we will be transitioning to a verbal society;

Trend #7 : The demand for global information is growing exponentially;

Trend #8 : The Stage is being set for a new era of Global Systems;

Trend #9 : We are transitioning from a product-based economy to an experience based economy;

Trend #10 : Libraries will transit from a centre of information to a centre of culture.

Breeding (2005), forecasted the following trends:

a. The Integrated Library System(ILS) will be reintegrated;

b. The business landscape will change;

c. Players in Broader industries will become involved;

d. Libraries will consolidate automation efforts and

e. The products and services from commercial vendors will continue do dominate.

Klein's (2005) top technology trends on LITA (Library and Information Technology Association) Blog (*http://litablog.org/2005/06/leo-kleins-top-technology-trends/*) illustrates CMS, Customised websites, Chat e-references, web standards and dynamic web content. Similarly Morgan (2006, *http://litablog.org*) traced features like web-blogs, social networking, open source s/w, meta-search standards, mass digitisation, digital resource management (DRM), licensed content, growing discontent with library catalogue and OCLC expansion as top technology trends in 2006 for American Library Association (ALA). Whitlatch (2006) in his article *Reference Futures* predicted 'outsourcing, web and knowledge counseling' as future scenario for library reference services.

Davis and Stephenson (2006) among other macroeconomic trends predict that ubiquitous access to information is changing the economics of knowledge. Knowledge is increasingly available and, at the same time, increasingly specialised. The most obvious manifestation of this trend is the rise of search engines (such as Google, yahoo), which make an almost infinite amount of information available instantaneously. Access to knowledge has become almost universal. Yet the transformation is much more profound than simply broad access. New models of knowledge production, access, distribution, and ownership are emerging. We are seeing the rise of open-source approaches to knowledge development as communities, not individuals, become responsible for innovations.

The 2006 handbook published by National Accreditation and Assessment Council (NAAC, 2006) - an official accrediting body of Government of India, contains case studies of best practices in use of IT in Library and Information services practiced in leading libraries in India. They are: total automation, campus-wide access, broadband/leased Internet access, library webpage, web OPAC, web access to digital resources, all time access to e-resources, use of open standards, institutional depositories, consortium networking, online user feedback/reservations, CD-Net/Mirror servers, digitisation of manuscript/special collections, electronic surveillance and RFID.

Mallery (2007) who carried out the survey on technology innovation in libraries for Association of College and Research Libraries (ACRL, *http://www.acrl.org*) reports that: blogs, wikis, podcasting, web 2.0, librarian 2.0, RSS, IM reference, wireless, Information commons, media centre, MP3 audio lectures, institutional repositories, Open URL resolver, Open Archives Initiative, NCSU's Endeca, are some of the recent innovations in libraries.

Besides, the following are a few of the technologies emerged in Library and information Management systems:

* Implementation of wireless and mobile technologies for all time remote/campus-wide access,
* Interlibrary loan modules integrated into the circulation system
* Bar-coded library transactions,
* web site development, web-programming and management of the same, integration of web OPAC and integration of multi language on single platform,
* Access to OPAC's via mobile devices such as wireless PDA's
* Production and Use of e-books and e-journals,

* Computer integrated telephony for sending reminders and information on reservations to users
* Services for distance learning students, disabled/handicapped
* RFID for security, circulation and inventory management systems;
* Technology education, training and instructional/education technology to support teaching and learning, and
* Development of technology centres and promotion of information literacy.
* Emergence of open source software (OSS) such as Koha, e-prints, Green Stone Digital Library (GSDL), DSpace etc.
* Emergence of federated search engines such as Project MUSE to integrate several database searches with different login requirements.

4. DRIVING FORCES BEHIND IT INNOVATIONS IN ACADEMIC LIBRARIES

There are many driving forces that are responsible for IT innovations in libraries. The forces can be graphically represented as in Fig 1.

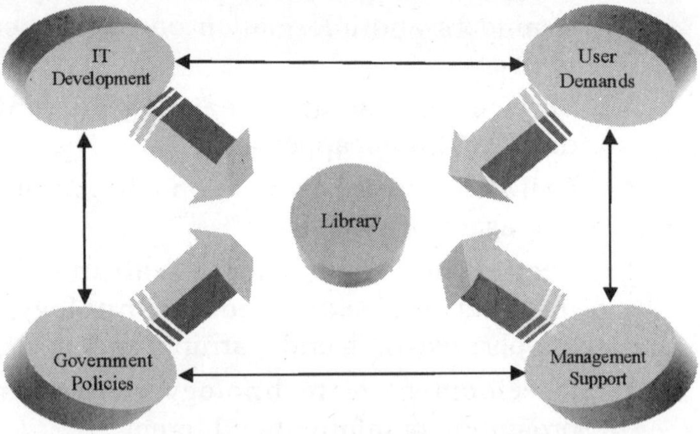

Fig. 1. Drivers of technology in libraries

The intertwined or interrelated key drivers on development of IT in libraries are research and developments in technology, Government policies, Management's attitude/support in implementing new technologies and user Expectations/demands.

Developments in IT: Ayers (2004) while explaining the dynamics of technology defines characteristics of IT as: i) everywhere and nowhere; ii) brash young industry; iii) highly unstable; iv) new competitors continually emerge; v) possibility of great profits; vi) work performed by anonymous teams; vii) obsolescence built in; viii) virtually instant results necessary; and ix) designed to be transparent. The trends described as earlier also reinforce the fast developments in IT which need to be addressed by libraries.

The major findings of Pew Internet Research Study (Horrigan, 2007) reveal that:

* 8% of Americans are deep users of the participatory Web and mobile applications;

* Another 23% are heavy, pragmatic tech adopters – they use gadgets to keep up with social networks or be productive at work;
* 10% rely on mobile devices for voice, texting, or entertainment;
* 10% use information gadgets, but find it a hassle;
* 49% of Americans occasionally use modern gadgetry and many others bristle at electronic connectivity (in connection with social networking)

Government Policies : the central and state Government policies do have direct impact on technology development and implementation in the country. The Government's initiatives/policies on infrastructure improvement, establishment of INDEST, INFLIBNET's e-consortia, NAAC/NBA/AICTE's norms/ standards on technology and e-resources in libraries, UGC's Infonet facility and its decision to provide grant to universities are some of the examples.

User Demands/Expectations : Baker (2006, p 5) describes the user demands/ expectations as "The emphasis is moving from provider to consumer, and the consumer must be better understood. Researchers emphasise quality through peer review – including as a mechanism for gaining "proper" recognition of their own work. Teachers are looking for stand-alone, reusable, infrastructure-backed resources, and for easy integration between ranges of resource types, perhaps through virtual and managed learning environment development. Student needs encompass a wide and diverse range of course and user types. "Traditional" face-to-face programmes will continue, but many students will be distance learners, looking for strong digital support in a blended learning environment that de-emphasises physical attendance at an institution".

Management Support : in an academic environment, library is the subsystem/supporting element of any academic or research organisation. The development of technology/infrastructure mainly depends on the priorities, policies and execution plans accomplished by the parent body. In the increasing competitive environment, the academic institutes are forced /motivated to adopt modern technological gadgets/devices in curriculum designing and teaching methodology in order to attract students. This has direct influence on development of supporting systems too. The students, faculty, infotech /Technology centre, members of library committee do play a significant role in adoption/implementation of IT products and services in academic libraries.

5. LIBRARY ISSUES IN IT DRIVEN ERA

Saurine (2000) points the new technologies and Internets have challenged traditional library services and practices. While the shape and nature of the resources to be organised and accessed may be changing radically, the basic functionality required of a library remains much as before, with digital libraries consisting of a set of core functions: assessment and acquisition, organisation and presentation of resources of all kinds, regardless of provenance or format, the whole underpinned by a set of management processes.

Sun Micro System's (2003) White Paper lists some of the issues faced by today's libraries to provide greater information access to users. They are:

* Need for trained staff in technology and traditional library disciplines;
* Investment in continuing education and budgetary restrictions;

* Physical and digital subscription resources are increasing in volume and cost;
* Growing popularity of Internet as research tool;
* Increased user expectation with widespread use of Internet and
* Need for library's link with other academic departments.

Loriene Roy and Bill Crowe (2006) the 2006 presidential candidates for American Library Association identified i) the need to engage library community with Google and commercial service providers, ii) the challenge of succession plan, iii) challenge of communicating library stories to outsiders, iv) need for continuing education and training for library workers, v) tailoring library services to respond to user needs, vi) increasing salaries and benefits of librarians as the issues facing the library community.

Mfrisque (2006) identifies basic IT skills for staff, knowledge of h/w ,s/w and trouble shooting, online help desk, ability to move/talk with customers, empowering staff, creating technical team, educating staff and users on use of technology and e-resources as some of the core competencies to be addressed by that the library professionals.

ACRL's 2007 (Mallery, 2007) Survey lists some of the prominent challenges or obstacles to library technology innovation. They are budget restrictions, administration, technology provision/implementation, InfoTech centre's priorities, semi skilled or untrained staff, faculty's non-cooperation, and inadequacies in infrastructure provisions.

6. CONCLUSION

The adoption and use of information and communication technologies depends on organisation's technology assets, their actions and their attitudes towards the same. The future upgrades and expansion of new technology will continue to change the world of learning. Institutions and libraries cannot just keep up; they have to explore and keep pace with new technology applicable for library setting. Library professionals need to embrace the current technologies to address the growing customer expectations and for their survival too. They need to be bold, ready but cautious about technology obsolescence while adopting technologies. They need to be alert in understanding and updating on current technologies in the field and attempt to induct them into their services.

Ranganathan's Fourth law "save the time of reader" holds good even today and keep striking LIS professionals for aligning library resources, facilities and services towards the common goal "serve the customer to his satisfaction". Technology is not an end by itself, it is just a tool towards the better and efficient customer service. It is the service people who make or mar the system. Hence, LIS professionals should not resists or lag behind to embrace the current technologies and devote them to make best use of it for serving academic community.

Finally,

Pusthakasthā cha yā vidya Parahasthe cha yaddhanam |
Kāryakaale samuthpanne Na sā vidya nā taddhanam ||

— (*Subhashitha*)

meaning,

Knowledge hidden in the book, Money in others' hand, If not put into use/available on time, Their presence/absence doesn't make any difference (waste).

REFERENCES

1. Ayers, Edward L (2004). The Academic Culture and the IT Culture: Their Effect on Teaching and Scholarship. *EDUCAUSE Review,* 39 (6), November/December, pp. 48-62. Available at http://www.informedlibrarian.com
2. Baker, David (2006). Digital Library Futures: a UK HE and FE Perspective. *Interlending & Document Supply,* 34 (1), pp. 4-8. Available at http://www.informedlibrarian.com
3. Breeding, Marshal (2005). Looking Towards the Future of Library Technology. *Computers in Libraries: Library Technology Guides,* 25 (25), May, pp. 39-42. Available at http://www.librarytechnology.org/ltg-displaytext.pl?RC-11414
4. Castells, M. (2001). The Internet Galaxy: Reflections on the Internet, Business, and Society. New York: Oxford University Press.
5. Davis, Ian and Stephenson, Elizabeth (2006): Ten Trends to Watch in 2006. *McKinsey Quarterly,* Web Premium Exclusive, January, pp. 1-5. Available at http://www.mckinseyquarterly.com (Accessed on May 2, 2007)
6. DiMaggio, P et al (2001). Social Implications of Internet. *Annual Review of Sociology,* 27, August, pp. 307-336.
7. Frey, Thomas (2005). The Future of Libraries Beginning the Great Transformation. Colorado: The DaVinci Inst, Available at http://www.davinciinstitute.com/page.php?ID=120
8. Horrigan, John B (2007). Typology of Information and Communication Technology Users. Report of Research Study Conducted by Research Team of PEW Internet & American Life Project, Washington during May 2007. Summary and Report Available at http://www.pewinternet.org) (Accessed on 10-5-2007)
9. Mallery, Mary (2007). ACRL 2007 Panel Session on Technology Innovation Survey Summary. Available at http://www.njla.org/njacrl/ACRL07TechInnovYesResults.doc
10. Maness, Jack M (2006). Library 2.0 Theory: Web 2.0 & its Implications for Libraries. *Webology,* 3 (2), June. Available at http://www.webology.ir/2006/v3n2/a25.html
11. Primary Research Group (2005). Best Practices of Academic

Library Technology Directors. Available at http://www.researchandmarkets.com/reportinfo.asp?report_id=296304

12. Sun Micro Systems Inc. (2006). Information Technology Advances in Libraries. A White Paper on Digital Library Technology Trends Prepared in 2003. Available at http://www.sun.com/edu/whitepapers/pdf/digital_library_trends.pdf
13. Whitlatch, Jo Bell (2006). The Future of Reference Services. Available at http://www.ala.org/ala/rusa/rusaprotools/futureofref/referencefutures.htm

25

Sustenance of Libraries in Digital Environment What & How To Do?

R. S. R. Varalakshmi

ABSTRACT

The changes in recorded media from paper to digital, the impact of Information & Communication Technology (ICT), pervasion of the Internet in scholarly communication, the changing user perception and self access to information are the challenges before the contemporary Library & Information Science (LIS) profession. To cope with the challenges of digital environment and sustain in the ever changing knowledge society Library & Information Centres (LIC) have to initiate new services. Library services do not involve the library resources alone; they have to deliver e-services in the context of a wider ICT – based provision. The article discusses the mode of organising services like aggregation, info literacy, Institutional Repositories (IR), webliography, etc. as some measures to meet the user demands and sustain in digital era.

1. INTRODUCTION

The vital role played by information and communication technologies in the development of digital environment revolutionised the way libraries handle information for centuries. The gathering, processing and storage of data, availability and ready access to information that may be extracted from such data are recognised all over the world as key resources. The ICT's offer increased efficiency in terms of time, human resources and cost; improved quality of information, greater flexibility and responsiveness, increased access and sharing, enhanced degree of user interaction to specific information, review and modify the needs as per the situation. More specifically the Internet takes firm roots in information storage, processing and dissemination – hitherto the core activities of libraries – and provides global access. The e-books, e-journals, e-reference sources, e-news, e-marketing, etc makes 42,000,000 Indians as users of the Internet with a use growth of 740.0% from 2000-2007. (Source: Internet World Stats, URL: http://www.internetworldstats.com/stats3.htm#asia). Owing to the new systems of information handling, the libraries are the less attractive centers of information / knowledge as the user can access his information at work place, at home and or at cyber café according to convenience. The ground reality is that the users prefer the ease of use, portability, affordability and access to wide range of subjects on the web over the rule bound library environment. How libraries can sustain under the impact of ICT and specifically the Internet? How to get our users back to the library? How to prove that the Internet can't be a replacement but only a supplement to libraries?

The electronic environment is not rosy, as it

appears to be. The major issue is content organization. The information is poorly structured on the web while libraries have successful methods for information processing and retrieval. The content mapping, semantic web, ontology are under experimental stages for the purpose of effective organisation and retrieval of web resources. Hence users are apparently in need of librarians to assist them in accessing pertinent and precise information. Therefore it is high time for library professionals to make their identity and prove their capabilities. They ought to remodel themselves to the digital reading devices and act as educators, aggregators, knowledge managers and in simple as cybrarians.

2. WHAT TO DO?

The librarians traditionally play an intermediary role in channelising knowledge / information that is hidden in the documents to the user community. Now the mode of recording media has changed to electronic, but the role of librarians is same as intermediary. To sustain in the emerging digital environment the libraries have to respond positively and grab every situation to make their identity and play a vital role as mediator.

* The electronic environment provides an opportunity for libraries to design and disseminate new services. The libraries have to explore the opportunities.
* The librarians have to highlight their expertise, abilities in organizing and enabling easy and pertinent access to digital resources.
* The libraries have to integrate its services suitable to electronic resources and netizens through sustainable and seamless

infrastructure.

* Provide bibliographic tools that permit easy searching and browsing.
* Develop tools that render and present content in user customized formats.
* They can develop embedded training modules to assist in information seeking.

3. HOW TO DO IT?

The librarians are expected to initiate a variety of new services or traditional services in new form to serve their community. The aim is to promote their sources, material and manpower, through a variety of products and services. Some products and services the librarians can develop with the existing infrastructure facilities are discussed below.

3.1. Institutional Repositories (IR)

The higher educational and research institutes generate significant number of internal research publications of high value. These publications constitute their 'intellectual capital'. The libraries have to play a vital role in digitising and networking the intellectual out put of the institutions. There is a fundamental change in the role of libraries as leaders of the scholarly record. Now the scholarly communication and publishing is in digital form hence it is comparatively easy for the libraries to collect digital information and, organise and provide access on campus networks. Unless they take part in canalising the digital communication, the libraries will not have a future in digital era. Hence the mission has to be collecting, managing and preserving the scholarly record. For this the librarians have to be proactive in capturing the research and scholarly material. "In particular, in the past five years the trend towards online, digital publishing and sharing of digital research data has exploded on campus." (Smith, MacKanzie 2004). As a result the institutional repository concept has taken its roots and adopted by a number of libraries through out the world.

The higher educational and research institutes produce substantial quantity of research output as published books, research articles, research reports, conference/seminar proceedings, dissertations, teaching notes, lab manuals etc. A portion of this output gets published in peer-reviewed journals, (international and national) which might not have been accessed by members of university if they are not procured. The remaining might be for limited circulation or remain as informal communication. Hence by organising institutionally generated information accessible online for on campus and global users, the institutes can get several advantages.

* Improved 'visibility' to the intellectual out put of institutions and the results of investment.
* Interoperable repository supports the researcher's ability to search seamlessly; facilitate interdisciplinary research and discovery.
* The heterogeneous data of repositories can be mined for new thoughts with a global platform.
* The digital repositories contribute for a sound protection and preservation of institutions' intellectual property.
* It enhances access by removing access barriers, which in turn improves research capacity including the collaborative research.

* Brings together the intellectual output and the organisation which otherwise get separated in conventional publishing system.

Procedure : Bailey Jr, Charles W (2005) has listed possible activities of reference librarian in institutional repositories. However in Indian context where the libraries are being managed with minimum manpower the core procedure in developing IR can be –

* Create IR policies and procedures and pretest for their adoptability
* Design an effective and easy to use IR and user interface
* Conduct awareness and training programmes to inform publisher policies and licensing options
* Initiate digitising or gather digital collections and encourage self-archiving by members
* Nominate review committee to check the authenticity of publications
* Create metadata and repository of scholarly publications
* Make the repository operational for browse and search

Hitherto libraries acquired copyrighted documents but the IR requires handling copyrighted material with different licensing policies as listed at *RoMEO Project* (Rights MEtadata for Open archiving) (www.romeo.org). The use studies may be a regular policy to get feed back and improve the repository.

A major development has been the inter-operability framework provided by the Open Archives Initiative (OAI - www.openarchives.org). The framework, through the protocol for metadata harvesting (OAI-

PMH), enables different digital libraries to expose their metadata for purposes of automatic metadata extraction from all participating digital libraries and building various services, including a central metadata index and search system.

Requirements : Basic system design requires server platform support and web server support, along with the following requisites:

Hardware :

* ***Computer***: Intel Pentium 4, Clock Speed 3.0 Ghz;
* 1 MB L2 Cache; 800 MHz FSB
* 512 MB PC 2700 ECC DDR RAM
* 2X36 GB ULTRA 320 SCSI HDD *(OR)* 3X80 GB Serial ATA HDD
* 2X 10/100 Mbps LAN Card
* DVD – RW
* Intel Advance Graphic cards; integrated audio
* Serial and Parallel I/O Ports
* WINDOWS software
* *Scanner:* A4 Size, Flat Bed, 24 Bit Colour Scanners
* 4800x9600 dpi; USB Connectivity
* Bundled with OCR Software
* *Printer:* HP Laser jet 1020
* UPS

Software : There are a number of digital library software available as open source that include *Archimede, Arno, Cern Document Server Software, DSpace, Eprints, Fedora, GSDL, i-Tor, MyCoRe, OPUS.* However in India *DSpace, E-Prints, Greenstone and Fedora* are more in use and one should get training in the chosen software. All these have the required features of supporting all document formats, multilingual, indexing, search and retrieval, access management and security, usage management and reporting etc. The choice of software depends on the size and nature of collection, technologies and technical expertise available, nature and strength of users and the services to be offered.

Network : Intranet and Internet facilities are essential for implementation of IRs to provide internal and external access. Nowadays almost all libraries have the Internet connectivity and Intranet through campus network as they are providing access to e-consortia. The existing provisions can be utilised for connecting the digital repository to the stakeholders.

3.2 OPEN ACCESS PUBLISHING

The technological change opened up another means to use digital technologies for the creator to be the publisher. A significant amount of information is available in electronic form and attempts have been made to provide access to these through network file sharing, web, etc. Researchers and librarians have considered the impact of digital media on scholarly communication. Optimum utilisation and realisation of this development will provide wider access to scholarly communication and reduce the problems of periodical subscriptions. This has lead to the development of open access publishing.

"Open Access is the free online availability of digital content. It is best known and most feasible for peer-reviewed scientific and scholarly articles, which scholars willingly publish without expectation of payment." (Wikipedia). Open Access is a property of individual works, not necessarily journals or publishers. Thus, Open Access is online access to 'public domain' scientific literature, without access charge to readers or libraries.

In spite of the availability of millions of data as free access on the web, majority of the users in our country are not able to make optimum utilisation. Probable reasons may be lack of awareness, non-availability of net access for long hours and lack of time. Hence the librarian has to play the role of an aggregator, collect the freely available information on the web, categorise, organise and index and disseminate to the relevant individuals or groups.

There are number of directories and websites that lead to the open access books, journals, reference sources, conference proceedings etc. Some examples are:

Open Access Journals : Directory of Open Access Journals (www.doaj.org), BioMed Central (www.biomedcentral.com/browse/journals/), PubMed (http://www.ncbi.nlm.nih.gov/sites/entrez) Open J-Gate of Informatics India (http://www.openj-gate.org/index.asp);

Free e-books : World eBook Fair (http://worldebookfair.com/), Free Books (http://www.e-book.com.au), Abbaci books (http://www.abacci.com/books/default.asp), FreeTechBooks.com(http://www.freetechbooks.com/ index.php), Ebooks4free (http://www.ebooks4free.net), Free Novels Online and Free Online Cyberbooks (http://www.starry.com/free-online-novels/index.htm), Audiobooks for free(http://www.audiobooksforfree.com); Sripriya (2007) has listed the websites for ***e-reference sources***: Internet Public Library-Reference: (http://www.ipl.org/div/subject/browse/ref00.00.00), Internet Library For Librarians (http://www.itcompany.com/inforetriever/

),D-Lib-ReadyReference: (http://www.dlib.org/reference.html), Kathy Schrock's Guide for Educators - Ready Reference & Copyright (http://school.discoveryeducation.com/schrockguide/referenc.html); Purdue University Libraries - Quick Reference: (http://www.lib.purdue.edu/eresources/readyref/), LSU Libraries - Ready Reference (http://www.lib.lsu.edu/ref/readyref.html), Ready Reference (http://als.lib.wi.us/ReadyReference.html), Electronic Reference Sources (Rutgers University Libraries) (http://www.libraries.rutgers.edu/rul/rr_gateway/e_ref_shelf/e_ref_shelf.shtml). Professional websites BUBL Link, Infolibrarian, informed librarian etc. will also provide related information.

The procedure is similar to preparing a documentation list or a trend report but additionally providing full text access.

* The librarians can download articles on specific themes from the free web resources.
* Aggregate them as per theme / topic and maintain folders.
* Make them available for user's or forward them to concerned faculty, researchers / scientists.

Such value added services will facilitate the higher order user satisfaction, the ultimate aim of any library. Further such value added services enhance the image of the professional as 'reactive and creative'.

3.3. Webliography

Librarians are familiar with the compilation of bibliographies. LIS professionals at national and local level have made significant contribution for the bibliographical control of print documents. Similar control mechanism is required for electronic documents named as webliography, coined by Dr. James Frankel, 2000. The webliography presents a wide range of electronic resources related to a specific subject that are freely available on the Internet. Webliography denotes an enumerative list of hypertext links surrounding a common subject or theme following standard citation guidelines.

To develop a webliography, Dariush Alimohammadi suggested the following phases:

* Selecting the topic; it is the first and of course an important phase.
* Searching the Web; the Net should be navigated by using one of the popular Internet search tools like Google.
* Browsing and selecting the best ones among retrieved hits following the criteria for web site evaluation
* Creating a web page; some software like Microsoft FrontPage, Netscape Composer and Dream weaver can be manipulated.
* Writing an introduction; preparing a table of content to help user to navigate the subject gateway easier.
* Producing the body; Body or the main part of the webliography consists of a list of Internet sites, which have been equipped with qualitative annotations. It includes several records/web sites containing each of two to three fields like title, annotation (Critical description) and URL establishing hyperlinks;
* Preparing an index; the index should be comprised of several keywords extracted from the text of the body (annotations).

* Transforming the manipulated file, for example from Microsoft FrontPage to an HTML document in order to prepare it to be published on the World Wide Web;
* Publishing the webliography by uploading it on the server; the designer can enter meta-tags to the source code of the webliography in order to increase its searchability.

Indeed the librarians are familiar with compilation of subject bibliographies in anticipation or on demand. Hence compilation of webliography is not a big task for them, provided they have seamless Internet accessibility.

3.4. Information Literacy

Information literacy is not a new concept to LIS, rather an extension of deep-rooted user education / orientation service. Information literacy is the ability to recognise information needed and then locate, evaluate, and effectively use needed information. As it forms the basic skill to access information, the librarians need to constitute a new paradigm for libraries.

The technologies offer an opportunity to the users to have self-access to information without intermediaries. However the 2006 e-readiness rankings of The Economist rates India as 58 out of 68 countries and the Internet Use and Populations Statistics for Asia reveal that Indian users for Internet are 9.6% ranking third after 37.1% China and 19.8% of Japan. Therefore, to make use of technology based e-resources, the user has to be trained in technological skills to recognise, locate, compare, organise and synthesise information on the web.

The information literacy instruction can be taken

in phased manner to impart basic skills of information handling. The contents may include :

* skills to interact with Internet and use various net based services;
* information search tools and strategies;
* use of the available consortia, databases etc.;
* use of digital collections – open access publications, digital repositories, digital archives;
* e-publishing through wikis and web writing.

The training methods vary depending on the course structure and the level of users. There are a number of models available for imparting information literacy. The more popular strategies are the introductory course, stand-alone course, integrated with curriculum and online tutorials, each having its own benefits.

Introductory course : The libraries are following this method for a long time as initiation of freshman for an introduction to library environment. With the complexities of information environment a new approach to old concerns is necessary. Any type of library can adopt this method.

Stand-alone course: In this method the course is strictly devoted to teach information literacy skills. Information literacy component added to a discipline specific course.

Integrated with curriculum : This method is linked to academic programmes and hence suitable in academic libraries. Majority of Universities in USA adopted this method. The customised tutorials are integrated with course assignments so that the student can develop information competencies. Some are devising a separate credit course for information literacy as part of curriculum.

Online course : Online tutorials are available on the net in the use of e-mail, create web page, blogs, search strategies etc. These tutorials can be made use in combination with other methods. This method pre supposes self-learning skills and basic ICT skills.

The trainer can chose combination of the methods and can follow a blend of theory and practical sessions to impart the content. Librarians are well placed to have a key role in information literacy programmes as teachers. With implementation of information literacy programmes the librarians develop skilled users having knowledge of access to world of information.

4. CONCLUSION

The LIS profession has acquired rich experiences from the days of clay tablets to print on paper to electronic records; from the role of custodian to professional to that of digital librarian or cybrarian. Therefore the design and development of electronic and web based services has to be taken as one of the key challenges to sustain in emerging knowledge society ruled by digital documents. The librarian has to develop new products and services to connect users with required information. To achieve this target, he has to act as intermediary, enabler, aggregator, trainer, team leader, manager and so on...all in one...or else a robot may take his place.

REFERENCES

1. Alimohammadi, Dariush (2004). Designing Webliographies in an Effective and Simple Manner: A Step by Step Process. *Webology,* 1(1). Available at *http://www.webology.ir/2004/v1n1/a2.html*
2. Asia Internet Usage and World Stats (2007). Internet World

Stats - Usage and Population Statistics. Available at http://www.internetworldstats.com/stats3.htm#asia. (Accessed on 19-09-2007)

3. Bailey, Charles W., Jr.(2005). The Role of Reference Librarians in Institutional Repositories. *Reference Services Review,* 33 (3), pp. 259-267.

4. Smith, MacKanzie (2004). Libraries in the Lead: Institutional Repository Phenomenon. Available at http://www.vala.org.au/vala2004/2004pdfs/69Smith.PDF. (Accessed on 15-09-2007)

5. Sripriya, S. Ready Reference Websites. Posted on *LIS FORUM,* Dt 09-09-07.

6. The Economist (2006). The 2006 e-readiness rankings - a White Paper from The Economist Intelligence Unit. Available at http://graphics.eiu.com/files/ad_pdfs/2006 Ereadiness_Ranking_WP.pdf (Accessed on 14-11-2006)

26
Biometric Technology for Network Security

Rekha Rani Varghese

ABSTRACT

In information technology, biometrics refers to technologies that measure and analyse human body characteristics, such as fingerprints, eye retinas and irises, voice patterns, facial patterns and hand measurements, for authentication purposes. Biometric Authentication has been heralded as the future of security systems, a verification system that not only drastically reduces the risks of the systems security being compromised but also eliminates the need for much of the traditional security overhead. The most obvious use of biometrics for network security is for secure workstation logons for a workstation connected to a network. The use of biometrics in networks as an authentication feature is gaining momentum. However, the widespread use and acceptance of biometrics is, at this current time, still in its babyhood. The effectiveness of a biometric authentication system is for the most part dependant on the requirements of the network and the chosen biometric. However, as technology improves and costs come down we may well see a change in this as demand for more secure networks increases.

1. INTRODUCTION

Biometrics is becoming an interesting topic now in regards to computer and network security; however the ideas of biometrics have been around for many years. Possibly the first known example of biometrics in practice was a form of finger printing being used in China in the 14th century. With regard to computer networks, the network security relies on one of three approaches for identification - what you have, what you know or who you are. Previous forms of identifiers relied on what you have or what you know or both. Personal Identification Numbers (PINs) were one of the first methods used for identification. There are also methods that involve passwords and physical tokens e.g. smart cards. There are a number of problems associated with this kind of identification. People forget passwords, lose tokens, reuse passwords, write them down, tokens can get stolen. The recognition of the above does not mean the identification of the person providing it - they could be presented by anybody. Here comes the importance of Biometric Technology. Biometric security offers a different method of authentication by using something that is far more unique than a password – ourselves. Biometric recognition technologies are finding increasing use in a wide range of business process applications, libraries and information centers wherever the accurate identification or verification of an individual is essential to security, access, asset protection or personnel tracking.

2. WHAT IS BIOMETRICS

The terms “Biometrics” and “Biometry” have been

used since early in the 20th century to refer to the field of development of statistical and mathematical methods applicable to data analysis problems in the biological sciences. Biometrics may be defined as "the science and technology of measuring and analysing biological data." In information technology, biometrics refers to technologies that measure and analyse human body characteristics, such as fingerprints, eye retinas and irises, voice patterns, facial patterns and hand measurements, for authentication purposes. Authentication by biometric verification is becoming increasingly common in corporate and public security systems, consumer electronics and point of sale (POS) applications. Identification requires comparing an individual's biometric templates with a set of many stored profiles and finding the best match. In contrast, authentication involves a one-to-one matching of an individual's live reading and his or her stored profile. The latter case asks the question "Is this person who he or she claims to be?" In addition to security, the driving force behind biometric verification has been convenience.

With regard to technology, Biometrics is the term given to the use of biological traits or behavioural characteristics to identify an individual. Biometric identification uses some unique physiological or behavioural characteristic, not shared by any other individual, to positively identify an individual. In computer security, biometrics refers to authentication techniques that rely on measurable physical characteristics that can be automatically checked. A biometric system is essentially a pattern recognition system enabling identification by means of a UNIQUE physical or behavioural characteristic to unequivocally link an individual to an action or transaction.

Biometrics unequivocally link an individual to an action or transaction while offering the benefits of preventing use of ID tokens by unauthorised users, providing proof against loss or theft, convenience of use, high accuracy, low cost and secure audit control. The chief virtue of biometric authenticators is that they are intrinsically linked to an individual, and are therefore hard to fake. In Libraries an authentication token such as a card can be borrowed, lost, or stolen. An individual can easily compromise a knowledge-based authenticator by passing this knowledge to another person or being observed while entering it. Anyone who obtains an authentication token or a knowledge-based authenticator can fool the system into believing that he or she is the authentic user. In contrast, biometric authentication systems can be 'spoofed' only with great difficulty. Biometrics provide a convenient additional level of security to current methods of verification as provided by the use of PINs or passwords in conjunction with identification devices typified by ID cards (in various formats), encryption keys and digital signature.

3. BIOMETRICS AND COMPUTER SECURITY

Passwords are easily broken. Security cards can be lost or stolen. What other options do we have? The answer might be Biometrics. With the advent of e-commerce brings increased pressure on IT managers to provide partners and customers with means of identification to access corporate networks. This results in a deluge of passwords and means of access, which are often forgotten, misused or lost. With the increased population accessing these networks the risk of attacks on the networks is increased. Companies are turning to Biometric Systems to bring tighter security to their computer networks. This security offers increased confidence levels for users of the network, providing the system is correctly implemented and utilised. The Network can be exploited fully without fear of a security breach. Biometric secure Systems on the web would make the popular targets of banking data, business intelligence, credit card numbers, medical information and other personal data transactions on the web more secure and thus increase the population's confidence in using these methods, increasing e-commerce confidence and thus enabling it to reach its full potential.

The fundamental argument for using biometrics for network authentication is the increase in security while eliminating the extras such as PIN, passwords and smart cards, which can get into the wrong hands and do a lot of damage to a network, which is then not able to run at its full capacity until the security breach has been amended. In the workplace passwords and logins are often passed between co-workers, written down for convenience or reused multiple times for different networks. Biometric logins would make it unfeasible for anyone, other than the intended login, to login to the network. So for every worker, if they were to use the network an account must be set up for them. The workers cannot forget their password, which may be one of several passwords, because their password into the system is a physiological trait.

The most obvious use of biometrics for network security is for secure workstation logons for a workstation connected to a network. Each workstation requires some software support for biometric identification of the user as well as, depending on the biometric being used, some hardware device. The cost of hardware devices is one thing that may lead to the widespread use of voice biometric security identification, especially among companies and organisations on a low budget. Hardware device such as computer mice with built in thumbprint readers would be the next step up. These devices would be more expensive to implement on several computers, as each machine would require its own hardware device.

One way that biometrically verified logons would be implemented is using a centralised system (particularly using voice biometrics). Such a system would be ideal for implementing secure remote logons by mobile users. Remote network access enables tele-working, which has been promised by the 'e' community for a long time, especially with the arrival of broadband access from the home. It is also important for field employees who travel all over for the company, yet need access to company resources. Biometric identification used along with a secure connection (a problem that is entirely separate to that of Biometrics) to the network makes this once vulnerable aspect of networking more secure. A host of networking associated companies has recently added biometric authentication features to their products. Companies such as Novell, Baltimore Technologies are some of the first to take advantage of biometric scheme. Keyware Technologies LBV (Layered Biometrics Verification) Internet Toolkit will allow software providers to add biometric voice and fingerprint authentication to traditional security applications that protect Internet servers. Keyware is targeting companies who deal with e-commerce applications requiring high levels of security. Keyware's LBV software can integrate several biometric identification features into an application, and is compatible with Microsoft Internet Explorer 4.01 and higher and with Microsoft's Information Server. The layered security levels can provide most value for companies needing high levels of security.

Biometric Authentication has been heralded as the future of security systems, a verification system that not only drastically reduces the risks of the systems security being compromised but also eliminates the need for much of the traditional security overhead. In recent years biometric authentication systems have become more prolific as numerous manufacturers of biometric sensing devices and middle-ware providers have entered the market. Having met with particular success in restricting physical access in high-security environments it is curious to note that this success has not been echoed where network authentication is concerned

4. TYPES OF BIOMETRIC ENCRYPTION

All biometric devices work by matching an individual's features to the one recorded in the device's memory. This one-to-one comparison mode of operation is known as verification of identity of the "verify" operational mode. The user must identify him/herself to the device by way of a personal number or card so that his or her identity may also be corroborated by the device. The bio identifier technologies that register and compare these characteristics may be further divided into three categories: Behavioral Traits, Topological Traits and Discrete Traits.

Behavioural Traits are habituated activities which a person does in a regular, learned or otherwise consistent manner. Examples are handwriting, keyboard dynamics and voice verification. Topological Traits are unique, superficial, physiological characteristics which remain reasonably stable enough throughout an individual's lifetime to serve as bio-identifiers. Among these are fingerprints, hand geometry and facial features. Discrete Traits are characteristics which are neither behavioural nor topological. Discrete traits may not be acquired without the knowledge and consent of users nor be used to track persons. Retinal vasculature is an example of a discrete trait.

5. MAJOR ISSUES REGARDING BIOMETRIC IDENTIFICATION

Biometric user authentication techniques require a user to present identifying information based on an unchangeable personal feature. There are several practical problems associated with biometrics. Some of these technologies are not yet on the market. In addition, not all marketed technologies are equally effective, and it is often hard to determine which technique is the most suitable for a given application since no two vendors use the same reference specifications. Also, the ability of different technologies to withstand environmental hazards such as dirt and vandalism over long periods of time has not been determined. Cost is another practical issue. Appropriate hardware and software for registering and evaluating biometric data must be purchased and installed in every system. Users must be enrolled individually; perhaps at a substantial labour cost. Another problem is that not every biometric authentication technique may be completely spoof-proof. If biometric data are stolen or sold, it may be possible to use them to execute a successful masquerade. A perpetrator might be able to build spoofing devices, such as fake hands for a hand geometry reader or a synthetic speech generator that matches a particular voice profile. More realistically, a skilled hacker might be able to feed a biometric digital signal directly into a system, circumventing the normal 'reading' process entirely. This problem is especially serious because of the intrinsic linkage between individuals and their biometric authenticators.

6. CONCLUSION

Though the field is still in its infancy, many people believe that biometrics will play a critical role in future computers, and especially in electronic commerce. Personal computers of the future might include a fingerprint scanner where you could place your index finger. The computer would analyse your fingerprint to determine who you are and, based on your identity, authorise you different levels of access. The use of biometrics in networks as an authentication feature is gaining momentum. However the widespread use and acceptance of biometrics is, at this current time, still in its babyhood. The effectiveness of a biometric authentication system is for the most part dependant on the requirements of the network and the chosen biometric. However as technology improves and costs come down we may well see a change in this as demand for more secure networks increases. An indication of what may be to come may be found in Microsoft's recent announcement that they are to include biometric authentication software with forthcoming releases.

REFERENCES

1. Biometrics: Definition. Available at http :// searchsecurity.techtarget.com/sDefinition/0,,sid14_gci211666,00.html (Accessed December 22nd 2006)
2. Biometrics. Available at http://www.webopedia.com/TERM/B/biometrics.html. (Accessed January 2nd 2007)
3. Biometrics. Available at http://www.biometrics.org (Accessed on January 4th 2007)

4. What is biometrics? Security Industry Association. Available at http://www.siaonline.org/groups/biometrics_whatis.cfm (Accessed January 3rd 2007)

5. What is Biometric Technology? Available at www.axbiometrics.com/whatbiometric.htm (Accessed December 22nd 2006

27
Digital Library Security & Competencies of Library Professionals

Shilpi Verma
K. L. Mahawar
Rekha Verma

ABSTRACT

In today's modern world libraries are in transition phase from traditional to digital library. Digital library security techniques such as cryptography, Digital signatures, Firewalls, Digital watermarking, Steganography are used for secure and effective distribution of digital assets to the end users. Protection of information resource is as necessary as any other resource of organisation. Library professional's competencies are also changing from document management to e-sources management.

1. INTRODUCTION

In today's dynamic environment, libraries are becoming intermediaries, rather than storehouse of information, as we have entered in the information age. We are using information from several years, but now people have started recognising the value of information. Now a days information is stored in digitised forms in the libraries and it is accessible through networks.

2. DIGITAL LIBRARY

Digital library is defined as "A focused collection of digital objects, including text, video, audio, along with methods for access and retrieval, and for selection, organisation, and maintenance of the collection." (Ian Witten and David Bainbridge).

As we can say Digital library has a collection of texts, documents, images, sound, software, etc. collected for the specified information needs of the users. Digital library contributed greatly to the development of IT. It helps in information access techniques that can enable efficient searches of large distributed information repositories, and more efficient processing and retrieval of information. Digital imaging technologies create an entirely new form of information dissemination. It involves transforming the very concept of format rather than creating a document, photograph or map on a different medium. Their importance from the educational, social and economic point of view is already evident.

Digital library security and data protection is very necessary. Like on the Internet security it is needed to prevent unauthorized changes to your web sites. Security administrators face the risk that an attacker will be able to break into the network. There must be a *secure communication link* for data transmission between interconnected host computer systems of the network. Data security procedures are essential for preservation and *integrity* of the resource by preventing alteration or loss. It is important to note that not all digital resources will require identical levels of security.

Likewise, both publisher and reader will require that the content is authentic, i.e. that is has been really published by the given publisher, and that it is intact, i.e. that nobody has added to or deleted from the package. To be secure from eavesdroppers, the content never should be transmitted and stored in a readable format. It is often forgotten, but these authenticity and integrity requirements are not only applicable to the content, but also to a contract offer which may accompany the content and which states the terms and conditions under which a reader may use the content. The publisher may want to prove that the reader has accepted the terms, and the reader may want to have a signed copy of what he or is entitled to do.

A variety of tools is available to help the Librarian to implement the security plan, including encryption tools, route and packets filtering and firewalls. Every library must have their own security plans and policies. The internal security plans should be distributed to everyone who uses the facilities, with written guidance for library employees on the proper use of passwords.

There must be a proper *authentication* before a user can access a terminal, an online application, or the network environment. Unauthorized use should deactivate or lock a terminal. Digital content management requires technologies for all these aspects:

* Asserting intellectual property rights;
* Protecting intellectual property;
* Managing the intellectual property value chain;
* Efficient storage and retrieval of digital assets;

* Verifying the source of the assets (authentication)
* Secure distribution of digital assets to end users;
* Effective distribution of digital assets to end users.

For protection of intellectual property and authentication, secure distribution of digital assets, several methods of security are used:

3. SECURITY TECHNIQUES

A. Cryptography : Cryptography is the art of secret writing. The basic service provided by cryptography is the ability to send information between participants in a way that prevents others from reading it. It is a technique of encoding and decoding message, so that they are not understood by anybody except the sender and the intended receiver. The sender and recipient of the message decide on an encoding and decoding scheme and use it for communication. This process is completed by Encryption and Decryption. Encryption is the translation of data into a secret code, a method of scrambling information. The original text is called as plaintext. When it is encrypted, it is called **Cipher text.** It's the most effective security device because you must have a specific key to unlock the data. Any digital data can be encrypted included e-mail messages, telephone calls, movies, pictures and computer files.

Based on the number of keys used for encryption and decryption, Cryptography can be divided into two categories.

(i) Symmetric (Secret Key) Encryption

(ii) Asymmetric (Public Key) Encryption

(i) Symmetric (Secret Key) Encryption : Here the sender uses the secret key (a large binary number) algorithm to mathematically encrypt the communication and the recipient uses the same key to decrypt it. Both the parties must agree upon the key before any transmission begins, and nobody else should know about it. Secret key encryption is relatively fast and small.

(ii) Asymmetric (Public Key) Encryption : Public Key cryptography uses a public key and a private key that are mathematically tied together. In this type of Cryptography two different keys (called as a key pair) are used. Using this method a message is encrypted with a public key, and the private key is used to decrypt the same message. No other key can decrypt the message not even the first original key. In this scheme every communicating party needs just a key pair for communicating with any number of other communicating parties. Before the invention of, Public key Cryptography it was virtually impossible to provide key management to large scale networks. Public key encryption however is bulky and slow, it does not easily encrypt a file once for a number of different people.

B. Digital Signatures : Digital signature is a code that can be attached to an electronically transmitted message that uniquely identifies the sender. Just we sign a check, we can sign a computer-generated document or message. The purpose of Digital Signature is to guarantee that the individual sending the message really is who he or she claims to be. Other important feature supported by digital signature is non-repudiation. i.e. a sender can not refuse having sent a message. Adding a signature to a message validates the integrity of the message. It confirms that the message has not been altered since you signed it because any change to the message after you sign will invalidate the signature.

C. Firewalls : A Firewall means that sits between your internet network and the rest of the network and attempts to prevent bad things from happening without preventing good things from happening. It is a system or group of systems that enforces an access control policy between two networks. It can be compared with a sentry standing outside an important person's house. This sentry usually keeps an eye on and physically checks every person that enters into or comes out of the house. It can be divided into 2 types:

1. Packet filter
2. Application Gateways

Packet filter : Packet Filter applies a set of rules to each packet and based on the outcome, decides to either forward or discard the packet. If packet is not acceptable, it is dropped at the firewall.

Application Gateways : Another way to protect your vulnerable network is by use of an application level gateway. It is also called as a proxy server. This is because it acts like a proxy and decides about the flow of application level traffic. The gateway could have two network adaptors and act as a router, but more often it is placed between two packet-filtering firewalls. A proxy firewall makes it more difficult for hackers on the outside to exploit vulnerabilities on systems inside the firewall.

D. Digital Watermarking : watermarking, a pattern of bits inserted into a digital image, audio or video file that identifies the file's copyright information (author, rights, etc.).Unlike printed watermarks, which are intended to be somewhat visible, digital watermarks are designed to be completely invisible, or in the case of audio clips, inaudible. Moreover, the actual bits representing the watermark must be scattered throughout the file in such a way that they cannot be identified and manipulated. And finally, the digital watermark must be robust enough so that it can withstand normal changes to the file, such as reductions from lossy compression algorithms. This ownership information may take one of two forms: the watermark may identify the originator of the material, or it may identify the recipient (the end-user or library) to whom the material was given.

E. Steganography : Steganography is the practice of hiding message in such a manner that its very existence is concealed. This is done by embedding the message in such a manner that its very existence is concealed, such as document, image, sound recording, or video. Anyone knowing that the medium contains a secret code can readily extract the message, assuming the method of encoding is known. For everyone else, the message will be completely invisible.

Digital Security supports the mission of the organization and it is an integral element of sound management. Protecting information resource can be as important to a library as protecting other resources such as money, physical assets, and employees. Digital security should be cost effective .The resource spent on security should be appropriate and proportionate to the value of and degree of reliance on the information systems being protected.

4. COMPETENCIES REQUIRED

The change in library and information centers demand a significant change in the role of library professionals, the role will have to be redefined.

Corrall, S. and Brewerton, A. proposed a

professional competence model, which consists of six parts that include (1) generic personal skills (communication, problem-solving, etc.), (2) professional/specialist information skills (collection development and management, knowledge organisation, etc.), (3) IT skills, (4) business and management skills (accounting, budgeting and costing, marketing, etc.), (5) organisational knowledge and subject understanding (culture and climate, terminology of the field, etc.), and (6) personal work behavior (achievement/results orientation, leadership/ initiative, strategic perspective, etc.)

Some of the competencies required by library professionals can be stated as follows:

* Ability to provide literature search service on e-resources,
* Ability to search efficiently and effectively and save results and download in print or digital media,
* Ability to select, acquire, process, use and shelve e-sources,
* Knowledge of human resource management, time management, financial management, system design & analysis and statistical databases,
* Knowledge of search engines, web security techniques and telecommunication networks and channels,
* Marketing skills, liaison and negotiating skills,
* Ability to convey the effect of synergistic approach to higher authority through constant flow of information.

Digital security is constrained by societal factors. Security can enhance privacy and the free flow of information by protecting the confidentiality, integrity, and the availability of information. It requires a comprehensive and integrated approach. Digital security responsibilities and accountability should be made explicit. The Library professional's role is changing from custodian to navigator of information. The responsibilities of librarians have become crucial. The universities, the national libraries, the professional societies and international organisations have the responsibility to develop and organise courses, workshops, seminars, conferences etc. to ensure that librarian understand and applies appropriate technique of today and tomorrow, instead of rely on the traditional method of past.

REFERENCES

1. Curtin, Foley, Sen and Morin (1999). Information Technology: the Breaking Wave. New Delhi: Tata McGraw Hill
2. Denning, D. (1999). Information Warfare Security. Singapore: Addison Wesley
3. Haykin, Simon (2001). Communication Systems. Singapore: John Wiley & Sons
4. Kaufman, Perlman and Speciner (2003). Network Security. Delhi: Pearson Education
5. Raina, Gupta, and Gaur (2005). Library Management: Trends and Opportunities. New Delhi: Excel Books
6. Shim, Qureshi and Siegel (2001). "The International Handbook of Computer Security". New Delhi: Harnandi Publishers & Distributors
7. Sheila Corrall, Antony Brewerton (1999). The New Professional's Handbook: Your Guide to Information Service Management. London: Library Association Publishing, p.289 & 291.
8. Digital Libraries: Digital Asset Management. Available at www.ima.umn.edu/multimedia/winter/m6.html
9. Safeguarding Digital Library Contents and Users. Available at www.dlib.org/dlib/december97/ibm/121otspiech.html.
10. Going Digital: Issues in Digitization for Public Libraries. Available at www.ukoln.ac.uk/public/earl/issuepapers/digitisation.h tml.
11. ERCIM News. Available at www.ercim.org/publication/ercim_news/enw27/introdl .html.

28
Competencies of Library & Information Professionals in the Digital Age

K. P. Vijayakumar

ABSTRACT

This paper highlights the changes in the information environment and its impact on all sectors, particularly, institutions of higher education and research centres. Sustantiating on this focal point, it emphasises that the library and information professionals have a moral responsibility to rise to the occasion and equip themselves to play the role of skilful communicators, net navigators, IT gatekeepers, information brokers, information consultants and educators.

1. INTRODUCTION

Traditionally, university libraries have been perceived as the 'heart of the university' where scholarly resources are acquired, organised and preserved and where learning and research take place. These traditional library functions have not changed or diminished but the role of libraries has expanded to a large extent in the recent years to accommodate not only print collections but on-site services also. As a result, libraries are in the midst of refocusing their fundamental programmatic mission. Activities once regarded as fundamental to library operations are being replaced by new services and new ways of providing services to achieve greater efficiency. These changes make it obligatory on the part of library management to contemplate on changes in the quantity, qualification and skills of their staff.

The application of information technology (IT) has played a key role in focusing attention on manpower. Over the years, some people, especially university administrators assumed that automation would reduce the overall cost of library operations but this has not been the case. Automation and the proliferation of IT as well as new technologies for accessing and acquiring information have produced significant changes in staffing patterns and job assignments. It will continue to be a major catalyst for more changes in the future. Implementation of automation systems has provided a strong incentive for libraries to embark on staffing studies to determine a more appropriate staff configuration and their qualification and skills.

2. CHANGES IN THE HIGHER EDUCATION SECTOR

Deekle and de Klerk have summarised the emerging trends in higher education which have major implications for academic libraries.[1] More significant ones are the following:

* Advances in telecommunications and computer technology.
* Changes in curricula which recognise the interrelationship of academic disciplines.

* Increases in user demand for prompt and responsive information service.
* A frustrating sense of information overloads for both faculty and student clientele.
* A corresponding need for greater user discretion and selectivity amid the glut of information.
* Funding and spatial constraints which limit acquisitions, storage and service options.
* A need for effective administrative responsiveness toward fund raising and consortia requirements, and
* The management issues associated with changing organisational structures and staffing in response to changing needs of users.

The reactions of the authors to these changing trends have been different. Thompson predicted the end of academic libraries as far back as 1982.[2] But the fact remains that much of what he has predicted have not come true. Wilson only suggested a redesigning of the university libraries in the context of the changed parameter.[3] Brophy attempted to portray a generic model for the library which combines the traditional, hybrid and electronic in one and the same so as to serve 'the common mission' to enable users to get access to whatever information they need.[4] Ackeroyd, on the other hand, is quite clear in his vision of the future academic libraries.[5] He envisions that:

* Libraries will become functions rather than places.
* Libraries will become user-focused rather than collection-centred.

* Information will become cheap, but of questionable quality.
* Users will be more distributed, yet we will need to know more about them.
* Libraries will add value to information to provide more appropriate resources.
* The core processes of organising information will diversify into creating user-focused, personalised systems addressing all kinds of information.
* Libraries will comprise a mixture of professionals with changing boundaries and alliances.
* Routine work will be shed in the pursuit of improving the student experience.

It is a fact that staff responsibilities have dramatically changed over the past few decades. Association of Research Libraries (ARL) statistics indicates that the greatest increase in professional hiring over the last few decades involves 'functional specialists' defined by ARL as "...media specialists, or experts in management fields such as personnel, fiscal matters, systems, preservation etc." Only 55 percent of the functional specialists possess that badge of professional librarianship, the MLS degree.[6] Steele and Guha pose a number of questions as to the new role of librarians in the changing information scenario. "Are we leaders, supporters, participants, supplicants or mere spectators in the inexorable process of globalisation? Are librarians to be archival museum keepers, Internet subject facilitators, web masters, metadata creators, virtual university content providers, electronic information entrepreneurs?"[7] Then they try to provide the answers also. In the information society of the future the ability to manage knowledge in different ways is essential. The traditional skills of librarianship will either be transformed and/or supplemented. Employees will be involved in a life-long learning process; be flexible to work in a variety of projects and areas; be able to process and apply information to the satisfaction of their user communities; and be able to market information and have a high level of expertise in appropriate information technologies. A shift in paradigm of working styles, meshing traditional library approaches to information provision, will occur.

Some tasks that are to be taken up in libraries due to the changing information scene are related to the traditional library departments, but some are new. Roitberg lists the following jobs as some of the daunting tasks library professionals are forced to take up now.[8]

* Licensing electronic journals is related to the periodicals section which is a labour intensive and time-consuming job;
* Linking the electronic journals to the library homepage;
* Imparting reader's services by electronic means;
* Constant checking of new journals and e-journal collections as to their contents, format and method of linking;
* Conducting user education as to the use of new services and facilities;
* Maintaining and updating of library homepage which requires a lot of effort;
* Dealing constantly with new missions, new technologies, to partners to compete with; and

* Constant pressure to proceed and not to be left behind.

3. COMPETENCES

Restructuring is leading many libraries to rethink individual job qualifications and other requirements. Such restructuring of the libraries and the library manpower is likely to lead many of the academic libraries to have an expanded concept of manpower. Thus, there may be a more diverse and perhaps larger workforce in terms of number and type of professionals where the jobs and qualifications are rethought on a regular basis. It is high time that Indian libraries thought of restructuring the workforce in the light of the induction of new technologies.

Developed countries started thinking of the competencies to be possessed by various professionals in the 21st century way back in 1990s.The Special Libraries Association (SLA) in 1996 produced a document identifying the competencies required by professionals in the next century.[9] They have divided the competencies into two categories — professional competencies and personal competencies.

The first category is related to the professionals' knowledge of the information resources, information technology, management and research and the ability to apply these areas of knowledge for the successful performance of the duties and responsibilities. The second category i.e. personal competencies refer to the set of skills, attitudes and values that enable them to function efficiently and effectively. These include good communication skills, life-long learning skills, skills for value addition, adaptability and ability to survive in the changing scenario. The document contains details of the skills mentioned.

Nick Moore divides the information professionals into three categories and outlines their skills and roles.[10] The three categories according to him are:

a. **Creators :** those who design and develop products and services, e.g., content developers

b. **Communicators :** those who are adept in identifying, locating, analysing and interpreting information like subject specialists, and

c. **Consolidators :** those who select, analyse and synthesise information like researchers.

The Library and information Commission of UK assigns more roles for the information professionals in the 21st century.[11] They are Net navigator, IT gatekeeper, Information Consultant, Information Manager, Knowledge Management Specialist etc. The skills or competencies expected of the professionals are quite obvious from the roles given tom them.

In order to be a knowledge management specialist, a professional has to play a number of roles and therefore has to be multi-faceted. The roles are that of (1) Business professional (2) Technology manager (3) Content organiser (4) Communicator and (4) Change agent (5) Entrepreneur and (6) Team player.[12] Accordingly various commentators have provided a checklist of the skills to be possessed by professionals. At the same time, they also stress the point that the skills acquired by the professionals have to be complemented by personal qualities and abilities.

It is a fact that we are very slow to respond to the changes taking place in the information scenario as is evidenced by the lack of literature in the area. In this backdrop the author has attempted a survey of the basic qualifications possessed by the university library professionals in Kerala and the additional skills acquired afterwards by attending various training programmes.

4. QUALIFICATION AND SKILLS OF LIS PROFESSIONALS IN UNIVERSITY LIBRARIES

The study of the qualifications and additional skills acquired by the professionals covered the entire professional staff of the five major university library systems in the state viz. Kerala University Library (KUL), Calicut University Library (CUL), Cochin University of Science and Technology Library (CUSATL), M G University Library (MGUL) and Kerala Agricultural University Library (KAUL). The library systems consist of the central library, the departmental libraries, the study centre libraries and the constituent colleges, if any.

4.1. General qualification

The basic qualification prescribed for the entry level post i.e. the post of Library Assistant / Professional Assistant Grade 2 in all the university libraries in Kerala is a basic degree in any discipline with degree in Library and Information Science.

While about 60 percent of the professionals are post-graduates, more than four percent possess higher qualifications like M. Phil. or Ph. D. degree in subjects other than Library and Information Science.

4.2 Professional qualification

The analysis of professional qualification shows that while more than 76 percent possess post graduate degree or higher qualifications in LIS, only a little more than 23 percent have bachelors degree which is the entry level qualification prescribed by the universities as is evident from Table 2 :

Table 1. General qualification of the professionals

Qualification	*Name of the University*					*Total*
	KUL	*CUL*	*CUSATL*	*MGUL*	*KAUL*	
Graduation	19(23.17%)	18(42.86%)	18(52.94%)	14(37.84%)	4(30.77%)	73(35.10%)
Post-graduation	59(71.95%)	23(54.76%)	14(41.18%)	21(56.76%)	9(69.23%)	126(60.58%)
M. Phil.	3(3.66%)	—	1(2.94%)	2(5.41%)	—	6(2.88%)
Ph. D.	1(1.22%)	1(2.30%)	1(2.94%)	—	—	3(1.44%)
Total	**82(100%)**	**42(100%)**	**34(100%)**	**37(100%)**	**13(100%)**	**208(100%)**

Table 2. Professional Qualification of the Staff

Professional Qualification	*Name of the University*					*Total*
	KUL	***CUL***	***CUSATL***	***MGUL***	***KAUL***	
BLISc	22(26.83%)	7(16.67%)	8(23.53%)	9(24.33%)	3(23.08%)	49(23.56%)
MLISc	59(71.95%)	30(71.43%)	24(70.59%)	27(72.97%)	7(53.84%)	147(70.67%)
M.Phil./Ph. D	1(1.22%)	5(11.9%)	2(5.88%)	1(2.7%)	3(23. 08%)	12(5.77%)
Total	**82(100%)**	**42(100%)**	**34(100%)**	**37(100%)**	**13(100%)**	**208(100%)**

It is quite interesting to note that the percentage of those who possess BLISc degree alone remains more or less the same in all universities, except Calicut University. The percentage of those who possess M. Phil. or Ph.D. is more in Agricultural University, followed by Calicut. Further analysis shows that in Calicut out of the five professionals with higher qualifications, four are with doctorates and one with M. Phil. This has further led to the mode of study resorted to for taking professional degrees.

While the percentage of staff with bachelor's degree through distance education mode is only 3.85, their corresponding figure with master's degree through this mode is 52.83. This quite natural because those who are employed prefer distance mode to regular classes for acquiring higher qualifications.

4.3. Additional qualifications of the staff

An attempt to study the additional qualifications or skills acquired by the staff members through programmes of more than one month duration revealed that many people have tried to update their knowledge and sharpen their skill by attending various means. The results are given in Table 3.

Table 3. Additional qualifications/skills acquired by the staff

Sl. No.	*Programme*	*Frequency*
1	Computer basics	14 (6.73%)
2	Database management	3 (1.44%)
3	DCA/PGDCA/PGDIT	12 (5.77%)
4	Hardware/Networking	3 (1.44%)
5	Library automation	8 (3.85%)

6	Programming languages	6 (2.88%)
7	Software Packages	24 (11.54 %)
8	Others	6 (2.88%)
	Total	76 (36.54 %)
	Missing System	132 (63.46%)
	Total	**208 (100%)**

Only 36.54 percent of the staff has undergone any formal training programme of more than one month duration. Of these, the largest share is for software packages followed by training programmes concerned with computer basics. The number of persons who have undergone PGDCA/DCA/PGDIT courses is 12 (5.8 %). But the fact remains that more than 63 percent of the professionals have not attended any programme of such duration, except the refresher courses and orientation programmes of Academic Staff Colleges which are general in nature and mandatory for those who belong to the UGC stream.

It can be seen that nobody has gone for any short term training or for formal qualification in Management despite the fact that university libraries are emerging as big institutions in terms of the 3 Ms – men, money and materials. In other words, those who have tried to acquire additional qualifications or skills have done so only in the IT related areas and nothing else. On the other hand, the developments in the information scenario demands development of skills in communication – both oral and written —, negotiation, problem-solving methodologies, project and programme management, management of the institution and management of the self (time management, continuous professional development etc.) in addition to IT understanding. Nobody seems to care about such things in Kerala.

The experience in UK and USA is quite different. There the information professionals have got a penchant for MBA programmes in addition to the professional qualifications. According to Corral and Brewerton, such programmes have the added benefit of exposure to perspectives and experiences beyond the LIS sector while usually providing opportunities through practical assignments for participants to apply general management theories and techniques to their own work situation.[13] The popularity of more specialized Masters Degree programmes like M.Sc. in Human Resource Management, Electronic Information Management, Information Systems etc. in UK bear testimony to this fact. The latest in the list is Knowledge Management. Right here in India, the position in British Libraries is a pointer to the upcoming scenario. There a degree in Management is considered to be superior to a degree in Library and Information Science, if the selection process in them is taken as an indication.

Another trend that is catching up at the global level is mentoring. It is the process of getting trained under the close supervision and guidance of an expert senior. This practice is very much there in all established professions like Medicine, Engineering, Law, Accountancy, Company Secretaryship etc. There is a one-to-one relationship between the mentor and the learner. Unfortunately, this method is conspicuous by its absence in LIS profession either as part of the curriculum or as internship. It is very much possible once the Masters Degree course is converted to two year semesterized programme. Now that M. Phil. courses in LIS are becoming quite common in universities, the practice of submitting dissertations in partial fulfillment of the MLIS programme can be done away with and the internship or mentoring programme introduced for a fixed period, say one month or so.

5. CONCLUSION

Information Literacy (IL), which emphasizes life-long learning, has emerged as buzzword of the century. Library and Information Science professionals have to play a major in imparting IL programmes. This can be successfully done only if the professionals are bent on updating themselves. In absence of managerial skills they are likely to be sidelined and the governance of at least a few mammoth Library and Information Centres would be in the hands of other professionals as was the case by the turn of the 20th century. If the recurrence of the old story is to be prevented, librarians have a moral responsibility to rise to the occasion and equip themselves to play the role of skilful communicators, net navigators, IT gatekeepers, information brokers, information consultants and educators.

REFERENCES

1. Deekle, Peter V. and De Klerk, Ann (2002). Perceptions of Library Leadership in a Time of Change. *In:* Personnel Management in Library and Information Science / edited by M. A. Khan. New Delhi: Cosmo Publications, pp. 52 - 73.
2. Thompson, James (1982). The End of Libraries. London: Clive Bingley, p. 66.
3. Wilson, W. (1998). Redesigning the University Library in the Digital Age. *Journal of Documentation,* 54 (1), pp. 15 — 27.
4. Brophy, P. (2000). Towards a Generic Model of Information and Library Services in the Information Age. *Journal of Documentation,* 56 (2), pp. 161-184.
5. Akeroyd, John (2001). The Future of Academic Libraries. *Aslib Proceedings,* 53 (3) March, pp. 79-84.
6. Wilder, Stanley (2002). New Hires in Research Libraries, Demographic Trends and Hiring Problems. 221 ARL

Bimonthly Report, April. Available at http://arl.org/newsltr/221/newhires.htm (Accessed on 21-10-2005)

7. Steele, Colin and Guha, Mechthild. Staffing the Digital library in the 21st Century. Available at http://www. staff-lhtm. (Accessed on 30-11-2005)

8. Roitberg, Nurit (2000). The Influence of Electronic Library on Library Management: a Technological University Library Experience. *In:* Proceedings of the 66th IFLA Council and General Conference, Jerusalem, Israel, 13—18 August 2000. Available at http://www.ifla.org/IV/ifla66/papers/050-132e.htm (Accessed on 224-2006)

9. Special Libraries Association. Competencies for Special Librarians of the special Library, 1996. Available at http://www.sla.org/professional/competency.html (Accessed on 15-3-2007)

10. Moore, Nick (1996). Creators, Communicators and Consolidators: the New Information Professional. *Managing Information,* 3 (6), pp. 24-25.

11. Library and Information Commission (1998). Building the New Library Network: a Report to Government. Library and Information Commission, 235-237.

12. Corrall, Sheila and Brewerton, Antony (1999). The New Professional's Handbook. London: Library Association, p. 272.

13. Ibid, p. 274

29

Scholarly Communication in the Networked Environment Problems and Prospects

V. Vimalkumar

ABSTRACT

This article gives an over view of how popularity of World Wide Web and open access concepts challenge the existence of traditional scholarly communication. New publishing outlets such as blogs, wiki & podcasting facilitate agile communication channels for scholarly communication. Open access concepts in scholarly communication enable free access of knowledge. Research community and information professionals hope that scholarly communication through Internetmakes available wider access of knowledge.

1. INTRODUCTION

Scholarly communication is an integral part of research process, which has an important role in the social and economic development of our society. Traditional method of scholarly communication creates bottlenecks in the wide dissemination of research output. At the same time World Wide Web becoming popular medium for scholarly communication has opened up new outlets for publication of research output. Libraries and information professionals are also confronting challenges in handling scholarly knowledge due to copyright restrictions, financial constraints and time lag in the publication of primary research publications. This paper is an over view of the problems in traditional scholarly communication and new prospects put forwarded by Internet for the wider access of scholarly knowledge.

2. TURBULENCE IN SCHOLARLY COMMUNICATION

Current scholarly communication is not sufficient for the exchange of knowledge from research process. Researchers, reviewers, publishers, libraries and users are the main components; and journals are the main medium of communication in the existing system of scholarly communication. Publishers of the journals hold the ownership of the journal article in the present scenario and restrict the broad distribution of knowledge. The copyright conditions attached with traditional journal submission procedure hamper the exclusive rights of the author. Writers need special permission or payment to further use of his/ her scholarly work, i.e. production, distribution, public performance, public display and modification of the original work. These stringent conditions also affect the user's freedom to access the knowledge. Students, professionals, policy makers, and the general public are the stake holders of scholarly publications. This led to the erosion of copyright from the owner and narrows the chance of free access by public [1]. Developing countries including India spend a large sum of money for research activities in government and academic sector in the expectation that this research will address the social and economic development of the society. Knowledge emanated from public funded research fails to reach the stake holders due to the lack of proper national strategies for knowledge dispersion. The extensive users of research output are researchers itself and they need to access the existing knowledge in their field in order to undertake innovative research.

Increasing price, growth in the number of journals and insufficient budget allocation for periodicals prevent libraries to become archives of physical records of scholarly publications. Advent of electronic database services in certain extent give relief from maintaining the physical collection of journals in libraries. Subscription rate of electronic database service providers are high and not affordable to libraries in developing countries. Introduction of electronic journals in consortium basis with the aim of price consolation for libraries resulted in the access of titles do not need to support research and academic programmes[2].

3. NEW KID IN THE SCHOLARLY COMMUNICATION BLOCK

Non-friendly approaches of traditional scholarly knowledge dissemination lead researchers to think about new alternative models of scholarly publication. As the consequence of this, open access concept rooted in the scholarly publication through open access journals and open archives. Open access mean the free availability of peer-reviewed literature on the public Internet permitting any user to read, download, copy, distribute, print, search, or link to the full texts of the articles. Open access journals which are freely available online world wide and does not rely up on the traditional subscription based business model to generate revenue[3]. Open archive or an institutional repository is a publicly accessible repository of pre-print or post-prints of research output of an academic or research institute. Open access journals and open archives are affiliated to open access concepts in publication of scholarly literature.

Open access is not a new type of scholarly publication model; it's only a way for the dissemination of knowledge, retaining authors copyright to their scholarly works and keep users freedom to access it.

Peer review process is also applicable to open access journals. Open access literature is digital, online, free of charge, and free of most copyright and licensing restrictions[4]. Open access publication follows different business models like article processing fees, institutional membership, sponsorship and advertising for the free availability of scholarly literature. The publication costs for open access literature shift from the user (subscriber) to the content producer (author). In other words, a journal charge fees for dissemination of the content, not to access it, as in the traditional subscription models [5]. Copyright provisions of open access enable users seamless access (reading, downloading, copying, sharing, storing, printing, searching, and linking) of the full text of the work. Creative commons is a popular license used to publish scholarly literature in public domain and publishers can create their own license agreement to ensure the freedom in the access of knowledge.

4. DYNAMIC WEB AND SCHOLARLY COMMUNICATION

One of the visible features in World Wide Web in these days is the dynamic information content and increasing interactivity with users. Second generation of web (web 2.0) based services allow community participation in the creation and updating of information content in the web through online collaboration and sharing among users[6]. Wikis, Blogs, and Podcasts are the major services which ensures creation and free access of community generated information. These services not only influence the business and social life but are also changing the way of scholarly communication. Emergence of these easily accessible social tools attracts researchers to World Wide Web to build their communication platform. As the result of this, increasing number of people access Internet for the collection of research information.

Blogs are the popular easy to publish medium in World Wide Web. Using blog writer can also update the content and collect feed back from users. Authors of the research articles often include their works in their blog to get wider public attention and discussion; therefore it is easy to find new peer-reviewed literature by searching blogs. Bloggers are early birds because they are willing to cover preprints and conference presentations[7].

Wiki is a collaborative website whose content can be edited by anyone who has access to it[8]. It can be used to create a knowledge base encouraging collaboration of experts in a particular area. Wikipedia is a free wiki based encyclopedia project written collaboratively by volunteers[9]. Flu Wiki is an example of medical wiki which gives information about various types of influenza.

Podcasting is delivering audio content to iPods and other portable media players on demand, so that it can be listened to at the user's convenience. The main benefit of podcasting is that listeners can sync content to their media player and take it with them to listen whenever they want to. Because podcasts are typically saved in MP3 format, they can also be listened to on nearly any computer[10]. JournalJunkie is a free podcast service provider which gives medical professionals with immediate audio access to abstracts from the latest medical journals.

New technologies are enhancing scholar's abilities to report, review and distribute research results and are greatly increasing the accessibility of research, regardless of geographic location. New technologies allow easy access to and navigation of rich multimedia formats and the integration of text, sound, graphics and video, as well as increasing interactivity. These capabilities are also challenging traditional models of scholarly communication and questioning the very nature of the traditional vehicles for the dissemination of scholarly material[11]. The web 2.0 applications would be major medium of scholarly publication to free access of knowledge.

The integration of scattered open access digital scholarly material is now possible through the standards like Open Archive Initiative Protocol for Metadata Harvesting (OAI-PMH). This protocol helps to gather and retrieve scholarly information reside in various communities and institutions on open access software platform. Search engine giants like Google, Yahoo and Microsoft's decision to index open access materials in their search purview would be helpful for Internet users to reap the benefits of free scholarly materials.

5. SCHOLARLY COMMUNICATION MOVE ON WITH HOPE

New publishing outlets of scholarly communication in the World Wide Web attracts the attention of academics and researchers. At the same time open access advocates and volunteers are struggling to remove barriers against the free flow of scholarly information.

Call for free access of public funded research is strong in many countries. Federal Research Public Access Act (FRPAA), 2006 by US Senate is considered as a revolutionary effort in Government level, which facilitates open exchange of research findings. This bill suggests that agencies with research budgets of more than $100 million enact policy to ensure that articles generated through research funded by that agency are made available online within 6 months of publication. Another agitation is 'Petition for guaranteed public access to publicly-funded research results'[12] in research recommendations proposed in the EU's 'Study on the Economic and Technical Evolution of the Scientific Publication Markets of Europe'. Spontaneously many universities and research institutes adopt open access policies in their scholarly communication environment. More than twenty institutions in India adopted open access. The India Institute of Science is the first institute in India to adopt open access in India. IIM Kozhikode is the first management institute in India to set up an open access archive.

Increasing number of open access journals is another accreditation to the growing popularity of open access principles in scholarly communication. DOAJ (Directory of Open Access Journals) listed 2500 peer reviewed open access journals in 2006.

Author addendums from SPARC (Scholarly Publishing and Academic Resources Coalition), Boston Library Consortium, MIT, Science Commons and JISC help to relieve authors from the clutch of harmful copyright of publishers and bring back the exclusive rights. Author addendum is a legal instrument that modifies the publisher's agreement and allows keeping key rights of authors.

6. CONCLUSION

Traditional scholarly communication model is not favourable in the case of free access of knowledge. World Wide Web and its allied services become the most rational and fast channel for knowledge transfer. A free flowing stream of scholarly communication will reduce the role of scholarly authority in the progress of research. In the networked environment any one with access to the Web can participate in scholarly communication. Scholarly communication through World Wide Web needs gatekeepers to filter the public scholarly discourse[13]. Open access has the provisions to safeguard the rights of public to free access of knowledge. Information professionals need awareness and training to organise and storing of research output using open access repositories and digital libraries. The government and academic institutions are not serious enough to monitor the scholarly publishing behaviour of public funded research. Research community and users are under the belief that government intervention is necessary at least in public funded research publication to enable free access of knowledge.

REFERENCES

1. Carroll, Michael W. (2006). Author rights:. Using the SPARC Author Addendum to Secure your Rights. 2006. SPARC. Available at www.arl.org/sparc/author/addendum.html
2. Drake, Miriam A.. (2007). Scholarly Communication in Turmoil. *Information Today,* February.
3. Guide to Open Access Publishing and Scholarly Societies. July 2005. Budapest Open Access Initiative. Available at www.soros.org/openaccess/scholarly_guide.shtml
4. Suber, Peter (2004). A Very Brief Introduction to Open Access. December. Available at www.earlham.edu/~peters/fos/brief.htm
5. Hawkins, Donald T.(2005). Does Open Access Publishing Really Work in Practice? *Information Today,* January
6. Web 2.0. 2007. Available at http://en.wikipedia.org/wiki/Web_2.0
7. Suber, Peter (2007). Open Access in 2006. Available at www.earlham.edu/~peters/fos/newsletter/01-02-07.htm (Accessed on January 2, 2007)
8. Wiki. Answers.com. 2005. Available at www.answers.com/wiki
9. Wikipedia. Wikipedia. 2007.Available at http://en.wikipedia.org/wiki/Wikipedia
10. What is Podcasting?. Podcasting News. Available at www.podcastingnews.com/articles/What_is_Podcasting.html
11. Birdsall, Bill (2000) . Canadian Association of Research Libraries. Optimizing the Transformation of Knowledge Research: Towards a Canadian Research Strategy
12. Petition for Guaranteed Public Access to Publicly-funded Research Results." February 2007. Available at www.ec-petition.eu/
13. Chodorow, Stanley (2000). Scholarship & Scholarly communication in the Electronic Age. *EDUCAUSE Review,* January/February, pp. 86-92.

30
Web Based Knowledge Management in Digital Era

K. Vinitha
S. Kanthimathi
S. Sampath Kumar

ABSTRACT

To succeed in any venture, including business ventures, sufficient knowledge is required. Knowledge Management has become necessary as we have moved from a society where information was scarce to a society where there is an overload of information. The problem today is generally not about procuring information but deciding which information to use. The paper speaks on basic pattern relationship on data, information, knowledge and wisdom. Further discusses on the types, subject domain and need for Knowledge Management. Knowledge Management activities such as creation, transfer and storage in digital era is discussed. Paper highlights on the Web Based Knowledge Management and its advantage and requirement is also briefed in the article. Organisations should be careful in acquiring relevant data and processing those in an ever-changing business landscape. It is equally important for businesses to discard obsolete information and acquire the latest information to survive and stay competitive.

1. INTRODUCTION

Knowledge Management is the order of the day in organisations in general and in library and information centres in particular. The term of yester years was Information Management. This term came about when people realised that information is a resource that can and needs to be managed to be useful in an organisation.

When Ranganathan wrote that 'the Universe of subjects is synonymous to Universe of Knowledge', he became the first to identify knowledge management in libraries. Though claims may be there, from various other quarters of contributors, for the introduction of the term in library management, there cannot be any doubt about Ranganathan's originality of the claim. From this, the ideas of Information Analysis and information Planning came about. Organisations are now starting to look at "knowledge" as a resource as well. This requires ways for managing the knowledge in libraries of organisations.

2. KNOWLEDGE MANAGEMENT

Knowledge management can be defined as "the harnessing of a company's collective expertise wherever it resides and the distribution of that expertise to the right people at the right time. It's not a product but a process—the process of gathering, managing, and sharing employees' knowledge capital."

Knowledge management is a process that helps organisations to: *find, select, organize, disseminate, and transfer important information and expertise. Necessary for problems such as ,problem solving, dynamic learning, strategic planning and decision making.* Knowledge management *includes: management strategies, methods, and technology for leveraging intellectual capital and* know-how to achieve gains in human performance and competitiveness.

3. KNOWLEDGE MANAGEMENT - RELATED SUBJECT DOMAINS

Knowledge management draws from a wide range of disciplines and technologies. Cognitive science, Expert systems (ES), artificial intelligence (AI) and knowledge base management systems (KBMS). Computer-supported collaborative work, Technical writing, Document management, Decision support systems, Semantic networks, Relational and object databases, Simulation, Organisational science in particular.

Library and Information Science: One can find that card catalogs in libraries will help to find the right book when needed. The body of research and practice in classification and knowledge organisation that makes libraries work will be even more vital as inundated by information in business. Tools for thesaurus construction and controlled vocabularies are already helping to manage knowledge.

4. NEED FOR KNOWLEDGE MANAGEMENT

Why do we need to manage knowledge? Ann Macintosh of the Artificial Intelligence Applications Institute (University of Edinburgh) has written a "Position Paper on Knowledge Asset Management". According to him, the need for knowledge management is as follows:

* Any work is information and knowledge based.

* Organisations compete on the basis of knowledge.
* Lack of time to experience and acquire knowledge
* Need to manage increasing complexity
* Need for life-long learning is an inevitable reality
* To remain aligned with the dynamically changing needs of the environment
* The underlying premise is that 'best practices' of yesterday may not be taken for granted as 'best practices' of today or tomorrow. Hence, double loop learning, unlearning and relearning processes need to be designed into the organisational business processes.
* Knowledge management is necessary for organisations because what worked yesterday may or may not work tomorrow.
* To remain aligned with the dynamically changing needs of the business environment, organisations need to continuously assess their internal theories of business for ongoing effectiveness. That is the only viable means for ensuring that today's 'core competencies' do not become 'core rigidities' of tomorrow.

5. KNOWLEDGE MANAGEMENT METHODS

Knowledge Management methods can be categorised into two main groups:

* Those that move knowledge around the organisation
* Those that help create new knowledge

Methods that help move and create knowledge

include: Face-to-face communication methods, e.g. peer assist, lessons learnt reviews, knowledge fairs, computer-based communication methods, e.g. email, Lotus Notes, communities of practice , Storage-and-retrieval using computer systems, e.g. intranets, knowledge books and Knowledge-Based Systems, e.g. expert systems.

6. KNOWLEDGE MANAGEMENT ACTIVITIES

Knowledge management encompasses three major activities namely,

* Knowledge Creation
* Knowledge Transfer and
* Knowledge Storage

6.1. Knowledge Creation

The process of creating new knowledge requires that organisational members acknowledge the existence of useful data and information. They should then transform it, through some form of process, into insights. New knowledge is created through a continuous dialogue between tacit and explicit knowledge. The business provides the infrastructural support to creative individuals or provides the context for such individuals to create knowledge.

6.2. Knowledge Transfer

Knowledge transfer is about exchanging good ideas. Knowledge transfer can involve a range of methods- from seminars to media relations, from placements to partnerships - fundamentally it is a two-way process. By creating more of a dialogue between researchers and research users, the results of research are more likely to be applied in policy and practice. It is important to transfer knowledge between different members and areas of the organisation so that knowledge can be fully exploited.

6.3. Knowledge Storage

Once knowledge has been created, to be of long-term value to the organisation it must be stored for subsequent use by people in different parts of the organisation. However, knowledge storage is more than simply codifying knowledge and storing in databases, documents and the like. It is the embodiment of tacit knowledge into processes, practices, materials and culture. The process of storing knowledge for subsequent use may be similar to a type of 'organisational memory'. Organisational memory becomes more powerful when it, and its context, are stored in a form that makes it easily retrievable by staff and management who have need of it.

7. WEB BASED KNOWLEDGE MANAGEMENT

With recent development in Internet technology and its wider acceptance and popularity there are many products available today to facilitate knowledge sharing and coloration using web technologies. The main advantage of web-based technology is it can be deployed in Internet or in intranet within the organisation. Internet is also used to create a VPN (virtual private network) using Internet as medium of data transmission. We will discuss more about web based Knowledge Management system here. Organisations have used different platforms to deploy a Knowledge Management system but in all most all cases a web browser is used as client end tool to access the Knowledge Management system. The varied modes of e-transfer of knowledge include the following:

* Intranet
* Extranet

* Groupware
* E-mail/Knowledge transfer
* Newsgroups/Work-Flow Systems
* Chat Rooms
* Video Communication
* Group Calendaring/Scheduling
* Value Chain
* Web portals

The advantages of web based knowledge management system are that it is easy to maintain, changes can be done to the system easily, In client side any web browser can be used to access the server, user-frirendly and this is one of the major reasons to go for a web based Knowledge Management system. Any new employee joining the organisation can use the system with out any formal training on portal. Up gradation is also easy as one end at server the up gradation is to be done. The reach of the portal is not limited as any one can access from any part of the intranet or Internet. The access area of the portal increases with the expansion of the network.

8. REQUIREMENTS OF A WEB BASED KNOWLEDGE MANAGEMENT SYSTEM

8.1. WebServer

The hardware of the web server is to be decided based on the traffic, network configuration etc. Web server operating system is the part of the system which delivers the required files to the client browser after required processing. Web server is to be selected based on the scripting (programming) language, database supports etc. There are many web servers available in the market today and Microsoft's windows® server is a major player in the corporate market today. Windows 2003 server is the most recent one. In the other hand the Linux server is of great demand as a part of open source community. Window server usually runs IIS (Internet Information Server) as the web server and in the same way Linux server runs APACHE as the web server.

8.2. Programming Language and database

Depending on the server support the programming language can be selected. Some of the languages popularly used for scripting are Java Server Pages (JSP), ASP or ASP dot Net, PHP, Cold fusion, Perl, etc. Database support is a common requirement in such cases as details of files, members, system tracking etc are to be stored. Popular database for web applications are MySQL, MSSQL, Oracle etc. In the client side any web browser can be used to access the server. Popular browsers are MS Internet Explorer, Netscape Navigator, FireFox etc.

8.3. Network

An existing network can be used to develop a web based KM system. Internet also can be used for this with required access limitations. Organisations with offices in scattered geographical locations can use VPN (virtual private network) which uses internet to create a private network. In such a system organisation can keep its web server inside its premises and through VPN outside offices can access the server.

8.4. Knowledge Management Portal

One web portal can be developed using any internet hosting solutions and access can be restricted by login systems. Users with different levels of permission can access contributions / articles of different authors. This type of system helps in sharing best practices, experiments, innovations, failure stories etc. KM portals are developed with database support to keep the records of authors, members, access levels, visitor tracking and many other requirements. Usually all contributions of members passes through a veteran approval system before it goes to the public view or the member view. Members posting to the author, rating system, feedback of users' member's management, admin area etc are some of the features generally used in KM portal.

8.5. Web Based discussion Board or Forum

A virtual community can be created by using Web based discussion boards. Different sections or areas can be created to create different sections for discussions. Here the discussions are available for all in the organisation to view / post / reply to the topics. This is an ideal solution for branch offices, communities located in different geographical areas but having common area of interest. They can share there common problems, areas of concerns, experience and help each other in building a strong bond of networking. Little help from organisation in creating trust among members by organising face to face interactive sessions will encourage the members to actively participate in the forums.

9. CONCLUSION

There are many ready made scripts available in the market and one such system can be developed in house keeping in mind the requirements of the organisation. Web blogs are popular now a days and companies have utilised this tool to create awareness and evolve opinions on different issues. Blogs can be hosted in the company intranet or popular blog sites like blogspot.com can be used to give a platform to the employees to post their views. Many companies have their blogging policy also. Expert's database with profile updating can be kept for the public view and queries can be posted to specific experts based on the areas of domain and expertise of the exports. This helps in creating innovation and learning culture in an organisation.

Index

Behavioural Traits 362
Bibliometrics 303
- Bradford's Law 305
- Lotka's Law 306
- Zipf's Law 306
Biometrics 358
- Security 357
- System 358
Blog 193, 394
- Audio 196
- Text-only 196
Classification Schemes 54
Community Knowledge 265
Competitive Intelligence 250
- Activities 252
- Benefits 258
- Information Sources 254
- Objectives 252
- Problems 258
- Process 255
- Tools 253
Creative Commons 393
Cryptography 369
Cybermetrics 309
Cyberspace 261
Cyborg 132
Data 152
Digital Archiving 225, 228
- Imaging 367
- Information 316
- Library 131, 326, 367
- Literacy 293
- Longevity 317
- Preservation 224
- Resources 224
- Signature 370
- Products 127
- Watermarking 371
Discrete Traits 363
e-Books 349
e-Governance 180
e-Readiness Rank 180
e-Scholarship 143
- Editions 143
- Programme 141
- Publications 144
- Repository 142, 146
Electronic Database 213
- Information sources 212
- Journals 226
Explicit Knowledge 93, 153, 237
Faceted Classification 54
Federal Research Public Access Act 396
Firewall 371
Full-text Search 58

Globalization 282
Information 91, 152
- Delivery 45
- Literacy 188, 291, 352, 388
- Manager 4
- Organization 53
- Seeker 3
- Source 3
- Society 261, 283
- Technology 4, 127, 327, 334, 336
Information Communication Technology 177, 207, 269, 342
- Projects 181
- Dristee 182
- Gyandoot 181
- Invite 185
- NaiDisha 184
- Pravana 182
- Sristi 183
- Village Knowledge Centre 184
- Warna Wired Village 183
Informetrics 307
Institutional Repositories 344
Intellectual Property Right 227
International Archive 145
Internet 42, 45, 126, 176, 179, 212, 262, 325
Keyware 361
Knowledge 25, 63, 91, 152, 164
Knowledge Management 26, 64, 91, 113, 151, 154, 164, 234, 250, 263, 400
- Activities 403
- Advantages 247
- Analysis phase 30
- Approaches 25
- Assessment 28
- Challenges 75, 95, 118
- Codification Strategy 34
- Components 70, 92, 155
- Definition 236
- Design phase 32
- Features 69
- Future 85
- Growth and Development 115
- Impact 77
- Implementation 28
- Importance 72
- Initiation phase 30
- Initiatives 71
- Key elements 93
- Librarians 81, 94, 169
- Libraries 156, 166
- Merits 79
- Methods 402
- Need 401
- Objectives 68
- Personalization strategy 35
- Process 26, 94
- Professional skills 160
- Purpose 93
- Requisites 70
- Stages 238
- Strategies 33
- Successful factors 240
- Tools 72
- Web-based 404
Knowledge Society 175, 261, 284
Local Area Network 128
Librametrics 302
Librarianship 4

Library and Information Center 2
- Changes 4
- Future 133
Library Consortia 214, 218
Library and Information Professional 41, 375
- Cocooning 44
- Competencies 373, 380
- Ethics 43
- Future 48
- Human relation 46
- Placement 47
- Qualification 382
- Recognition 43
- Workplace 45
Library and Information Science
- Course 11
- Education 2, 8
- India 8
- Profession 7
- Schools 47
Metadata 322
Mobile Communication 271
Networking 128
Notation 56
Open Access 129, 393
- Archives 130, 393
- Journals 349
- Publishing 348
Organizational Knowledge 26
Pod-casting 395
Publishing Literacy 293
Research Literacy 293
Resource Literacy 293
Scholarly Communication 390
Scientometrics 308
Steganography 372
Tacit Knowledge 153, 238
Technology phobia 42
Tool Literacy 293
Topological Traits 362
Total Quality Management 100
University of California 141
Wide Area Network 128
Webliography 350
Weblog See Blog
Webometrics 311
Wiki 394
WiMAX 272
Wireless Technology 270
World Wide Web 195, 394